Peter T. De Simone is Associate Professor in the Department of History at Utica College, New York. He received his PhD from Ohio State University specializing in the Russian Orthodox Old Rite as well as Russian, European, and Religious history and has published in peer-reviewed journals and presented at conferences internationally on the Old Believers.

"In this valuable new book, Peter De Simone examines the world of the Old Believers in Imperial Russia, from the eighteenth century through the early twentieth century. These religious sectarians, despite the persecution they faced, played a prominent role in the country's social and economic life. Focusing on the Rogozhskoe community in Moscow, De Simone shows that Old Believer families were able to maintain their religious beliefs even as they established powerful merchant dynasties. His work makes a major contribution to Russian religious history and to the history of Imperial Russia more generally."

David L. Hoffmann, Distinguished
Professor of History, the Ohio State University

"A penetrating study of an Old Believer community in the heartland of Russia across three centuries. De Simone's special focus on the Rogozhskoe cemetery group in Moscow illuminates the social activity, sacred spaces and dogma, church architecture and self-identity of Old Rite communities as a whole. The book succeeds in enriching our understanding of the complexity of religious life and the dynamics of urban society in tsarist Russia."

Lucien Frary, Professor of History, Rider University, New Jersey

Library of Modern Russia

Building on I.B.Tauris' established record publishing Russian studies titles for both academic and general readers, the *Library of Modern Russia* will showcase the work of emerging and established writers who are setting new agendas in the field.

At a time when potentially dangerous misconceptions and misunderstandings about Russia abound, titles in the series will shed fresh light and nuance on Russian history. Volumes will take the idea of 'Russia' in its broadest, cultural sense and cover the entirety of the multi-ethnic lands that made up imperial Russia and the Soviet Union. Ranging in chronological scope from the Romanovs to the present day, the books will foster a community of scholars and readers devoted to a sharper understanding of the Russian experience, past and present.

New and forthcoming

Building Stalinism: The Moscow Canal and the Creation of Soviet Space, Cynthia A. Ruder
Criminal Subculture in the Gulag: Prisoner Society in the Stalinist Labour Camps, Mark Vincent
Dissident Histories in the Soviet Union: From De-Stalinization to Perestroika, Barbara Martin
Fascism in Manchuria: The Soviet–China Encounter in the 1930s, Susanne Hohler
Ideology and the Arts in the Soviet Union: The Establishment of Censorship and Control, Steven Richmond
Myth Making in the Soviet Union and Modern Russia: Remembering World War II in Brezhnev's Hero City, Vicky Davis
Nomads and Soviet Rule: Central Asia under Lenin and Stalin, Alun Thomas
Power and Conflict in Russia's Borderlands: The Post-Soviet Geopolitics of Dispute Resolution, Helena Rytövuori-Apunen
Power and Politics in Modern Chechnya: Ramzan Kadyrov and the New Digital Authoritarianism, Karena Avedissian
Russia in the Time of Cholera: Disease under Romanovs and Soviets, John P. Davis
Russian Pilgrimage to the Holy Land: Piety and Travel from the Middle Ages to the Revolution, Nikolaos Chrissidis
Science City, Siberia: Akademgorodok and the Late Soviet Politics of Expertise, Ksenia Tartachenko
Soviet Americana: The Cultural History of Russian and Ukrainian Americanists, Sergei I. Zhuk
Stalin's Economic Advisors: The Varga Institute and the Making of Soviet Foreign Policy, Kyung Deok Roh
The Communist Party in the Russian Civil War: A Political History, Gayle Lonergan
The Idea of Russia: The Life and Work of Dmitry Likhachev, Vladislav Zubok
Sport and Society in the Soviet Union: The Politics of Football after Stalin, Manfred Zeller
The Russian State and the People: Power, Corruption and the Individual in Putin's Russia, Geir Hønneland *et al.* (eds)
The Tsar's Armenians: A Minority in Late Imperial Russia, Onur Önol

THE OLD BELIEVERS IN IMPERIAL RUSSIA

Oppression, Opportunism and Religious Identity in Tsarist Moscow

PETER T. DE SIMONE

I.B. TAURIS
LONDON · NEW YORK

Published in 2018 by
I.B.Tauris & Co. Ltd
London • New York
www.ibtauris.com

Library of Modern Russia 21

ISBN: 978 1 78453 892 7
eISBN: 978 1 78672 422 9
ePDF: 978 1 78673 422 8

A full CIP record for this book is available from the British Library
A full CIP record is available from the Library of Congress

Library of Congress Catalog Card Number: available

Typeset in Garamond Three by OKS Prepress Services, Chennai, India
Printed and bound by CPI Group (UK) Ltd, Croydon, CR0 4YY

For Louis and Maureen

CONTENTS

List of Illustrations xi
Transliteration and Dates xiii
List of Abbreviations xiv
Acknowledgements xv

Introduction 1
Overview 6
Russia's Spiritual Development before the *Raskol* 8
The Old Believers' Defense of their Faith 13
The Rogozhskoe Old Believers and their Community 17
A Note on Sources 26

1. **Old Believers and the Opportunities of Imperial Russia** 28
Introduction 28
Opportunity Arises 30
The Conflict over Old Believer Identity 35
Rogozhskoe Cemetery's Founding and First Decades 42
The Rogozhskoe Old Believers and the Reimagining of Moscow, 1812–25 57
Rogozhskoe as a Center of the Old Rite 65
Conclusion 67

2. **Faith and Identity Under Siege, 1822–56** 69
Targeting the Old Rite 71
The Rogozhskoe Old Believers and the Founding of the Belokrinitskaya Hierarchy 78

Divide and Conquer 87
Conclusion 96

3. **Rogozhskoe in the Reform Era, 1856–1905** 97
Redefining the Old Rite in Rogozhskoe Cemetery 99
Community and Order in Rogozhskoe's Holy Moscow, 1856–1905 113
The Rogozhskoe Old Believers and the Era of Reform 119
A Community of Loyal Old Believers 136
Conclusion 146

4. **A New Beginning, 1905–17** 147
"Now we have a Church!" 149
Rogozhskoe after Religious Toleration 160
Governing the Community 169
Rogozhskoe as a Spiritual Center after Toleration 175
Rogozhskoe's New Generation 183
Rogozhskoe and the Efforts to Define the Old Rite after 1905 195
Conclusion 208

Epilogue and Conclusion Tragedy and New Challenges 210
Conclusions 213

Notes 216
Bibliography 246
Index 255

LIST OF ILLUSTRATIONS

Figure 1.1 Old Ritualist Intercession Chapel, Rogozhskoe Cemetery, 1883. Nikolai Naydenov, Album, *Views of Some Urban Areas, Temples, Notable Buildings and Other Structures*, Moscow, 1884. 49

Figure 1.2 Overview of the floor plan of the Intercession Cathedral. Courtesy of Peter T. De Simone. 50

Figure 1.3 Old Ritualist Nativity Chapel, 1883. Nikolai Naydenov, Album, *Views of Some Urban Areas, Temples, Notable Buildings and Other Structures*, Moscow, 1884. 51

Figure 1.4 Overview of the floor plan of Nativity Cathedral. Courtesy of Peter T. De Simone. 52

Figure 1.5 A portion of a map of Moscow in 1818 with highlighted box depicting Rogozhskoe Cemetery's location in relation to the rest of Moscow. From "Topographical Map of the Suburbs of Moscow, recorded by the officers of the Quartermaster 1818." Military Topographic Depot, 1823. 60

Figure 1.6 Detail of Rogozhskoe Cemetery, 1818. From "Topographical Map of the Suburbs of Moscow, recorded by the officers of the Quartermaster 1818." Military Topographic Depot, 1823. Detail courtesy of Peter T. De Simone. 60

Figure 2.1 Father Ivan (Ioann) Iastrebov, Russian Orthodox Old Rite Church. 81

Figure 2.2 Metropolitan Ambrose, Russian Orthodox Old Rite Church. 86

Figure 2.3 Nikolai Ivanovich Subbotin. Public Domain. 91

Figure 3.1 Ilarion Kabanov, "Xenos." *Okruzhnoe poslanie*, Moscow: E. Lissner and Iu. Roman, 1893. 105

Figure 3.2 Antonii (Shutov), Archbishop of Moscow and All Rus', 1870s. *Tserkov'*, 1908. 106

Figure 3.3 Ivan Shibaev, late nineteenth century *Tserkov'*, 1908. 127

Figure 3.4 Interior of Intercession Cathedral, Sherer, Nabgol'ts and Co., 1876. 133

Figure 3.5 Intercession Cathedral, Sherer, Nabgol'ts and Co., 1876. 134

Figure 3.6 A View of Rogozhskoe Cemetery, Sherer, Nabgol'ts and Co., 1876. 135

Figure 3.7 Old Rite Rogozhskoe Cemetery, 1886. Nikolai Naydenov, Album, *Pictures of Views of Locations, Buildings and Othere Structures*, Vol. 3, 1886. 145

Figure 4.1 Damage to the Intercession Cathedral altar space after their reopening, Nikifor Zenin, April 16, 1905. 154

Figure 4.2 Damage to the Intercession Cathedral altar space after their reopening, Nikifor Zenin, April 16, 1905. 155

Figure 4.3 Damage to the Nativity Cathedral's altars upon its reopening, Nikifor Zenin, April 16, 1905. 156

Figure 4.4 Damage to the Nativity Cathedral's altars upon its reopening, Nikifor Zenin, April 16, 1905. 157

Figure 4.5 Draft of the Rogozhskoe Bell Tower. F. F. Gornostaev and Z. I. Ivanov. *Tserkov'*, 1908. 164

Figure 4.6 Rogozhskoe Bell Tower Dedication Services on April 20, 1908. *Tserkov'*, 1908. 165

Figure 4.7 Mounting of the Rogozhskoe Bells. *Tserkov'*, 1908. 166

Figure 4.8 Rogozhskoe's Bell Tower, 1913. *Tserkov'*, 1913. 169

Figure 4.9 Rogozhskoe students after completing their exams. *Tserkov'*, 1912. 179

TRANSLITERATION AND DATES

For this work I have followed the Library of Congress system for transliteration. For naming individuals I have provided personal and family names. Patronymics appear where there is need to distinguish between individuals who share personal and family names. All dates prior to 1918 appear according to the Julian calendar, which trails the Gregorian calendar by 13 days. Dates from 1918 and after use the Gregorian calendar.

LIST OF ABBREVIATIONS

HRL	Hilandar Research Library and Resource Center for Medieval Slavic Studies
OPI GIM	Otdel Pis'mennikh Istochnikov Gosudarstvennogo Istoricheskogo Muzeia
PSZ	*Polnoe sobranie zakonov Rossiiskoi Imperii*
RGADA	Rossiiskii Gosudarstvennyi Arkhiv Drevnikh Aktov
RGB	Rossiiskaia Gosudarstvennaia Biblioteka
SobranieMVD	*Sobranie postanovlenii po chasti raskola*
SppcrSVS	*Sobranie postanovlenii po chasti raskola sostoiavshikhsia po vedomstvu Sv. Sinoda*
TsGAMO	Tsentral'nyi Gosudarstvennyi Arkhiv Moskovskoi Oblasti

ACKNOWLEDGEMENTS

The following work is the culmination of years of work that began in graduate school. I could not have completed this work without the enormous amounts of support I received from numerous people in my life. First, I wish to thank my graduate advisor, Dr. Nicholas Breyfogle of Ohio State University whose mentoring, patience, and insight continue to play a critical role in my academic and professional career. I also must thank Dr. David Hoffmann, Dr. Robin Judd, and Dr. Predrag Matejic also at Ohio State for their advice and help in building this project in its earliest stages. I am also eternally grateful to my colleagues and especially my fellow History Faculty at Utica College, Drs. Sherri Cash and David Wittner, who not only welcomed me with open arms into their small family, but have provided extremely valuable insight and discussion on how to shape the work presented here. Their help and continued support through this process made this possible as it opened up many doors in my research and professional career. This work could also not have been completed without the very understanding and very helpful aides of particularly the Russian State Library.

I am also very thankful to my children, Louis and Maureen, and my wife, Elizabeth, for their continued love, patience, support, and understanding while I completed my research and work. I would also like to give special thanks to my parents, Glenn and Patricia for their continuous support throughout my life and for inspiring me to never give up on my dreams, and instilling in me my love of history that led me to this moment.

Finally, I would like to thank my many friends who helped throughout this endeavor. Particularly, Dr. Christine Rydel and Dr. Edward Cole for not only introducing me to the amazing culture and history of Russia, but also helping me establish many valuable contacts for my research and work over these past decades. Furthermore, I also could not have completed this work without the support I received from friends and family over the years who readily offered to be eyes, ears, and even crutches through the highs and lows while I completed my work. To those passed, you are missed every day. However, for everyone in my life, I could not have done this without you.

INTRODUCTION

> the Council of 1666–1667, cursed and betrayed the ancient traditions of the Holy Church ... as a result the mainstream Church embarked on a false path and departed from the holy church and ancient piety, and violated the teachings of the gospel, the apostles and the Holy Fathers
>
> Feodor Permiakov[1]

> our ancestors grew a sense of responsibility not only for ourselves but for others... it is the Old Believers, and their religious phenomenon, that are most acquainted with the history of this spiritual feeling in Russia
>
> Vladimir Riabushinskii[2]

Since the mid-seventeenth century and into the twentieth century, the many groups collectively referred to as Russian Orthodox Old Believers directly challenged the very definitions of "Russian" and "Orthodox" in the Russian Empire.[3] The confrontation between authorities and the Old Believers remained ideological, cultural, and even physical as both sides regularly denounced one another as dangerous to the very essence of Russian Orthodoxy, Russian culture, and even the Russian state itself. The very idea of which group represented a more "pure" form of Russian Orthodoxy, and who served as torchbearers for Russia's cultural destiny, lay at the heart of the debate among the Old Believers and the Russian state and church authorities.

The Old Rite directly developed out of Russia's efforts to define and place Russian Orthodoxy in the larger history and traditions of Christendom. Beginning with the Byzantine Empire's collapse in 1453, Muscovy, a relatively new state recently independent of the Golden Horde's influence, spent the next two centuries attempting to create a unified sense of Russian Orthodoxy. The sixteenth century in particular witnessed a flowering of Russian spiritual thought along with efforts to establish Russia and its people as the inheritors of the one true, Ancient Christian Church. However, by the mid-seventeenth century, Russian Orthodoxy and Russian identity descended into religious chaos.

From 1653–6, Patriarch Nikon of Moscow began his first efforts to introduce a number of reforms designed to bring Russian Orthodoxy into liturgical conformity with the contemporary Greek Orthodox Church. Nikon's efforts witnessed many Russians' condemnation of the reforms as both an invalidation and a corruption of the purity of Russia's Orthodoxy because the Greeks' defeat to the Turks revealed God's displeasure for the Greek Church. However, Tsar Alexis's official adoption of Nikon's reforms and the outright rejection of the reforms by elements throughout Russia's laity and clergy resulted in what became the *raskol*, or schism, of the Russian Orthodox Church. This split directly gave rise to the formation of the religious groups collectively known as *staroobriadtsy*, Old Ritualists or Old Believers.

The Old Believers resisted both the Russian Orthodox Church and state authorities in an effort to maintain their understanding of Russian Orthodoxy. The Old Rite, while itself divided into different branches, spread throughout the Russian Empire and through all levels of Russian society. In the immediate aftermath of the split, many Old Believers fled to the far reaches of the vast Russian wilderness in order to escape from tax collectors and other state agents, who they now believed worked as agents of the Antichrist. However, many other Old Believers persevered and found social and economic success among the tradesmen and merchants of some of Russia's largest cities.

Moscow, in particular, offered the opportunity for Old Rite individuals and communities to thrive even while in plain sight of their oppressors. For urban Old Believers, and in Moscow especially as the "Old Capital," remaining in the open presented its own unique challenges. While the cities provided the Moscow Old Believers strong social and economic ties to one another as well as Russian society, it also made them easy targets for oppression. However, even while living openly as challengers to the official Church, through the eighteenth century, Moscow Old Believers gradually became some of the city's most influential and successful merchants and business owners. Ultimately then, the Moscow Old Believers demonstrated that they could be a part of two different ideological and cultural worlds: their own idealized world guided by the principles of their faith in the Old Rite, and the ever-changing world of contemporary Moscow. More importantly, for many Moscow Old Rite communities, their existence required them to find a means not only to embody their own perception of Old Rite and Russian "purity," but also to do so while remaining active members of the ever-changing world of Moscow and Russian society.

In this context, this work explores the specific Moscow Old Rite community that developed at Rogozhskoe Cemetery and the attempts to establish a physical and spiritual embodiment of their worldview shaped by their faith in the Old Rite. Named after the designated burial site for *popovtsy*, or priestly, Old Believers during the Moscow Plague in 1771, the Rogozhskoe Old Believers quickly established themselves as an epicenter of the entire priestly Old Rite movement throughout Russia and the world. To this end, Rogozhskoe Cemetery served as a direct representation of the community's attempts not only to define themselves within the Old Rite, but also present themselves as the true embodiment of Russian Orthodoxy and their idealized Russian cultural destiny.

Rogozhskoe Cemetery itself served as an evolving physical and ideological representation of the community's own understanding of their identity and duty to uphold, pre-*raskol* Russian Orthodoxy as an example for all of Russian society. Furthermore, Moscow served as both a physical and ideological medium, that I will identify as "Holy Moscow," in the Rogozhskoe Old Believers' efforts to form their ideology for and represent their community. Their efforts by no means remained static; instead the Rogozhskoe Old Believers actively and purposefully evolved through their history to define themselves morally, spiritually, culturally, socially, and economically within the Old Rite *and* the Russian Empire.

In the historiography of the Old Rite and the Old Believers, as well as Russian Orthodoxy as a whole, Rogozhskoe Cemetery remains largely overlooked. The works by historians Vladimir Makarov and Feodor Mel'nikov in the early twentieth century, and Elena Iukhimenko more recently, contribute the most comprehensive, although brief, general histories of Rogozhskoe Cemetery.[4] Therefore, I intend to bring Rogozhskoe Cemetery and its community of Old Believers into the larger historiographies of the Old Rite, Russian Orthodoxy, and religious minorities in Imperial Russia. Focus on the primary role of the cemetery also leads to several other contributions to the study of the Old Rite movement. Close attention to Rogozhskoe brings this priestly Old Believer community into the larger historiography of the Old Rite that has disproportionately focused on the more diverse *bezpopovtsy* (priestless) branch of the Old Rite. A study of Rogozhskoe Cemetery and its community will help provide more insight into a significant influence in the development of the priestly Old Rite within Russia.

However, most importantly, my study pays significant attention to the relationship between the Old Rite and Imperial Russian State; more specifically, it reframes the understanding of the Old Rite's relationship with the Russian Empire. Oftentimes, two common themes appear in previous histories of the Old Rite: first, they emphasize a story of persecution and survival; second, they present the Old Believers' as a story of preservation of a religious minority's faith and identity in the face of tsarist and Church oppression.[5] While themes of persecution and survival do appear in my narrative, I present the Rogozhskoe Old Believers' efforts and accomplishments to build their ideal community as a story of opportunity. As tsarist Russia changed not only politically but also socially, economically, and spiritually into the twentieth century, the Rogozhskoe community purposefully and carefully evolved their own self-identity and understanding of themselves to fit their immediate needs in order to champion the Old Rite while actively participating in contemporary Russian society. By shifting focus to a story of opportunity, I then tell a story of a highly successful religious community in an often-oppressive state. Rogozhskoe's success can be measured in two significant areas. First, the Rogozhskoe community boasted some of Imperial Russia's most economically successful and socially influential merchant and industrial dynasties. Second, throughout the community's history, Rogozhskoe Cemetery quickly became one of the most vital and influential spiritual centers within the entire Old Rite movement. Ultimately the cemetery helped to establish and then to serve as the primary site for the Old-Rite Belokrinitskaya Hierarchy to restore what the community eventually accepted as a true, Orthodox Church hierarchy.

Consequently, the idea that Rogozhskoe Cemetery became what I will call a "Holy Moscow" becomes central to my work. Rogozhskoe Cemetery, then, evolved into a symbolic, physical, and spiritual representation of the Rogozhskoe Old Believers' efforts to create and maintain some semblance of sacredness in a seemingly corrupt world. Within this context, Rogozhskoe's own walls served as both a physical and ideological manifestation of the boundaries between the community's public world and socio-economic activities with Moscow and Imperial Russia, and the private realm of their own manifestation of their idealized Orthodox community within the walls. Therefore, Rogozhskoe Cemetery became the embodiment of the community's own efforts to answer their own questions of how to live a proper, Christian life: how to balance their accumulation of wealth with efforts at salvation, the meaning of good deeds, the relationship between clergy and laity, and even their own place as a religious minority in an oppressive state.

Through such efforts, the Rogozhskoe Old Believers reflect a number of trends shared among many religious communities. As argued by scholars on religion such as Mircea Eliade and Emile Durkheim, many communities often use religion to shape their view of their spiritual as well as physical worlds. In their works, both scholars in particular emphasize how a community's religious beliefs help divide the world between what the community deems sacred and profane. For Durkheim, through a community's representation and then veneration of the sacred, they are able to express their faith and to represent themselves as the embodiment of their own ideal society.[6] For Eliade, religious communities only gain a real and meaningful awareness of their world when they formulate specific definitions of sacred and profane created in what he described as the hierophany – a community's ideal sense of the sacred.[7] In Eliade's concept of the hierophany, only through this ideal sacredness can a community gain any sense of value or purpose in their world in order to structure their own society to reflect what they believe is the ideal manifestation of this hierophany. Within this framework, I explain how the Rogozhskoe Old Believers created their interior and exterior boundaries physically as well as ideologically in order to present their idealized Orthodox community to the world. More specifically, I demonstrate that the "interior" of Rogozhskoe served as a reminder of the sacred – a space that served the sole purpose to reaffirm the community's ties to the Old

Rite and reaffirm their duty as protectors of their perceived pure Christian faith.

By contrast, the "exteriors" then served to separate the community physically and spiritually from the world outside. As I argue, this division was not only intentioned to prevent what the Rogozhskoe community could perceive as "corruption" from the impure world outside their walls, but also to remind their own members of the careful balance they maintained as a community between two worlds. For example, Rogozhskoe claimed many of Moscow and Russia's wealthiest merchant families as members. As some of Rogozhskoe's most visible and influential representatives, these merchant families were expected to separate their public lives as entrepreneurs from their spiritual lives in Rogozhskoe. While a number of families established some of Moscow's most celebrated homes, these same families often constructed smaller, simpler houses in or near Rogozhskoe to live in during Church holidays. For example, one of Rogozhskoe's most celebrated families and some of Russia's wealthiest industrialists, the Riabushinskiis, established their own cell (*kelya*) in Rogozhskoe in which all family members lived in during the Lenten period. In such cells, the Riabushinskii and other Rogozhskoe Old Believer merchant families devoted themselves entirely to their spiritual obligations and refused to take any part in their businesses during these periods.[8] Through the creation of separate spaces for the wealthy families to interact with the sacred and profane, the Rogozhskoe Old Believers found the means to find opportunities within Imperial Russian society to maintain and build their ideal community in the cultural heart of Russia: Moscow.

Overview

This book traces this tale of opportunity through the chapters ahead; exploring the history of Rogozhskoe Cemetery and its community of Old Believers in four major periods of their history. Using these moments, this book explains how the Rogozhskoe Old Believers used many available opportunities even in the face of persecution to shape their community as a reflection of their understanding of an ideal Moscow society in Imperial Russia.

The first chapter explores the situation many Old Believers, particularly in Moscow, faced in the period from the early eighteenth century to the early 1820s. This chapter explores how within a generation after the Church split, while no less ideologically or legislatively hostile toward the Old Rite, Peter the Great's more "diplomatic" approach toward Old Believers and their economic niches allowed for greater opportunities for many Old Rite communities to prosper economically and spiritually. This chapter sets up the major theme of opportunity for this entire work and eventually explains that, particularly for the Rogozhskoe Old Believers, Old Rite economic success provided the opportunities to establish flourishing communities in what is often historically portrayed as a period of oppression. A key factor to this success during this period became the state's inability to find an effective means to target Old Believers for persecution. As tsarist authorities quickly discovered, not only could Old Believers blend in with the rest of Russian society, but also, any oppression potentially disrupted many Old Rite communities' economic contributions to the Russian Empire. Within this setting, the chapter finally explores the origins of the Rogozhskoe Old Rite community and their presence as a major economic success and social influence in Moscow in the late eighteenth and early nineteenth centuries.

Chapters 2 and 3 focus on Rogozhskoe's interactions with Imperial Russia during a time of increased persecution by the tsarist state. As I explain in Chapter 2, Rogozhskoe, and in fact all Old Believers, found themselves targeted by Nicholas I's increasingly oppressive state, specifically because of their economic and social success. This intentional targeting of groups such as Rogozhskoe stemmed from tsarist and Church officials' perception that Old Rite success directly threatened "acceptable" Russian culture and society. The ideological and economic battles between groups such as Rogozhskoe and the tsarist and Church authorities continually forced the Rogozhskoe Old Believers to adapt the very understanding and purpose of their community. In particular, Rogozhskoe found itself in the middle of its own spiritual and ideological battle between the newly established Old Rite Belokrinitskaya Hierarchy, the first Old Believer-led Old Rite Orthodox Church hierarchy and the State's efforts to forcefully convert the community to mainstream Orthodoxy or the state-sponsored Old Rite hierarchy, *Edinoverie*.

Chapter 3 continues the story of the Rogozhskoe Old Believers' attempts to redefine their community within Imperial Russia's ever changing political and social situation during the Reform Era. A major theme in this chapter follows the Rogozhskoe Old Believers' efforts to use the opportunities of this era to assert themselves firmly as both the seat of the Belokrinitskaya Hierarchy in the Russian Empire, and also to champion themselves as loyal subjects of the Tsar in a period of increasing social and political turmoil. Russia's Reform Era witnessed an increased effort by the Rogozhskoe Old Believers to maintain their way of life economically, socially, religiously, and politically.

The final chapter explores the dramatic changes the Rogozhskoe Old Believers experienced following Nicholas II's decree on religious toleration for the Old Rite in 1905. Particularly, this chapter explains how the seeming end of persecution galvanized the community's efforts to present themselves as the physical and spiritual embodiment of "Holy Moscow" to the greater public. During this period, the Rogozhskoe community undertook new construction projects, expanded their charity institutions, and even established or restored many hospitals and cultural venues throughout Moscow. This chapter also looks at the influence some of Rogozhskoe's more affluent families such as the Morozovs and Riabushinskiis held not only in the community but also in Moscow and Imperial Russia, and ultimately served as living models of Rogozhskoe's Holy Moscow. This chapter presents the case that while the period of toleration only lasted just over a decade, these few short years witnessed the closest that the Rogozhskoe Old Believers came to realizing their ideal Holy Moscow.

Overall, this work reveals that the Rogozhskoe Old Believers' greatest historical attribute, in contrast to many other Old Rite communities, was that Rogozhskoe developed and evolved as a very visible representation of the entire Old Rite movement. While many Old Believers spread throughout the Russian Empire, and even the world, the Rogozhskoe community found opportunity for success in an often-oppressive state in the very heart of Russia's Old Capital. It would be Moscow, both the city and the very idea of Moscow, then that served as a means for the Rogozhskoe Old Believers to display their own ideals publically for all of Russia to see and ultimately present their own model of an ideal Russian society.

Russia's Spiritual Development before the *Raskol*

One of the main objections by Old Believers against the Nikonian Reforms in the mid-seventeenth century claimed that conforming

Russian Orthodoxy to the rituals and liturgical practices of the contemporary Greeks invalidated Russia's spiritual purity. Over the two centuries prior to Nikon's efforts, the Russian Orthodox Church and Russian state continually refined its understanding of their Orthodox faith. Furthermore, these debates of the fifteenth and sixteenth century seemingly established a divine destiny for *Russian* Orthodoxy as the sole remaining, pure form of Christianity left in the world. Therefore, Nikon's efforts to emulate the Greeks not only invited God's displeasure that led to Constantinople's capture, the reforms seemingly placed the Russian Orthodox Church, and the Russian state, as potentially subservient once again to the Greek Orthodox Church. Therefore, for the Old Rite, defense of the pre-Nikonian Church became tantamount to their very understanding of their faith, culture, and society as they believed themselves to be the defenders of *true* Russian Orthodoxy.

The most direct political and cultural explanation for the development of Russia's spiritual identity is that with the fall of Constantinople to the Ottomans in 1453, and the end of the Mongol Yoke in 1480, Russians found themselves as the sole, independent Orthodox Christian state. Over the next decades and centuries, Russians began a process to place themselves within the greater history of Christian spiritual and political history. Grand Prince Ivan III's (the Great) marriage in 1472 to Sophia Palaiologina, the niece of the last Byzantine Emperor Constantine XI, tied Russia's rulers to the Imperial Byzantine bloodline. Given these circumstances, Muscovy, then, needed to define its place and purpose in history. The historian Isabel de Madariaga explains that Sophia's presence introduced the political aura of the Byzantine Empire to Muscovy through insistence on using grand political and court ceremonies emulating Byzantine customs.[9] More importantly, however, de Madariaga sees Sophia's presence as crucial to Russia's political development thanks to Sophia's own insistence that Ivan firmly establish Moscow as the capital of an Orthodox Christian state; de Madariaga even claims that Sophia's influence drove Ivan to end tribute to the Golden Horde.[10]

The Byzantine Empire's collapse, however, played a major role in Russia's efforts to establish a greater sense of its spiritual destiny. As argued by the theologian Father John Meyendorff and the historians Michael Cherniavsky, Dmitri Stremooukhoff, and Gustav Alef, Russia's political and cultural path toward claiming their spiritual destiny began in the events following Constantinople's decision to recognize Roman

Primacy over Christendom at the Council of Florence in 1439 in a desperate bid to save Constantinople from the Ottomans. As word spread throughout the Russian lands about the agreed Union, the Russian Church took its first steps at spiritual independence by outrightly rejecting the Union, forcing clergy who supported papal supremacy to recant their support or face imprisonment. Vasili II, Grand Prince of Moscow, quickly deposed and imprisoned the Metropolitan Isidore of Kiev (Greek by birth) upon his return from the Council in 1441 because of the Metropolitan's role as one of the most ardent supporters of the Union.[11] As both Meyendorff and Cherniavsky argue, the Russians rejected the Union on both political and spiritual grounds. Since the Byzantine Empire seemed doomed to fall to the Turks, the Union only served the political elite in Constantinople; but for the Russians: "The Orthodox faith could not be betrayed for the sake of the questionable and problematic survival of a dying empire."[12]

The Council of Florence therefore serves as a critical moment in the development of Russian spiritual and political ideology. Horrified by the proceedings, one contemporary Russian critic wrote a letter addressing the Byzantine Emperor John VIII Palaeologus, "What have you done? You have exchanged light for darkness; instead of divine law you have received the Latin faith; instead of truth and righteousness, you have loved flattery and falsity."[13] However, the aftermath of Florence placed Russia on its path in establishing its own unique take on its spiritual destiny. With Metropolitan Isadore removed, Grand Prince Vasili demanded that Patriarch Metrophanes of Constantinople appoint a new, *Russian* Metropolitan.[14] However, Metrophanes, a supporter of the Union, declined to act, thereby leaving the Metropolitanate of Kiev vacant for nearly a decade.[15]

More importantly, Constantinople's role in the Union and Russia's rejection of Florence thereby left Russia as the apparent sole defender of the Byzantine legacy and Orthodox Christianity. For Orthodox Russians, Vasili II became "the new Constantine" a god-sent ruler to uphold the purity of their faith.[16] Furthermore, based on Vasili's actions, Russian Orthodoxy could proclaim that "It was the Grand Prince himself who by exposing heresy saved Orthodoxy in Russia; and it was Russia which was the only Orthodox country left in the world [...] the tragedy of Florence became the great triumph of the Grand Prince of Moscow."[17]

Russia's path toward spiritual autonomy therefore took a major step forward on December 5, 1448 when the Russian council of bishops, as instructed by Vasili, elected Iona as Metropolitan of All Russia. Iona's election produced two major consequences. First, Constantinople's inability to respond to Iona's election made *de facto* the Russian Orthodox Church autocephalous. Second, Iona's election firmly established Moscow as the seat of the Russian Orthodox Church by creating the Metropolitanate of Moscow and All Rus', thereby contributing to Muscovy's growing influence and dominance throughout the Russian lands.[18] Russia's refusal to recognize the Union of Florence, therefore, put the Russian state and Church on the path toward establishing their own social and political identity as successors to, rather than disciples of, the Byzantine legacy. For the Russians, Constantinople represented the very source of their understanding of society, religion, and politics. However, by agreeing to the Union of Florence, then, the Greeks appeared, to the Russians, to violate and abandon their own Roman-Byzantine traditions. The Greeks' falling into heresy therefore *required* that the Russian state and Russian Church rise as defenders of Orthodoxy in order to maintain the very foundations of their society.[19]

The Ottoman conquest of Constantinople in 1453 seemingly confirmed God's displeasure with the Greeks' turn toward the heresy of the Union of Florence. In the decades after the fall of Constantinople, a handful of Russian spiritual thinkers soon made concerted efforts to champion Russia's divine destiny as the sole, pure Christian state. One such effort stemmed from the writings of the hegumen of the Eleazarov Monastery near Pskov, Filofei, who is credited with composing two critical works that attempted to define Russia's spiritual and cultural destiny. The first, *The Legend of the White Cowl of Novgorod*, mirrored the fabled *Donation of Constantine*. In Filofei's account, Constantine the Great presented Pope Sylvester with a white cowl as recognition of the Pope's rule over the Christian Church. Eventually the last "Orthodox Pope" foresaw Rome's inevitable fall into heresy and sent the cowl to the Patriarch of Constantinople, who likewise sent the cowl to the bishop of Novgorod before the Greeks fell into heresy at the Council of Florence.[20] The passage of the White Cowl then seemingly legitimized Russia as part of the larger Rome-Constantinople line of succession.

However, Filofei's second work, remains to this day far more notable for it directly lays out the very foundations of what developed to be the Third Rome Doctrine. In a letter to the Grand Prince of Moscow, Vasili III, Filofei proclaims that only the Russian state remains as the one, true bastion of Christendom remaining in the world; he concludes with his now famous statement: "Two Romes have fallen. The third stands firm. There will not be a fourth. No one will replace your Christian tsardom."[21] Felofei's claims seemingly presented a new ideological destiny for Russia, its people, and Russian Orthodoxy to become the final defender of humanity and Orthodox Christendom until the End Times. Under such a concept, Russia's Third Rome both inherited the Roman-Byzantine legacy, and now remained as the last uncorrupted, ideal Christian society. Rome gave to Christendom law, order, and discipline, representing the paternal authority of the Father. Constantinople offered intellectual leadership as it focused its existence on combating heresy and developing an orthodox faith, representing the Logos in the Trinity.[22] Under Filofei's idea, the role of the Russian Orthodox state and its followers then serve as the chosen vessels of the Holy Spirit before the Second Coming.

Through the sixteenth century, Russia continued its efforts to define their own Orthodox spirituality and identity more precisely. One of the most important moments for the sixteenth century Russian Orthodox Church came in 1551 with the *Stoglavy Sobor*, called by Metropolitan Makary. Under the guidance of both Makary and Tsar Ivan IV (the Terrible), the *Stoglav* aimed to establish a uniform Russian Orthodoxy. Specifically, the *Stoglav* sought to standardize liturgical texts and church rituals, respond to the growing debate between the Possessor and Non-Possessor movements regarding monastic land ownership, and even determine the acceptability of certain forms of icon painting.[23]

The sixteenth century continued to see the Russian Orthodox Church's prestige rise in the Orthodox world, eventually culminating with the formation of the Patriarchate of Moscow. The first overtures made for the recognition of a Russian Patriarchate began under Ivan IV as a means to elevate Moscow's standing within both Russia and Christendom. While Ivan's efforts did not bare fruit, under his successor Feodor I, mostly because of the diplomacy and flattery of Boris Godunov (Fyodor's brother-in-law, *de facto* regent, and Ivan's former advisor), Patriarch Jeremias II of Constantinople, while visiting Moscow on a fundraising journey, consented to create the Russian Patriarchate. His decision resulted in the election of Job the Metropolitan of Moscow as the first Russian Patriarch on January 26, 1589.[24]

The combination of the *Stoglav* and the new Patriarchate of Moscow, then, completed the perceived *pure* form of Russian Orthodoxy and set a course for the divine destiny of Russia and its people. Free of the corruption of the Council of Florence and Greek treachery, Russians now held the duty to protect the purity of Russian Orthodoxy and succeed where their Greek predecessors failed. For the Russian religious mind, then, Russian Orthodoxy could remain strong and pure as long as no outside influence corrupted their faith. Any deviation from this Russian Orthodoxy surely meant the onset of the Apocalypse.

The Old Believers' Defense of their Faith

In the century after the *Stoglav*, Russia experienced a period of religious and political turmoil with the collapse of the Rurikid Dynasty and the upheaval of the Time of Troubles. However, the rise of the Romanovs appeared to place Russia back on the path toward spiritual and political stability. However, the mid-seventeenth century witnessed new challenges with the ascension of Nikon to the Russian Patriarchate. Once elected, Nikon's primary goal focused on bringing the Russian Orthodox Church into ritualistic and liturgical conformity with the seventeenth century Greek Church practices. However, with the introduction of Greek rituals and new translations to conform to Greek phrases and spelling, many Russians viewed Nikon's reforms as foreign violations of Russian Orthodoxy. Furthermore, conformity with contemporary Greek Orthodox rituals invalidated any sense of a spiritual destiny for Russia and its people.

For many devout Russians, only by rejecting the reforms could they prevent the corruption of their faith. Soon, Russian clergy and laity split in the *raskol* between Nikon's supporters and those who formed the groups known as the Old Believers, who rejected the reforms as a contradiction and corruption of Russian Orthodoxy, and consequently Russia's divine place in Christendom. For what became the Old Rite movement, the primary disagreements with the Nikonian reforms centered on making the sign of the cross with three fingers rather than two, and editing all Russian liturgical books to conform to the contemporary Greek books, which included significant spelling changes such as the spelling of "Jesus" from *Isus* to *Iisus*.[25] However, while the Old Rite maintained dogmatic conformity with the mainstream Church, the Old Believers now appeared not only as competition to the Russian Church, but also as an alternative culture set to define both Orthodoxy and Russianness itself.

While ultimately adopted, Nikon's first efforts at reform, the Church Council of 1654, saw many members outrightly reject his changes. However, after Nikon removed his most vocal and influential opponent, Bishop Pavel of Kolomna, and the resulting boycott of Pavel's supporters, Nikon replaced the openings on the council with his own supporters and easily gained approval for his reforms.[26] Even then, many clergy and laity refused to abide by the Nikonian reforms. Continued efforts at resistance ultimately forced Nikon to compromise and approve clergy to use the old practices and books if they chose. Ultimately, thanks to receiving so little support for his reforms, and growing tensions with Tsar Alexis, Nikon resigned as Patriarch on July 10, 1658 and imposed a self-exile.[27] To those who refused to accept the reforms, it appeared that Nikon's efforts would fail and Russian Orthodoxy remain free from Greek corruption and the seeming agent of Antichrist, Nikon.[28]

Unfortunately for Nikon's detractors, with the Patriarchate still vacant, Tsar Alexis, looking for a means to strengthen his own control and influence over the Church, approved and then adopted all of the Nikonian reforms in 1666. This action therefore placed anyone who opposed the reforms in violation of both Church and State.[29] Many of the first Old Believers soon changed their view to proclaim Alexis, not Nikon, was the true Antichrist. Some Old Believers even claimed that Alexis demonically possessed Nikon in order to corrupt Russian Orthodoxy.[30] For many in the Old Rite, from this moment forward, the Tsar and Russian State appeared openly in league with the Antichrist. This perceived union led many Old Believers to refuse to pledge their loyalty to the monarch; as a result, they created a continuous point of contention between the Old Rite and state into the twentieth century.[31]

While now considered threats to both Russian Orthodoxy and the Russian State, Old Believers utilized one of their key advantages: their ability to hide in plain sight among the rest of Russian society. In fact, tsarist and church authorities' inability to find a means to identify Old Believers from their own followers not only created issues to target

Old Believers for persecution, but also created historiographical issues in defining and identifying the Old Rite movement. Specifically, state and Church authorities described all Russians who opposed the Nikonian Church Reforms or the Church itself as *raskol'niki*. However, the blanket term for all "schismatics" clearly does not help identify groups or individual Old Believers since the designation of *raskol'niki* included any individuals or groups who protested against the Russian Orthodox Church, such as the *khlysty*, who appeared during the same period as the Old Believers, but remained entirely separate from the Old Rite movement.[32]

Historiographically then, my study follows the thesis of the historians Robert Crummey and Georg Michels that it is important to begin by distinguishing the *staroobriadtsy* from other groups recognized as *raskol'niki.* Most importantly, Old Believers remained dogmatically in conformity with the Russian Orthodox Church. However, while the Old Rite split between varying branches based on ritualistic differences, the Old Rite movement defined itself specifically through the rejection of Patriarch Nikon's reforms.[33]

Since the Old Rite's beginning, historians and theologians debated and interpreted why non-dogmatic reforms created such backlash among those who became Old Believers. To the church scholars Vasilii Andreev, Ivan Nil'skii, and Afanasi Shchapov, the *raskol* was not a religious dispute but instead a social and political protest against the authority of the state and Church. These scholars cite "ignorance" as the primary cause of protest since the *raskol'niki* did not understand that the reforms did not change church doctrine.[34] Along similar lines, Shchapov and Georg Michels argue that early Old Rite leaders protested more to promote their own personal goals and voice their grievances with either the Church or state.[35]

In contrast to the works by Nil'skii, Shchapov, Andreev, and Michels, historians of the Old Rite movement such as Michael Cherniavsky, Robert Crummey, and Serge Zenkovsky argue that religious issues *were* the primary cause guiding the *raskol*. The Old Believers saw any changes to Russian Orthodoxy as corrupting their faith. Ultimately then, my work builds on the arguments put forward by these historians that to the Old Rite, the Nikonian reforms directly risked or invalidated Russia's spiritual purity. The reforms became a true religious issue becacuse Nikon had sought to bring the Russian Church into uniformity with the *contemporary* Greek Orthodox Church. However, to the Russian religious mind, the

Greeks betrayed Orthodoxy at Florence. God's clear abandonment of Greek Orthodoxy came in the eventual sack of Constantinople in 1453. Would not emulating the Greek Church therefore invite God's wrath? Furthermore, for many religious Russians, spelling changes in books or ritualistic changes challenged the Russians' own understanding of the entire Christian Faith. Each of these scholars suggests that rejection of the reforms as a means to uphold Orthodoxy for the sake of the world, Christendom, and Russia, the intentional effort to protect Russian Orthodox purity and thereby the Russian state from corruption developed into the Old Rite movement.[36] Ultimately, such rhetoric by some of the first Old Believers helped attract support for the Old Rite.

Early Old Believers, such as the Archpriest Avvakum, quickly rose to the defense of pre-Nikonian Orthodoxy and Russian spiritual purity. While initially a friend and confidant of Nikon, a rivalry between the two developed based on Avvakum's popularity as the Archpriest even became the primary challenger for the Patriarchate in 1652. The rivalry between Avvakum and Nikon soon extended into the debate over Nikon's reforms with the former quickly becoming a target for persecution once the Tsar officially adopted the reforms. During his second forced exile to Siberia (1669 – 72), Avvakum began work on his *Vita*. Avvakum's work clearly brings out the mindset of the early Old Rite, especially when it betrays his animosity for Nikon and his reforms: "[Nikon] belched forth his venom."[37] Avvakum spares no words in his account of Nikon's abuses. Nikon's ordering those who resisted his authority shaved (considered near heresy at this time for man to shave his beard) and icons weeping foretold of Russia's impending misfortunes for betraying the true faith.[38]

Not surprisingly, members of the mainstream Russian Orthodox Church read the works of Avvakum and other Old Believers and blamed ignorance and superstition in the Old Rite movement for the *raskol*, not the defense of Russian Orthodoxy.[39] For the Russian Church and state, then, any effort to tolerate the Old Rite became unacceptable. Forced conversion or education to reveal the Old Rite's errors became the preferred methods for the Russian Orthodox Church to combat the Old Believers in the immediate aftermath of the church split.[40]

Yet, as argued by other early Old Believers, for the Old Rite, the defense of Orthodox purity became the central pillar in the movement's ideology. Robert Crummy highlights the works of Andrei and Semon

Denisov of the Vyg community and one of the Old Rite's early leaders, Avraami, that envisioned the movement as a defense of the Russia's cultural destiny through the Third Rome Doctrine.[41] As Crummy summarizes Avraami: "The shameful Council of Florence and the subsequent fall of the Byzantine Empire to the Turks demonstrated clearly the price of apostasy. By extension, the Russian church and the princes who guarded it had inherited the mantle of true ecumenical Christianity. In the best-known symbolic statement, Moscow had become the Third and last Rome. [. . .] the Greek Church offered not models to be emulated but cautionary tales of heresy, apostasy, and corruption to be avoided at all costs."[42]

To that point, the historians Donald Ostrowski, Daniel Rowland, and Marshall Poe argue that in the centuries after their break from the Church, while the Russian state never accepted or adopted the Third Rome Doctrine, Old Believers took to invoking a sense of defense for the Third Rome Doctrine in their literature to explain their understanding of their spiritual duty.[43] As Poe argues, tsarist and Church authorities openly disregarded the Third Rome Doctrine: "the doctrine was ignored by secular authorities, who were uninterested in its imperial implications, and it was later banned by clerics, who recognized it as an article of the heretical Old Believer faith. In the eighteenth century, 'Third Rome' survived in Old Believer writings, but it was almost entirely forgotten by mainstream Russian culture."[44] Furthermore, Rowland too acknowledges that tsarist and Church officials showed no effort to adopt the concept of the Third Rome Doctrine: "By the second half of the seventeenth century, [the concept of Moscow the Third Rome] was under attack and by the 1700s was discarded by everyone except the Old Believers, who of course used it to undermine the state rather than strengthen it."[45] Ideas such as the Third Rome Doctrine, then, eventually became a point of contention in which Old Believers, such as those at Rogozhskoe, challenged the very notion of both Russian Orthodoxy and Russian identity and which society truly embodied these parts of Russia's historical narrative.

The Rogozhskoe Old Believers and their Community

Building from this thinking, my work explores how the Rogozhskoe Old Believers in particular fit into the greater historiography that explains how Old Rite communities used their congregations to embody and defend their sense of Russian Orthodoxy purity. Specifically, Old Believers created ideological and physical presentations of their understanding of their own ethics and morals as a counterbalance to the seemingly corrupt world around them.[46] Within this historiography, Old Believer communities understood their own community, faith, identity, culture, morals, and history based on each separate community's experiences throughout Russia's geographic diversity. Therefore, all of these factors influenced Old Rite communities by how they developed their understanding of Russian history and Russian Orthodoxy.

For example, Robert Crummey's work, *Old Believers and the World of Antichrist*, looks at how the Vyg community of priestless Old Believers maintained their community in Russia's northern frontier from the early eighteenth to mid-nineteenth century. As Crummey reveals, the Russian wilderness provided the opportunity for the Vyg Old Believers to exist mostly free from outside interference. The Vyg Old Believers also sought means to emulate the disciplined lifestyle of monastic life, going so far as to organize themselves into two separate "men's" and "women's" settlements.[47] In *Old Believers, Religious Dissent and Gender in Russia*, Irina Paert focuses on priestless Old Believer communities in Saint Petersburg and Moscow from the late eighteenth to mid-nineteenth century as opposed to Old Rite experience in the wilderness, and addresses issues such as marriage and gender among urban Old Believers in their search for spiritual and communal morality.[48]

Scholars of the Old Rite further note the formation of a distinctive Old Believer "culture" based around communities' own sense of ethics and morals that shaped their very notions of faith, history, and even duty. For example, Crummy, using Clifford Geertz's concept of "cultural systems," notes that even while Old Believers and their communities differed across time and experience in Russia, Old Believers still shared many "fundamental" assumptions regarding their understanding of their Orthodoxy and its purpose.[49] Crummy highlights that in early Old Rite literature "Russia guarded the true Christian faith, any other Christian community that differed in belief of practice must have fallen into error;" and that Nikon's reforms "unmistakably implied that Russian Orthodoxy was not fully authentic and that the nation's practice of the faith was flawed."[50] Therefore, defense of Russian Orthodoxy provided the very foundations of any Old Believer community's sense of moral duty.

Similarly, the ethnographer Douglas Rogers explores communal formations in his study on the Old Rite community in Sepych in the Urals. Rogers explores how the community utilizes what he refers to as a "moralizing discourse" in which groups or individuals shaped their understanding of their history and ethnical objectives in an effort to create their ideal moral community.[51] Using such notions, Old Believer congregations then utilized such methods as a means to defend their faith in a world they believed to be corrupt. Morality, ethics, and shared culture all became the only perceived means to defend what they viewed as their incorruptible Russian Orthodoxy.

Such notions place the Rogozhskoe Old Believers and their community into my larger exploration of how Old Believers structured their communities as physical and ideological embodiments of their perceived pure faith. Specifically, I explore how the Rogozhskoe Old Believers utilized the opportunities presented to them to develop their senses of morality and spirituality while maintaining a very active and public presence in what they believed to be a corrupt world. I argue that the Rogozhskoe Old Believers used any opportunity available to them to build on what they viewed as a Holy Moscow to serve as a model community for both the priestly Old Rite and Russian society.

The Rogozhskoe community's efforts to build their pure Old Rite community appear through a number of elements. First, as for all Old Rite communities, the Rogozhskoe Old Believers staunchly defended and maintained their devotion to the pre-Nikonian rituals and liturgical books as the core of their Orthodoxy. However, as part of the priestly branch of the Old Rite, a major distinguishing component of their own faith was the need to maintain an active clergy. To this end, Rogozhskoe quickly became a center, known both to other Old Believers as well as to tsarist authorities, for "runaway" or defrocked Orthodox priests who agreed to conduct services using the pre-Nikonian rituals and liturgical books. However, such practices made Rogozhskoe a primary target for persecution at the hands of tsarist and Church officials. The Rogozhskoe Old Believers then needed to use their influence and resources to their best of their ability to maintain a clergy, even going so far as to create their own. As I describe in Chapters 2 and 3, the Rogozhskoe Old Believers made great efforts not only to maintain a clergy but also to recreate a new Old-Rite Church hierarchy by aiding in the creation of the Belokrinitskaya Hierarchy in the mid-nineteenth century. As my study reveals, maintaining some tie to a clergy became a critical component for the Rogozhskoe Old Believers' own understanding of the Old Rite and community. Therefore, one of the defining characteristics of the Rogozhskoe Old Believer's own construct of a Holy Moscow was the community's need for an Old Rite clerical hierarchy.

Second, as an Old Rite community, the Rogozhskoe Old Believers presented their community as their defense of *pure* Russian Orthodoxy and its divine historical purpose. Particularly toward the end of the Imperial Era, as argued by some of the more prominent Rogozhskoe members, such as Vladimir Riabushinskii, the community understood the Old Rite as a faith that defended Russian history and tradition against the incursions of Western and other foreign corruptions. In that regard, Rogozhskoe's wealthy merchants in particular viewed their morality as superior to their European and Westernized Russian counterparts because of their emphasis on the use of capital and wealth for charity over self-indulgence. For the Rogozhskoe Old Believers then, Christian values such as charity, patronage, and love for Russian tradition became the community's attempt both to restore and to maintain their idealized Orthodox community.

As a key example, some of Rogozhskoe's prominent members such as Vladimir Riabushinskii, Ivan Kirillov, and Vasili Senatov, writing in the late nineteenth and early twentieth century, argued that the Old Rite embodied the cultural and historical ideals of the Third Rome Doctrine. Stressing that the Old Rite remained the sole embodiment of not only the Third Rome Doctrine, but of Russian cultural and national identity as well, these authors argued that Nikon's efforts and Tsar Alexis's adoption of the reforms both corrupted Russian Orthodoxy and completely negated its historical destiny.[52] Riabushinskii further stresses the Old Rite's duty to preserve Orthodoxy and Russianness after Nikon's reform took effect.

> As to the reasons behind Nikon's "greekification" one only needs to look at his character – it was his love of power [. . .] the old prayer books were declared corrupt, evil, full of errors, clearly concluding for the people: All of the Russian Church Hierarchs of the previous centuries, including the most famous, respected,

> even the most beloved saints, have obviously been all, without exception, either heretics or ignorant. [...] Therefore, for the enlightenment of the Russian spirit one must understand the meaning of the Old Believers and need to consider what role they played in the history of Russian culture [...] for it is the Old Believers, and their religious phenomenon, that are most acquainted with the history of this spiritual feeling in Russia, especially in the period from the late seventeenth century to the present day, and therefore it becomes all the more important to gain a proper understanding of Russian Orthodoxy, and indeed Russian reality.[53]

In their own writings, Kirillov and Senatov use phrases such as "national mourning" and "oppression of the Russian idea" to describe the Nikonian Reforms' effects on Russia's spiritual destiny.[54] For the Rogozhskoe Old Believers, pre-Nikonian Russian Orthodoxy was the *true* embodiment of Russianness. This Orthodoxy therefore distinguished itself and Russia from its Western counterparts through maintaining a strict devotion to their understanding of Christian piety and morality.

For the Rogozhskoe Old Believers, one of the most physical and ideological representations of this morality became the community's ties to charity. Rogozhskoe's charitable efforts, in fact, directly challenged and even surpassed state and Russian Orthodox Church efforts to provide for Moscow's sick and impoverished. Ultimately, the Rogozhskoe Old Believers used charity as a means to present their community as the true embodiment of Orthodox morality in a world of corruption. As described in Chapters 1, 3, and 4, particularly among Rogozhskoe's members of the merchantry, the entire community shared a common ideology that one of God's greatest gifts is love and charity.[55] For example, Timofei Prokhorov, of the eponymous cotton-manufacturing dynasty, wrote in the early nineteenth century: "wealth is bad and pure evil;" he argued that wealth often blinded the wealthy from both God and their Christian duty to provide for the less fortunate.[56] As the Rogozhskoe historian, Vladimir Makarov, argued in the early twentieth century, charity provided the means by which the Rogozhskoe Old Believers clearly distanced themselves from Russia's westernized nobility and directly challenged what they viewed as Western corruptions and abuse in the use of capital for exploitation.[57] Vladimir Riabushinskii, for example, blamed Peter the Great's Westernization for introducing a foreign culture and lack of morals to the Russian nobility that favored individual social or political advancement more on a family's wealth and property than on their contribution to Russian society.[58]

Finally, the underlying principle of my study demonstrates that a critical component in the Rogozhskoe Old Believer's efforts in building their idealized community relied on their adaptability. Specifically, the Rogozhskoe Old Believers used any and every opportunity available to them to adapt themselves and the Rogozhskoe Cemetery physically, spiritually, socially, and economically as both a part of the Old Rite and the changing world of Imperial Russia. To this end, one of Rogozhskoe's most important traits lay in the community's ability to maintain, predominately through their use of communal space and the public sphere, their devotion to the Old Rite while they actively participated in Moscow and Imperial Russian society.[59] This ability, in fact, places the Rogozhskoe Old Believers, into a larger historical paradox numerous historians of the Old Rite note in their works: Old Believers became what Irina Paert refers to as "agents of modernity." Specifically, that while the Old Rite movement presented itself as a defense of Russian Orthodoxy and Russian cultural purity, communities such as Rogozhskoe and its members, took on leading roles as many of Russia's earliest and successful entrepreneurs, industrialists, and patrons of the arts.[60]

Roy Robson explores how Old Rite communities in Late Tsarist Russia utilized sacred spaces to reflect their duality of championing "traditional" Russia while actively participating in Russia's rapid transformation during this period. Robson argues that in the period following the *ukaz* on religious toleration in 1905, "[Old Believers] sought to integrate their own views with the emerging modern society, culture, and politics of the period."[61] In regard to the period prior to 1905, Robson continues: "In legislating how the exterior of an Old Believer temple had to appear but ignoring the interior, previous centuries of imperial law had fostered a dichotomous relationship between the outside of an Old Believer structure and its inside design. This phenomenon created a curious aspect of Old Believer buildings – while tradition mandated a strict interpretation of liturgical space indoors, the outside of Old Believer buildings varied in light of legal problems, local conditions, and regional aesthetic."[62]

My work further argues that the Rogozhskoe Old Believers exemplified the pattern Robson describes as they continually evolved their spiritual ideology and physical structures to reflect the societal changes around them. Chapters 3 and 4 in particular focus on the rapid changes the Rogozhskoe community undertook in relation to their physical and sacred spaces in efforts to place their Holy Moscow within contemporary Russian society. Chapter 3, for example, focuses on how the Rogozhskoe Old Believers attempted to redefine their sacred spaces following the government's forced closure of the community's altars in 1856. The second half of the nineteenth century challenged Rogozhskoe's ability to physically use their sacred spaces or present them as models of their community to the outside world. Therefore, the Rogozhskoe Old Believers saw their struggle to reclaim their Holy Spaces as integral to their understanding of their duty to uphold a purer Russian Orthodoxy while at the same time to display their community as loyal to the tsarist state in this period of turmoil. My work therefore presents the idea that the Rogozhskoe Old Believers' concepts of their community was an ever evolving idea that preserved their devotion to the Old Rite, but allowed the community to remain an active part of Moscow and the Russian Empire.

Finally, while adaption and opportunism shaped the Rogozhskoe Old Believers' sense of morality for their community, for many of Rogozhskoe's prominent business and merchant families, this same morality became the very heart of their approach to their businesses and their wealth–both existed for the betterment of society as a whole. Many historical studies of families such as the Morozovs, Rakhmanovs, and Riabushinskiis either overlook or outrightly dismiss how these families reflected the values of the Rogozhskoe community.[63] Historians such as William Blackwell and Jo Ann Ruckman, in fact, present the idea that some Old Rite individuals intentionally broke away from their communal traditions in order to become leaders of Russian capitalism. However, a major argument in Chapters 3 and 4 maintains that in actuality, these families fully embraced their role as community leaders and even championed themselves as the public embodiment of the Rogozhskoe Old Believers' ideals of a proper Christian society and Russia's cultural destiny.

Ultimately for the Rogozhskoe Old Believers, their identity and ideology was shaped directly by their shared experiences as a community. This phenomenon, then, places Rogozhskoe into the larger historiography that looks at how religious minorities in Imperial Russia organized themselves not only for survival, but to shape their idealized society. For example, Crummey, Paert, and Robson all explain how community formation shaped Old Believer identity and their understanding of their place within the Old Rite, Russia, and Christianity. Robson, for example, argues that Old Believers' ability to establish communities that shaped and governed social and religious affairs allowed these same communities to respond more easily to the changing world around them.[64] Crummey, too, posits that because the Old Rite was not recognized by the state, "[Old Believer communities] governed their own affairs independent of any hierarchical structure or national organization."[65] Crummey further argues that such independence allowed Old Believers to create communities founded on parish, or secular, autonomy to shape and define their social and religious affairs. Furthermore, such autonomy allowed Old Rite communities to organize themselves as their vision for defense of the Old Rite while they actively participated in Imperial Russian society, economics, and culture.[66]

Community formation especially played a critical role for religious minorities throughout the Russian Empire. Rogozhskoe firmly fits into this larger narrative of a minority community who needed to define their self-identity and their relationship with state and Church authorities. In particular, Christian minorities, including Old Believers, who did not belong to the Russian Orthodox Church, faced some level of persecution throughout the tsarist period. However, these minority groups formed communities not only to maintain their faith, but also to form their own narratives with their own interactions with the tsarist state. In some instances, the state encouraged or forced migration of particular religious groups to specific regions of the empire. The historian Nicholas Breyfogle, uses his work *Heretics and Colonizers*, to explore how groups such as the Dukhobors, Molokans, and Subbotniks forged communities designed to preserve their unique views of Christian morality and spirituality while becoming a key colonizing force in Transcaucasia for Imperial Russia in the nineteenth century.[67] As Breyfogle reveals, while distinctly different in terms of ideology and ritual, each group defined itself in communal terms, for each believed itself to uphold "the true Christian faith." However, for the tsarist authorities, these same groups, even while targeted for persecution, ultimately became a potential "Russifying" colonizing force for what they viewed as a heretical state.[68]

The historians Heather Coleman and Sergei Zhuk also focus on the role community identity formation played in religious groups such as the Russian Baptists, the Shalaputs, and Stundists. In comparison to the Old Rite and other Russian religious minority sects, as Protestant sects, these groups faced significant challenges: in particular how to integrate into Russian society as members of an extremely *western* religious tradition. Coleman argues that Baptist communities emphasized an ideal that "one could be at once Russian and non-Orthodox and, later, both Baptists and socialist."[69] As both Coleman and Zhuk note, a key adaptation among Protestant communities promoted an increased notion of spiritual fulfillment through evangelization and proselytism in response to the continuous social and political turmoil in the late Imperial Era.[70]

Conversely, Vera Shevzov reveals that Russian Orthodox communities during the Late Tsarist Period also wished to define their spirituality and self-identity more accurately. In her work, *Russian Orthodoxy on the Eve of Revolution*, Shevzov explains how Orthodox communities attempted to maintain their "sacred community" in the face of Russia's social and political turmoil from 1861 to 1917.[71] Shevzov argues that Russian Orthodox laity were not "silent observers" to the changes around them; they challenged long held definitions and understanding of the "Orthodox community" and the Church's authority over their spirituality and how they expressed their faith.[72]

As previous historical works revealed then, many religious communities throughout the Russian Empire's vast territory used their faith as a critical component in the formation of their own ideal community. As my work reveals, while the Rogozhskoe Old Believers identified with the larger Old Rite movement, which viewed itself as the one pure form of Russian Orthodoxy, the community desired to recreate their understanding of the spiritual and physical Third Rome Doctrine. Ultimately then, I place Rogozhskoe Cemetery and community into this larger historical story in which Imperial Russia's societal and political struggles inspired many communities to turn to their faith to shape their self-identity and govern their public interactions. In the case of the

Rogozhskoe Old Believers, this turn to their faith culminated in their effort to establish their community as an idealized Holy Moscow, designed to uphold Old Rite and serve as a moral example for all Russian society.

A Note on Sources

In this work I refer to a wide range of sources, the most important of which is the Rogozhskoe Cemetery archives housed in the Russian State Library. Confiscated by Soviet authorities in 1923 from the Rogozhskoe Cemetery community, this extensive collection holds numerous private documents from the Rogozhskoe community and the Archbishop of Moscow and All Rus' of the Belokrinitskaya Hierarchy. These documents include financial records, collection records of icons and other relics, telegrams, letters, donations, census records for the community's almshouse, personal accounts of community meetings and events, and other materials from the second quarter of the nineteenth century to the early 1920s. Other archival materials from the Moscow Secret Committee on Old Believers held in the Russian State Archive of Early Acts, which contains communications, inquiries, and meeting notes by tsarist and Russian Orthodox Church officials in Moscow regarding the activities of the Rogozhskoe Old Believers in the second quarter of the nineteenth century, also makes up a large portion of the materials I used in my work.

This study also uses collections of published documents collected from Rogozhskoe Cemetery by nineteenth century Russian historians and religious scholars, most notably Nikolai Subbotin and Nikolai Popov. This work also incorporates the personal publications of Rogozhskoe individuals such as Vladimir Riabushinskii as well as other Old Believer publications such as *Tserkov'* and *Slovo Tserkvi*, journals printed and owned by Rogozhskoe members. *Tserkov'* and *Slovo Tserkvi* serve as the centerpiece in the history of Moscow Old Rite publishing because Rogozhskoe served as a printing and distribution center for these journals, in which their published articles regularly provided an extensive look at the many events and concerns that shaped Rogozhskoe and its community. A final source of notably rare published Old Believer documents, books, and materials that benefitted my research are held in the Pimen Sofronov Collection at the Hilandar Research Library at Ohio State University.

Use of these sources creates an internal look at how the Rogozhskoe Old Believers developed their community and identity in their conflicts with the state and Church as authorities responded to the Rogozhskoe Old Believers' efforts to build and define their community. Ultimately then, these documents provide a greater understanding of how the Rogozhskoe Old Believers not only defined themselves but also marked out their place in the Russian Empire and Christianity, in response to political, social, economic, and cultural changes in Imperial Russia.

CHAPTER 1

OLD BELIEVERS AND THE OPPORTUNITIES OF IMPERIAL RUSSIA

Introduction

In the century following the *raskol*, the Old Rite movement spread throughout the Russian Empire, with many Old Believers hoping to find refuge from persecution in Russia's vast wilderness. However, other Old Believers remained in some of Russia's major cities, primarily because of the significant number of merchants who adhered to the Old Rite and desired to maintain their family businesses. Moscow, in particular, remained home for many Old Believers of both the priestly and priestless sects with many prominent Moscow merchants and shopkeepers as part of their community. By the mid-eighteenth century, many Moscow Old Believers continued to flourish thanks to the state's increased efforts since the time of Peter the Great to utilize the many economic niches Old Rite members claimed, such as their influence among urban merchants.

During this period, the Moscow Old Believers found themselves in a particularly advantageous position in a new era of opportunity beginning with the reigns of Peter III and Catherine the Great. While Peter's reign remained brief before his overthrow by Catherine, both attempted to institute the first efforts of what could be called minor toleration of the Old Rite. This "toleration" more reflected Catherine's larger efforts to introduce some social reform as part of her Enlightened Despotism. In any case, Old Believers did find new opportunities to express themselves and organize their communities more freely.

The Moscow Old Believers utilized the new opportunities of Catherine's early reign to their advantage to expand their influence. However, the devastation of the Moscow Plague of 1770–1 provided the Moscow Old Believers the first true opportunity to establish their own communities that embodied their Old Rite ideals. In an effort to provide care for both Old Believers and other victims of the plague, Moscow Old Believers petitioned tsarist authorities for approval to establish gated, quarantined communities to prevent the further spread of plague and to provide burials for their community members. The petitioners offered to create and administer medical facilities and supervise quarantines for victims of the plague, both healthy and sick; and most important, they maintained religious structures and cemeteries to ensure that Old Believer victims received proper burial services in the Old Rites. Approved by tsarist authorities in Saint Petersburg, the Moscow Old Believers received permission to build two communal religious complexes, Rogozhskoe Cemetery for priestly Old Believers and Preobrazhenskoe Cemetery for the priestless Old Believers. Using this major opportunity, the Rogozhskoe Old Believers built their ideal spiritual and physical manifestation of an Old Rite community devoted entirely to their ideological worldview.[1]

The Rogozhskoe Old Believers' early history witnessed two key moments that influenced the physical and ideological understanding of their new Holy Moscow. The first was the community's founding in the devastating Moscow plague in 1771. In the aftermath of the plague, the Rogozhskoe Old Believers quickly established themselves as a successful and well-respected community in Moscow, in the Old Rite throughout the empire, and even with authorities back in Saint Petersburg. In the decades that followed, the Rogozhskoe Old Believers quickly set out to make Rogozhskoe Cemetery a physical embodiment of their idealized Orthodox society and even challenged the many restrictions in place against the Old Rite.

Rogozhskoe's second critical moment arose in the aftermath of Moscow's destruction at the hands of Napoleon's invasion and the Moscow Fire of 1812. Many opportunities for spiritual and ideological growth appeared for Rogozhskoe Cemetery, which quickly gained renown for Rogozhskoe's charitable efforts to help rebuild the city and reestablish normal commerce in the region. The opportunities in this period allowed Rogozhskoe to flourish. Rogozhskoe earned even more respect with Moscow and tsarist authorities alike as a model community; however, at the same time its sterling reputation inspired severe jealousy in those who viewed the community's success as a direct threat to the mainstream Russian Orthodox Church.

Opportunity Arises

The greatest advantage and opportunity for the Old Rite by the early eighteenth century was that the movement made up a significant, but ultimately unknown, percentage of Russia's population.[2] The fact that the tsarist state continuously struggled to find a means to distinguish Old Believers from "acceptable" Russian society ultimately became the primary means of survival for the movement. While targeted for persecution, many Old Believers utilized two effective methods to escape detection and defend their faith. The first option for Old Believers was to escape into Russia's vast wilderness and live on the periphery of the empire, out of the reach of state and Church intervention. The second option for Old Believers was to hide in plain sight and present themselves officially as members of the Russian Orthodox Church, while they observed the Old Rite in the privacy of their homes and communities. Both options presented the Old Believers with the opportunity to practice their faith with minimal threat from the state or Church authorities, as long as they remained undiscovered. Yet in the case of some Moscow priestly and priestless Old Believers, the urbaites among them chose to remain visible as merchants, shopkeepers, and textile manufacturers; consequently they became one of the most public and successful populations of Old Believers throughout Russia.

The history of the Rogozhskoe Old Believers and their interactions with the Russian state places them prominently in the larger history of the relationship between religious minorities and the tsarist state. Old Believers comprised only one group living within the multi-ethnic, multi-confessional Russian Empire, in which tsarist authorities willingly allowed minorities to contribute to the benefit of the empire.[3] Often historians, other scholars, and analysts in other disciplines portrayed tsarist Russia as staunchly unmoving and oppressive toward minority groups. While various periods in Russian history did witness such oppression, it does not make up the whole picture. Specifically, when placing the interaction between the Old Rite and Tsarist Russia into the larger history of other European states' approaches toward Christian minorities, Tsarist Russia's flexibility toward the Old Rite surprisingly sets this interplay apart from some of the far more intolerant approaches to religious dissent in Western Europe in the Early Modern Era.

One such comparative example appears in Catholic France's approach toward the Huguenots, by far one of the least accommodating interactions between a state and a Christian minority group in the aftermath of the Protestant Reformation. Like the Old Rite in Russia a century later, the Huguenots attracted followers from all levels of French society for various religious and political reasons. However, because of their faith, the Huguenot minority found themselves brutally targeted by state authorities and the Catholic population. Unlike the Old Believers in Russia, however, the Huguenots and French Catholics could not establish a meaningful, flexible coexistence. Rather, as both sides claimed to be the sole path toward God's salvation, violence or outright extermination became the sole means for either Catholics or Huguenots to define their understanding of divine truth.[4]

Like the Old Rite, Huguenotism claimed to represent the one, true Christian faith. However, in the French historical context, the Huguenots became distinctly different from mainstream Catholic French society; whereas the Old Rite still presented itself as part of Russian society. The French Catholic state's inability to accept religious pluralism thereby required an extermination of Huguenotism. To Catholic France, toleration for the Huguenots became synonymous with weakness.[5] Inability to accept a duality of French culture and society thereby encouraged French Catholics across all classes to view any toleration of the Huguenots as undermining France itself regardless of Huguenots potential economic and social influences.[6] Louis XIV's revocation of the Edict of Nantes in 1685 in favor of the Edict of Fontainebleau illegalized Protestantism, and thus cemented France's approach to religious pluralism. Huguenots therefore only had the options to accept conversion or face punishment at the hands of the state; consequently many Huguenots sought asylum outside of France.[7]

While Tsarist Russia did persecute and punish religious dissent, particularly toward Orthodox dissenters like the Old Believers,

Russia's ultimate goals with their approach toward religious policies appear more flexible by comparison witih policies throughout Western Europe. Over the course of the eighteenth century, the Russian Empire took a particularly "tolerable" approach toward the many religious minorities out of the "imperatives of empire building."[8] Therefore, although religious minorities' conversion to Russian Orthodoxy remained the preferred goal for tsarist and Church officials alike, authorities adapted their policies to allow minorities to contribute to the state economically and socially and at the same time maintain their traditional faith.

This particular approach of the state to interaction with the Old Rite began under Peter the Great and his model of absolutism. Peter broke with many of his predecessors' traditions, among them his view of religious matters, both in his personal spirituality as well as in his approach to the Russian Orthodox Church. In the Russian mindset, as previously seen in Vasili II's rejection of the Council of Florence, the position of the Tsar embodied the spirituality of the entire people and required the Tsar to be the first defender of Orthodoxy. However, Peter shattered the perception of the Tsar's "natural piety," in his many seemingly questionable actions; for example, smoking, his favoritism toward foreign customs and cultures, and most notably the well-known frivolous acts he committed with his "All Drunken Council of Fools and Jesters."[9] Peter's debauchery not only encouraged the rise of many enemies throughout Russia, but also encouraged critics, such as the Old Believers, to proclaim Peter as the Antichrist.

The Russian Orthodox Church counted itself among Peter's detractors, viewing Peter's antics with concern as he criticized the Church as an entity based on superstition. Presumably an Orthodox believer, Peter chose to approach religion with more rationalism than his predecessors.[10] More specifically, Peter saw the Orthodox Church as a compliant tool in his empire and under his rule as Tsar. Ultimately, Peter's creation of the Most Holy Synod in 1721 firmly placed the Russian Orthodox Church under state control. Peter's efforts officially ended the office of Patriarch of Moscow, which remained vacant until 1917; thus he made the Church completely subservient to the State.[11] By making the Church a tool of state authority rather than allowing it to remain a completely autonomous entity, Peter created the groundwork for a more flexible relationship between religious minorities and the state, whose economic and social priorities now took precedent over religious conformity.

Beginning with Peter the Great, and throughout the first half of the eighteenth century, authorities enacted laws both to identify Old Believers and to make their devotion to the Old Rite profitable to the state. The most well-known legislation targeting Old Believers came from Peter's infamous beard taxes, dress taxes, and double poll tax.[12] This policy toward the Old Rite served two purposes: create legislation to identify Old Believers based on their adherence to traditional Russian culture, and to use their devotion to their faith to bring in new sources of revenue for Peter's state. From Peter's efforts, the state saw such legislation as only beneficial. Either, Old Believers provided taxes for the state, or hopefully convert to the Russian Orthodox Church and abandon the Old Rite to avoid taxation.

However, Peter's legislation faced immediate problems. The most notable issue lay in the fact that Old Believers remained ardent adherents to traditional Russian culture, particularly in appearance and dress. With no distinguishing physical features to separate Old Believers from the majority of Russia's peasant and commoner population, Old Believers could often escape targeting under the new legislation. Thanks to their ability to hide in plain sight, Peter's taxes could never work as intended since most Old Believers simply blended in with the dominant Russian peasant culture.

The primary target, then, for legislation such as Peter's became the most visible bastions of the Old Rite, Old Believer merchants and communities in urban and production centers. However, even without the ability to camouflage themselves among the rest of Russia's population, wealthy Old Rite families and communities could often circumvent taxation and any other restrictions placed on them. In particular, one of the most successful and easiest methods, bribery of state and Church officials, became common to avoid registration for things such as the double tax.[13] Yet tsarist Russia proved flexible in its approach to Old Rite communities if they could contribute, primarily economically, to the state. For example, in order to encourage increased economic growth with mining of raw materials, increased production of manufactured goods, and creation of means to trade, tsarist authorities and some Old Believers established mutually beneficial relationships. Two such examples of this symbiosis in practice can clearly be found in the case of the Vyg Old Believer community and the special treatment for the Demidov metallurgical empire in the Urals, which played a critical role in Russian iron production.[14]

Because of this new approach, and even while identified as religious dissenters, Old Believers used these opportunities to maintain and expand their businesses, trades, and industries throughout the Russian Empire. Moscow in particular benefited from the relaxed approach toward the Old Rite. The economic foundations of Old Rite communities in Moscow stretched back to the *raskol* and into the early eighteenth century. For example, many members of the Moscow *Streltsy* regiments belonged to the Old Rite and maintained shops or trades while not on campaign.[15] Many Moscow Old Believer families owned shops, worked alongside other Old Believers in various trades, or belonged to the Moscow merchantry.[16] Peter's more flexible approach to the Old Rite in the early eighteenth century only encouraged more Old Believers to migrate to Moscow throughout the century for new economic opportunities, and many benefited from a favorable relationship with the Russian state because of their economic influence. Already holding many important business and personal relationships with city and state authorities, many of these Old Believers eventually became the founders of the future Rogozhskoe Cemetery.

The Old Rite however, was not the sole minority group to benefit from some form of legal flexibility with the Russian state. Prior to the schism, the mid-sixteenth century conquest of Tatar lands along the Volga River brought in many Muslim subjects and placed Orthodoxy and Islam into direct contact in the Russian state. Using "pragmatic flexibility," the Russian state cooperated with Muslim elites, to whom they guaranteed privileges in return for promises of military duty and economic stability in their regions.[17] Most critical for the Russian state, Volga Tatars nearly exclusively controlled trade along the Volga River.[18] Ultimately, because of their role in Volga trade, as well as significant control over regional businesses in honey and beeswax production, the Volga Tatars became major contributors to Russia's international trade as English and Dutch traders to Persia utilized the trade routes through Russia, in order to circumvent the Ottoman Empire.[19]

Similar relationships developed between the Russian state and other minority communities throughout the eighteenth and nineteenth centuries as specific groups contributed in different sectors of Russia's economy.[20] Like the Old Believer communities such as Vyg in the North, many ethnic and religious groups found opportunities to maintain and grow their preexisting businesses, trades, and industries since the Russian state desired to maintain economic stability in these regions. For example, the incorporation of Polish and Ukrainian lands witnessed Polish, but especially Jewish, merchants and entrepreneurs becoming major influences in the Imperial Russian economy. With such preferential treatment, Jewish merchants controlled roughly 30 per cent of the textile industry throughout Ukraine by the 1830s.[21] This economic advantage under Imperial Russia contributed to the Jewish merchants' ability to dominate commerce within the Pale of Settlement and thereby strengthen trade among the contiguous countries of Russia, Germany, and Austria.[22]

The Russian Empire's approach toward religious and even ethnic minorities thereby allowed specific groups to find opportunities to maintain their faith as well as flourish socially and economically through a symbiotic relationship with the Russian State. The flexibility of the Russian secular authorities toward select groups such as the Old Believers, Tatars, and Jewish merchants allowed these groups to contribute to Russia's economic development; at the same time they did not compromise their own cultural loyalties and values. Such precedent thereby provided the priestly Moscow Old Believers the eventual opportunity to nurture Rogozhskoe Cemetery's social and economic success.

The Conflict over Old Believer Identity

While targeted persecution remained part of the narrative in the relationship between tsarist authorities and the Old Rite, selective flexibility still provided numerous opportunities for Old Rite communities to thrive. However, the most important factor that shaped interactions between tsarist Russia and the Old Rite became the effort to control the very definitions of Old Believer identity. Since the first years of the split, the State and Church in particular, as well as Old Believers themselves, needed a means to best identify Old Rite adherents. In order to do so, both sides attempted to answer a number of questions, specially: who are the Old Believers? How do Old Believers fit into Russian society? How do Old Believers fit into the larger Orthodox and Christian world? In attempting to answer these questions, both Old Believers and authorities often arrived at conflicting conclusions about the characteristics of the Old Rite and its followers.

In terms of cultural self-identity, Old Believers championed themselves as ardent defenders and examples of traditional Russian culture. Spiritually, however, Old Believers themselves could not provide a universal definition of "*staroobriadtsy*." Even within the larger branches of the priestly and priestless groups, Old Believers often held many different interpretations of their own faith, as well as their place in the world. Individual Old Believer communities, such as the priestless congregations founded in Vyg and the Moscow Preobrazhenskoe Cemetery, as well as priestly denominations such as Rogozhskoe Cemetery, defined their own understanding of their place in Russia and Christendom based on how their own unique needs and settings changed over time.[23]

In the broadest sense, the only common identifying characteristic of the Old Rite remained that it formed as a direct response to and rejection of the liturgical and ritualistic changes introduced by Patriarch Nikon. Individual Old Believer groups, or *soglasie*, held varying beliefs and understandings of what it meant to be an "Old Believer." However, by far the most important factor in Old Rite self-identity is that the vast majority of Old Believers, regardless of sect, recognized one another as members of the Old Rite owing to their mutual rejection of the Nikonian Reforms and their shared persecution under state and Church authorities.[24]

A good example of this shared identity defines the often-cordial relationship between members of the priestless Preobrazhenskoe Cemetery and priestly Rogozhskoe Cemetery in Moscow. While divided over the issue of a clerical hierarchy, the members of both sects held much in common: in particular, ties to the Moscow merchantry and similar restrictions placed on the communities by the tsarist government.[25] Following the tsarist authorities' forced closure of the Rogozhskoe temples in the mid-nineteenth century, the bonds between these two differing Old Rite communities tightened as the Preobrazhenskoe Old Believers allowed the Rogozhskoe community to pray in their chapels on holidays and other special occasions.[26]

In the minds of all Old Believers, only they maintained the original purity of the Orthodox Church against what they viewed as "Western" corruptions of Russian Orthodoxy. Within this mindset, Old Believers not only placed themselves against the mainstream Russian Orthodox Church, but also instituted a culture and practice of resistance to the secular, tsarist authorities who continually adopted more and more aspects of western culture after Peter the Great's introduction of Westernization. For many Old Believers, they now represented the sole defenders of true *Russian* culture and identity as well. Therefore, in the most general of definitions, while all Old Believers identified themselves as part of Russian culture, they remained outside of mainstream society as targets of spiritual and civil oppression.

While Old Believers at least could identify with one another based on some common characteristics, conversely the tsarist and church leaders regularly struggled to determine how to identify, and thereby restrict, the Old Rite movement throughout the eighteenth and nineteenth centuries. In terms of the State and Church's first efforts to identify Old Believers as *raskol'niki*, schismatics, the term ultimately incorporated anyone who did not follow the proper Orthodox belief, or *pravoverie*.[27] Even this definition proved problematic because the State and Church also struggled to identify their own understanding of *pravoverie*; such confusion ultimately exacerbated the authorities' problem of identifying the difference between misguided members of the Orthodox Church, religious groups that had no connection to the events of the *raskol*, and the Old Rite believers.

In the tsarist state's opinion, Old Believers refused to follow the Russian Orthodox Church out of ignorance and thereby required targeted education and encouragement to return to the mainstream church.[28] The problem then became recognizing the best method of ending the *raskol* and bringing Old Believers back into the state-supported church. Therefore, tsarist and church officials needed to determine exactly who belonged to the Old Rite and how many lived in the Russian Empire. As a result, the Russian state attempted to define both the "norm" and what was "irregular" for Russian society and Orthodoxy, but also influenced the definition of the "self" dissenter populations.[29] Such forced definitions naturally led to a point of contention between the Old Rite and the State itself and only exacerbated the conflicts between them since Old Believers' self-identity now grew out of rejection of the "official" identifying language.[30]

However, Russia's own vast Empire, as well as the fact that Old Believers remained indistinguishable physically and socially from traditional Russian culture, provided numerous opportunities for Old Believers either to escape persecution or to disguise themselves among the general population. These factors ensured that state categorization and attempts at identifying *raskol'niki*, failed throughout the eighteenth century. This predicament made it nearly impossible for the State to enforce legislation, such as the "double-tax" and "beard tax," which were designed specifically to identify, persecute, and ultimately encourage Old Believers to rejoin the Russian Orthodox Church.[31] Despite legislation enacted by Empress Anne in 1735 that required all Old Believers to attend confession once each year to register as Old Believers and pay all necessary taxes, many Old Believers simply presented themselves as members of the mainstream Church to avoid both registration and taxation.[32] The inability to force an identity on the Old Rite ultimately made many members of the movement impossible to target for persecution. Therefore, the "invisible character" of the Old Rite created significant concern among State and Church authorities.[33]

As the eighteenth century progressed, tsarist authorities not only attempted to understand the Old Rite, but accepted it as a permanent fixture in the Russian Empire; albeit a fixture that still required some state intervention and control. One such effort began with the onset of a more moderate approach toward governing Russia's vast, multi-confessional state during the reigns of Peter III and Catherine II. Believing superstition – not political, civil, or religious dissent – to be the cause of the *raskol*, in her "graciousness" Catherine ended the policy of the double tax and the use of the term *raskol'niki* to classify Old Believers as part of her policy of religious toleration.[34] After removing the term *raskol'nik*, which Old Believers saw as derogatory, tsarist authorities used *staroobriadtsy*, Old Ritualists, to describe followers of the Old Rite movement. Ultimately, the new definition forced the State to be even more precise in its own designation of who belonged to this category of Old Believer, rather than to other unofficial Christian factions throughout the Russian Empire.[35]

However, even with the opportunities provided by Catherine's toleration, the relationship between Old Believers and Imperial Russia still witnessed points of conflict regarding Old Rite loyalty and identity. For example, the outbreak of the Pugachev Rebellion in the Urals from 1773–4 renewed suspicions about Old Believer loyalty. In the immediate aftermath of what became "the most prolonged, widespread, and destructive uprising against an indigenous Old Regime prior to 1789,"[36] Catherine remained convinced that Pugachev's success came from an extensive conspiracy, possibly with cooperation from the Old Rite. In fact, Pugachev not only attracted Old Believers to his following, but was also rumored to be an Old Believer himself; Catherine herself concluded that, "he surely corresponds with schismatics in Moscow, but their names are unknown."[37] While authorities never definitively tied the Old Rite to the Pugachev Rebellion, even after extensive interrogation of Pugachev and his followers, the event revealed that the tsarist state still feared the unknown abilities and presence of the Old Rite in Russia.

A major challenge for Catherinian Russia ultimately then remained the same that faced Peter the Great: how to encourage Old Believers to contribute to the stability of the state. Under the weight of this persistent enigma, Catherinian Russia witnessed the next evolution in tsarist efforts to define and identify the Old Rite. Following Catherine's example of a more moderate approach toward the Old Rite, bishops within the Russian Orthodox Church determined to reach out to the Old Believers in order to bring them back into communion with the dominant Church hierarchy rather than attempt to define the Old Rite as a community outside of the accepted Russian Orthodox Church. As a result the first attempt to create a state-approved Old Rite, *Edinoverie*, or "Unity in Faith," came into being.

As both a term and as a movement, *Edinoverie* recognized that while Old Believers and the Post-Nikonian Church varied primarily in the practice of rituals, they shared the same faith and dogmas. However, the very concept of "*Edinoverie*" speaks to the larger historical experience of Russian Orthodoxy throughout its existence. The Russian Orthodox Church had been anything but a monolithic faith; that is, from its inception, Russian Orthodoxy existed in a state of *Edinoverie* with itself.[38] The history of Russian Orthodoxy followed the history of a collection of followers who all believed and protected the same faith and same dogmas, yet they always lacked unanimous acceptance or practice of Church rituals. In fact, Russian Orthodoxy's lack of ritual consensus became one of the primary issues that Patriarch Nikon strove to correct with his reforms.

This paradox of Russian Orthodoxy evolved into the major influence that led to the formation of *Edinoverie*: the realization among some late-eighteenth century clergy and scholars that the Old Right and Russian Orthodox Church existed in a state of "natural *Edinoverie*."[39] In the atmosphere created by Catherine's semi-tolerance toward the Old Rite, Church leaders such as Metropolitan Platon of Moscow, ultimately realized that Old Believers were not different from their Orthodox counterparts. More importantly, both shared the dogmas and the same Faith.[40] Consequently tsarist efforts to identify Old Believers turned into attempts to include the Old Rite as part of the larger Russian Orthodox Church.

In 1765, early in Catherine's reign, while serving in her court as religious tutor to her son Paul, Platon published "An exhortation to the truth and hope of the Gospel of Love," his sermon that gave birth to *Edinoverie*. In this sermon Platon laid the groundwork for his future desire to bring the Old Rite and Russian Orthodox Church together when he became Metropolitan of Moscow. In his discourse, Platon states his belief that as long as unity in faith and unity in dogma existed between the Old Rite and the Russian Orthodox Church, ritual differences did not truly divide the Church: "Ceremonies themselves cannot divide the faithful."[41] Platon's approach toward the Old Rite served as a major influence in his future career as Metropolitan of Moscow; under his Metropolitanate both the Rogozhskoe and Preobrazhenskoe Old Believer communities received permission to build their first chapels in 1771.

Church leaders attempted to develop a general idea of what *Edinoverie* could offer to the Old Rite: namely, the ability to recognize Old Rite churches legally as churches (rather than chapels) and the right for Old Rite communities to obtain legally ordained priests trained in the Old Rite.[42] In exchange, the Old Rite Church and community would fall under the administration of the Russian Orthodox Church and Holy Synod.[43] Many Old Rite communities rejected the offer because placing them under the authority of the Holy Synod contradicted the very foundations of their identity and faith. However, Old Believers used this opportunity to begin a dialogue with tsarist Russia with the hope of gaining greater religious freedom.

By the end of the eighteenth century, seeing *Edinoverie* as a potential stepping stone in enhancing their own spiritual existence, many Old

Rite communities, Rogozhskoe Cemetery included, regularly petitioned tsarist and Church authorities with two major requests. First, Old Rite communities wished to recommend their own candidates to be ordained as priests, rather than be forced to accept priests approved by the Holy Synod. This concession would allow Old Believers the ability to select their own spiritual leaders who understood the Old Rite as an actual member of the movement. Second, and most significant to many Old Rite communities, they requested the creation and recognition of an Old Rite Bishopric.[44] An Old Rite bishop, ideally, would serve as the spiritual bridge between the Old Believers and their Orthodox brethren. Furthermore, an officially recognized and ordained Old Rite bishop would bring the Old Rite back into full communion with the Russian Orthodox Church hierarchy. An Old Rite bishopric would create an independent branch within the Russian Orthodox Church and allow the bishop to ordain as many Old Rite priests as needed. Ultimately, the request to create an Old Rite Bishopric would guarantee that Old Believers returning to the Church hierarchy would still maintain some autonomy and self-identity, rather than rely on the Holy Synod or Russian Orthodox Church to approve the appointment of a priest or control the number of priests available.

As advocates of *Edinoverie* sought to place the Old Rite under more strict control of the Holy Synod, the creation of an Old Rite bishop appeared contradictory to these aims. However, to tsarist authorities, *Edinoverie* seemingly offered the best means to control the Old Rite and better define the Old Believers' place in the Russian Empire. Therefore, in August 1785, an imperial decree established *Edinoverie* under the conditions to legally and spiritually recognize Old Rite communities and churches if they placed themselves under the jurisdiction of the Holy Synod and Russian Orthodox Church.[45] Catherine's successor, and Platon's pupil, Paul saw *Edinoverie* as a useful tool and desired to make it more appealing to the Old Rite, occasionally inviting Old Believers to meet with him and listen to their suggestions and requests.[46] In a display of his own toleration toward Old Believers, on March 12, 1798, Paul issued an imperial decree that ordered all Russian Orthodox bishops to ordain priests in the Old Rite and permitted the construction of Old Rite Churches.[47] However, Paul did not yield to other concessions, and refused to create a new bishopric in the hopes that Old Believers would ultimately join *Edinoverie*.

With the creation of *Edinoverie*, the State sought a complete redefinition of the relationship between Old Believers and the State. However, as *Edinoverie* was "partly Old Believer and partly Russian Orthodox, partly of the schism and partly of the Church,"[48] the movement only created further confusion of Old Believer identity. Specifically, *Edinoverie* created a division between "loyal" (from the state's perspective) Old Believers who accepted union with the Orthodox Church, and the disloyal who refused to accept union.[49] More problematic for efforts at defining the Old Rite, *Edinoverie* enjoyed only limited success. Because its formal adoption revealed that many Old Believers' refused to submit themselves to the Russian Orthodox Church, tsarist authorities turned *Edinoverie* into a social and religious weapon against the many Old Rite communities, such as Rogozhskoe Cemetery, that remained outside of the Church hierarchy.

Furthermore, the very existence of *Edinoverie* and the *edinovertsy* (the term for Old Believers who joined *Edinoverie*) directly challenged the identity of Old Believers everywhere. While the issue between the Old Rite and the Russian Orthodox Church hinged on which group upheld the "pure" form of Orthodoxy, *Edinoverie* created the problem of defining the "pure" form of the Old Rite. Rogozhskoe and other Old Believer communities, particularly *popovtsy* communities, now would not only have to define themselves within the greater movement of the Old Rite and Orthodoxy, but also defend their faith and identity against the encroachment of the *state-defined* branch of Old Believers in *Edinoverie*.

Rogozhskoe Cemetery's Founding and First Decades

Catherine's first steps toward a more tolerable approach toward Old Believers began when she upheld Peter III's 1762 decree of toleration for the Old Rite. To Catherine, the reasoning for toleration argued that the Old Rite did not base itself in political treason or heresy, but rather superstition.[50] Catherine further amended her decree on religious toleration in December 1762. The new decree encouraged Old Believers living abroad to return to Russia, and those living throughout the Russian wilderness to settle in urban centers.[51] Furthermore, Catherine's decree ended many of the "Old Rite taxes" established under Peter the Great such as the dreaded double tax as well as taxes that required Old Believers to maintain their beards and traditional Russian dress as identifying markers of the Old Rite.[52]

Catherine's new approach toward the Old Rite had two specific goals. First, she hoped that with fewer restrictions and less punishment by way of taxation, Old Believers would have greater opportunity to become more active in Russian society and thereby make the Old Rite a much more visible entity throughout the Empire. With such policies, officials hoped to get a greater sense of the influence and strength of the Old Rite throughout the Empire. Second, Catherine's new policy encouraged Old Believers to contribute to Russia's economic and urban growth, as well as create a potential "Russian" element for colonization or inhabitation of some of Russia's least populated regions. To achieve these goals, Catherine's remodeled Old Rite policies instituted a series of restriction within conditions on toleration. First, Old Believers living *within* Russia in 1762 received permission to move where they chose; or in the case of Old Believer serfs, simply to seek permission to move. The second stipulation restricted Old Believers who returned from abroad to settle only in designated regions near Tobol'sk, Omsk, Saratov, along the Samara River near Orenburg, and near Belogorod.[53]

Moscow in particular benefited from the ease on restrictions on Old Believer rights and settlements. Both the established Moscow Old Believers and those coming from the Moscow countryside saw Catherine's toleration as a moment of opportunity. For the established merchants, freedom of movement provided the prospect to aid their spiritual brethren through either purchasing freedom for Old Believer serfs, or providing charity or funds for Old Believers to leave the countryside and move to Moscow.[54] While a sense of loyalty and common identity as Old Believers played a significant role in their patronage, by funding the mobility of former serfs and peasants, Moscow Old Rite merchants found a means to increase their own labor force for their enterprises while maintaining their sense of Christian duty and morality.[55]

For the rural Old Believers, Catherine's toleration policies provided access to potential social and economic opportunities. Moscow experienced an influx of both priestly and priestless Old Believers that pushed their combined numbers in the city into at least tens of thousands.[56] Yet, contrary to Catherine's goal to make the Old Rite more visible, some Old Believers feared that the new polices concealed a ploy to attack the Old Rite and refused registration as members of the Old Rite.[57] Yet Moscow's Old Rite population continued to grow.

By the second half of the eighteenth century, the Moscow priestly Old Believers, many of the future founders of Rogozhskoe Cemetery, developed communities near the Donskoi Monastery in the south and near the Tver' Gates in the north-west suburbs of Moscow.[58] These groups of families shared religious bonds as well as economic ties for many worked together either as merchants or shopkeepers. However, while their professions allowed them to interact with the public, these early communities often gathered in private houses to conduct religious services and hide their priests by moving them among families.[59] As rural Old Believers migrated to Moscow, they often found refuge within these communities to escape detection, or even relied on the influence and wealth of the merchant families to protect them.

However, many groups other than the Old Believers also were moving into Moscow and thereby contributed to the crowded and disorganized conditions in the city. By Catherine's reign, Moscow's prestige had dwindled to near nonexistent among Russia's nobility and particularly the Imperial Court, all who viewed Moscow as a backwater, filthy town reminiscent of Russia's regressive past.[60] To add to Moscow's troubles, poor record keeping of the numbers of migrants or new inhabitants created a "floating" population found predominately in the suburbs of Moscow.[61] The collection of census figures became so problematic that by 1770, no one could even arrive at consensus on the total number of inhabitants in Moscow: various sources place the number of Moscow's inhabitants anywhere from the police statistics of 152,190 to numbers as high as 500,000 by tsarist officials.[62]

Such disorganization proved devastating in 1771 when an outbreak of bubonic plague devastated Moscow and sent city and tsarist officials scrambling for any means to combat the plague and maintain order in the ensuing chaos. As the historian Alexander Martin argues, the ensuing crisis in Moscow and the public's outright disorganization and rebelliousness toward any efforts at control, only reaffirmed Catherine's own disgust with Moscow, an entity contrary to her own views of enlightened society.[63] As the plague continued with seemingly little aid from authorities, Moscow found itself on the precipice of self-destruction.

Like the rest of the city's population, Old Believers in Moscow suffered from the combined devastation of the plague and often overly strict quarantine restrictions created by Moscow authorities that regularly prevented food and medical supplies from reaching areas of the city for days at a time.[64] Following the Plague Riot in September 1771, Catherine appointed Count Grigori Orlov to head a commission to restore order throughout the city. Under Orlov's watch, the situation in Moscow improved because officials instituted a number of public work projects and increased distribution of food and medical care for the citizenry.[65]

Ultimately, in what became one of the most important opportunities for the Moscow Old Believers, the Plague Commission appealed directly to Moscow's wealthy merchants for financial and material assistance in combating the plague. As a means of offering assistance, both priestly and priestless Moscow Old Believers petitioned the Senate, Orlov, and city officials for permission to establish their own, Old Believer-exclusive quarantines and cemeteries. With guarantees from the Old Rite petitioners that these communities would be fully constructed, guarded, staffed, provisioned, and administered without the need for state aid, Orlov and Petr Eropkin, the Lieutenant-General and acting Governor of Moscow, sent the petition with their approval on to the Senate.[66] On December 8, 1771 the Senate, in-turn, designated 24 hectares of land one mile east of Moscow in the village of Novoandronovka and between the roads to Vladimir and Ryazan as Old Rite property, the nascent Rogozhskoe Cemetery.[67]

This ruling provided the first opportunity that the Moscow priestly Old Believers needed to begin building their own idealized community based on their own specific morals and values. Rogozhskoe Cemetery soon gave the priestly Old Believers in Moscow and the surrounding area, and all Muscovites who sought the aid of the community (including non-Old Believers), access to medical aid, charity, and religious services meant to comfort the victims of the plague, as well as provide a quarantine to prevent further spread of disease. Yet Rogozhskoe also served a much greater purpose to its founders and community: the opportunity to build a community devoted to the traditions and ideals of the Old Rite.

Rogozhskoe Cemetery represented many things to its community of priestly Old Believers. Primarily, Rogozhskoe and its structures offered protection to its community physically and spiritually from the world outside its boundaries. Initially the community provided protection from the ravages of the plague and the genuine fear that Old Believer victims might not receive proper medical attention, or Old Rite religious or burial services. In the months immediately following Rogozhskoe's founding, the priestly Old Believers began construction of the first structures at the cemetery, which initially included an infirmary, some living facilities, an almshouse, and a wall surrounding the new construction.[68] To fulfil their spiritual needs, the community held religious services in private chapels built within the almshouse and infirmary.

Rogozhskoe belonged to two worlds: spiritual and secular. Because of the community's ties to the Moscow merchantry and the State's restriction on Old Rite structures, the group had to stylize their settlement as a sanctuary for the Old Rite and as a part of the contemporary Moscow in which they lived. In order for Rogozhskoe to preserve its ideals, creating and protecting the spaces inside of Rogozhskoe Cemetery became vital for the community's self-identity. However, as a religious minority already distrusted by tsarist and Church authorities, the Rogozhskoe Old Believers cautiously adapted their use of external demonstrations of their piety. The true issue for the Rogozhskoe Old Believers became not only how to "protect" their identity, their ideal, and their understanding of sacred space, but also how to *remind its own members* of the boundaries between their sacred world and the profane world outside of Rogozhskoe's walls.

Rogozhskoe's walls served as the community's first boundaries. Part of the original quarantine construction protected the community from the plague, yet Rogozhskoe's walls represented much more. Eventually surrounding the entire area of Rogozhskoe Cemetery, the walls served as a true divide between communal interior sacred and exterior spaces. For example, to prevent any backlash from authorities, the community itself restricted all displays of Old Rite spirituality to its interior land. Therefore, religious ceremonies regularly performed openly by the Russian Orthodox Church, such as burial services and holiday celebrations, remained within Rogozhskoe's walls.[69] Furthermore, within Rogozhskoe's walls, the community adopted practices reflective of monastic life.[70] Whereas Rogozhskoe merchants and other parishioners were expected and encouraged to maintain their livelihoods and interact with the world outside Rogozhskoe, the interior remained sacred ground, reserved for practicing and upholding the traditions and expectations of the Old Rite. For example, many successful merchants comprised a portion of its community; nevertheless, the Rogozhskoe Old Believers expected all families to maintain homes near Rogozhskoe during many of the religious holidays and fasting periods, especially the Great Lent, in order to devote themselves to their spiritual duties.[71]

However, the very heart of the community needed its spiritual spaces where members could practice their faith. The Rogozhskoe Old Believers viewed their new physical buildings no differently because they needed specifically designated structures as a place to carry on their spiritual lives. However, after the schism, tsarist and church law forbade the construction of Old Rite religious buildings without special permission. Any structures that violated these laws faced possible destruction. However, with their population growing and their economic and social influence in Moscow on the rise, the Rogozhskoe Old Believers received permission in 1776 from Moscow authorities to build their first chapel at the cemetery so that the community could hold burial services for its members.[72] Dedicated to Saint Nicholas, the one-story structure was constructed of wood.[73] While the Russian Orthodox Church and tsarist authorities often attempted to stall or actually prevent such construction efforts, Rogozhskoe Cemetery, in only five years since its founding, was known throughout Moscow as a major charitable center for Muscovites of all denominations.[74] Ultimately then, Rogozhskoe's continued expansion of its charitable foundations, such as the community's almshouses and medical facilities, brought the community both legal and spiritual protection from authorities thanks to the community's recognition for upholding the Christian value of charity.

Rogozhskoe's image as a charitable institution, as well as the vast amount of wealth distributed among its members, prompted the authorities to grant more privileges to the Rogozhskoe Old Believers. For example, in 1791 the Rogozhskoe Old Believers petitioned the Governor-General of Moscow, Prince Alexander Prozorovskii, for the right to construct a large temple dedicated to the Intercession of the Holy Virgin built in stone on the community's grounds.[75] Such a request proved momentous for it contradicted Russian laws that only permitted Old Believers to construct wooden chapels; previously Orthodox rules prohibited performing the Divine Liturgy in chapels as a means to prevent Old Believers from access to the Divine Liturgy. Even under Catherinian toleration, Church and tsarist decrees only recognized

Old Believer religious structures as chapels. This restriction legally forbade Old Believers from performing services other than Vespers, Matins, and Hours; for the main services, the church had to be constructed in stone, a right only reserved for the construction of permanent, Orthodox churches.[76] Therefore, the request to construct an Old Rite temple out of stone was extremely bold and reveals just how far the Rogozhskoe Old Believers were willing to challenge the tsarist state in creating their Holy Moscow. Yet citing that the only law regarding the construction of Old Believer buildings within Moscow dated to 1722 and only required for a community to petition for approval for the construction of any structure, as well as noting that the parishioners at Rogozhskoe numbered nearly 20,000, Prince Prozorovskii approved the community's request.[77]

The Rogozhskoe Old Believers soon put into motion the construction of their new temple, Intercession Cathedral. However, the cathedral represented much more than a means to meet Rogozhskoe's spiritual need; the Intercession Cathedral now served as a permanent monument to Rogozhskoe's Holy Moscow. The Rogozhskoe Old Believers soon hired an architect by the name of Kazakov to build a grand cathedral that reflected their worldview. The original design for the Intercession Cathedral provides a significant look into the Rogozhskoe Old Believers' understanding of their community's ties to pre-Nikonian Orthodoxy. Specifically, the planned size of Rogozhskoe's Intercession Cathedral surpassed the Dormition Cathedral in the Moscow Kremlin. At the time, the Dormition Cathedral was still one of the largest cathedrals in Moscow and historically recognized as the Mother Church and seat of Orthodoxy of Muscovite Era Russia. Even in the Imperial Era, the Dormition Cathedral retained its significance as the site of the coronation of the Tsars.[78] Rogozhskoe took their plans even further; during initial construction, builders modified Kazakov's plans to increase the size of the cathedral as well as change the number of domes from one to five, the same as the Dormition Cathedral.[79] The Intercession Cathedral, then, directly challenged the historical narrative of the Dormition Cathedral held in both Moscow and Russian culture.[80]

Such symbolism, however, was not lost on church authorities in Moscow who immediately brought the situation to Catherine's attention with their demands to end Rogozhskoe's construction efforts.[81] Following orders directly from Catherine herself, Prozorovskii oversaw the destruction of the Intercession Cathedral's foundations. However, Catherine did grant permission to the Rogozhskoe Old Believers to rebuild the temple in stone, but only with direct supervision by the Moscow authorities.[82]

Because tsarist and Church officials proved themselves more than willing to intervene in the physical and symbolic construction of their ideal community, the Rogozhskoe Old Believers realized that they needed to adapt their approach for presenting their model of Holy Moscow. To that end, the Rogozhskoe Old Believers sought a means to combine their devotion to the Old Rite and their Holy Moscow and at the same time to display their ties to contemporary Russia. The new Intercession Cathedral ultimately served as a melding of the two worlds between which Rogozhskoe remained trapped. While still large in size, and with only one dome, the cathedral's exterior now reflected the popular architectural styles throughout Russia at the time with traces of

Figure 1.1 Old Ritualist Intercession Chapel, Rogozhskoe Cemetery, 1883. Nikolai Naydenov, Album, *Views of Some Urban Areas, Temples, Notable Buildings and Other Structures*, Moscow, 1884.

baroque and neoclassical styles. However, the Intercession Cathedral remained topped by the true symbol of a traditional Russian Orthodox Church, an onion dome.[83]

As Rogozhskoe grew, the community petitioned the Moscow Governor-General Alexander Bekleshov in 1804 to construct a second stone temple.[84] Under the leadership of the merchant Ilya Sheviakov, Rogozhskoe began construction on the structure designed by Ivan Zhukov, and subsequently dedicated as the Church of the Nativity. Combined with the Intercession Cathedral and Saint Nicholas chapel, the latest temple represented the completion of Rogozhskoe's own Cathedral Square. The Church of the Nativity would serve as a winter cathedral because the Intercession Cathedral's large size made it ineffective and expensive to heat in cold weather.

Using the experience they gained when building the Intercession Cathedral, the Rogozhskoe Old Believers designed the Church of the Nativity as another example of mixing of external contemporary architectural styles with an interior devoted to traditional Old Rite styling and iconography. The Church of the Nativity reflected the neoclassical, or Empire, style that gained popularity under Alexander I. Constructed in the shape of a Latin cross, and topped with a large dome and colonnade, the Church of the Nativity's exterior exemplified

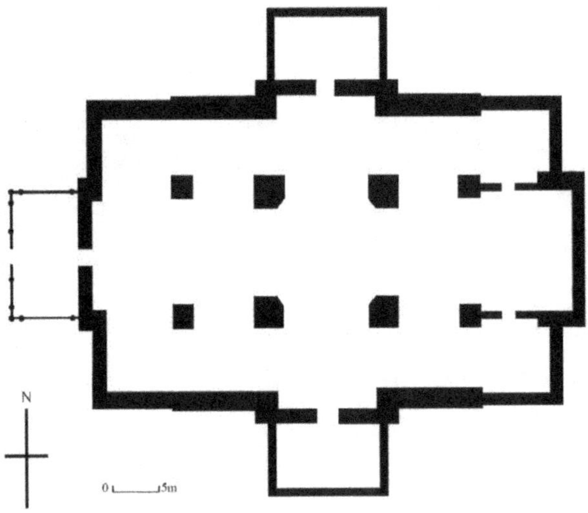

Figure 1.2 Overview of the floor plan of the Intercession Cathedral.

the Rogozhskoe community's ties and connection to the rest of Moscow as well as to the greater Russian Empire through its use of the popular architectural styles of the day. Similar to the Intercession Cathedral, the only external "Russian" aspect of the Church of the Nativity was the addition of a small, golden cupola on top of the distinctively neoclassical dome. However, like the Intercession Cathedral, the Church of the Nativity served as a division between the sacred space *within* the temple and the profane, non-Old Rite, outside world (Illustrations 3 and 4).

Externally Rogozhskoe's cathedrals emulated the popular architectural trends of the late-eighteenth and early nineteenth century Moscow. However, the cathedrals' interiors reflected the style of fifteenth, sixteenth and seventeenth century Russian churches, highlighted by the exclusive use of icons and antiquities from those periods collected by Rogozhskoe's members. For Rogozhskoe, the cathedral interiors remained sacred spaces and became testaments to the community's devotion to their Old Rite

Figure 1.3 Old Ritualist Nativity Chapel, 1883. Nikolai Naydenov, Album, *Views of Some Urban Areas, Temples, Notable Buildings and Other Structures*, Moscow, 1884.

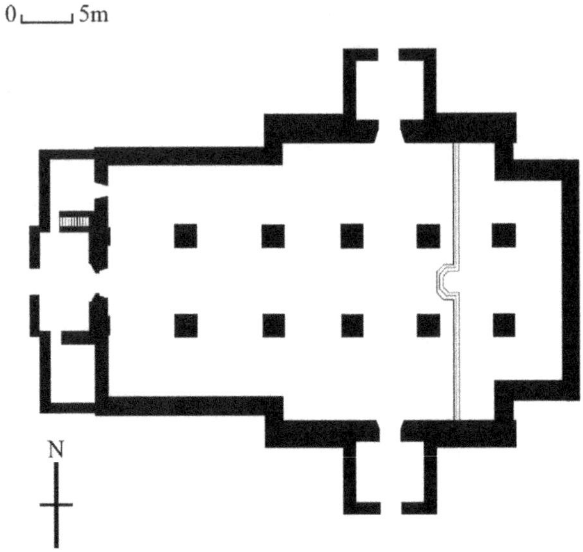

Figure 1.4 Overview of the floor plan of the Nativity Cathedral.

spirituality. According to the nineteenth century Old Believer historian Pavel Mel'nikov, "[The Intercession Cathedral] is beautifully decorated. The icons are excellent examples of the ancient styles – Rublev, Stroganov and others, gilded in rich silver with precious stones and pearls, silver chandeliers and candlesticks with large shrouded candles, a large iconostasis and magnificent and panels – all testified as to the zeal, and the wealth of the Rogozhskoe parishioners."[85]

The Rogozhskoe Cathedrals' interiors glorified the community's own understanding and devotion to the Old Rite. Along with housing Rogozhskoe's ever-growing collections of antique icons donated or purchased for the community by wealthy patrons, the Rogozhskoe Old Believers decorated the interior of the Intercession and Nativity Cathedrals in pre-Nikonian style frescoes and paintings.[86] Covering the interior walls with icons dating as far back as the thirteenth and fourteenth centuries and with wall frescos reflecting the styles of the Old Russian schools of icon painting served as yet another means for the Old Believer community to reject the spiritual and cultural changes introduced by Nikon and, later, the Holy Synod. The new Cathedrals, then, served to represent Rogozhskoe's own identity as a community devoted to preserving their faith in the world around them; while internally devoted to Old Rite ideas of sacredness, externally the cathedrals reflected the community's ties to the rest of Imperial Moscow.

The ability to divide their community physically and ideologically between the external world and their sacred interiors helped maintain the community's sense that they protected the sacredness of the Old Rite. Not only did Rogozhskoe Cemetery need to shield its parishioners from the perceived spiritual corruption of the outside world, the Old Believers also needed to guard what they viewed as sacred representations of their faith: icons, frescoes, other church decorations, as well as ancient Russian manuscripts. For example, the community's continuously growing icon collection remained a source of pride for the Rogozhskoe Old Believers throughout their history. For them this precious icon collection not only represented their efforts at preserving the icons themselves, but also an effort to preserve sacred treasures as well as their faith and Russian history. As the Rogozhskoe historian Makarov later claimed, "In the course of those early decades, there were hardly any churches in Russia that could claim as many precious treasures as collected for Rogozhskoe's cathedrals: particularly the ancient icons [...] all of which spoke to the ineffable affection, zeal, and love of the cemetery's parishioners."[87] Rogozhskoe quickly established itself as a center for the collection of Russian religious relics, icons, and ancient Russian manuscripts. Rogozhskoe's wealthiest merchant families of the early nineteenth century such as the Gol'skiis, Shelaputins, Rakhmanovs, and Tsarskiis, and those that came later in the community's history such as the Morozovs, Riabushinskiis and Soldatenkovs, spent fortunes to purchase and refurbish numerous traditional Russian religious and cultural antiquities. Eventually, over the course of the nineteenth century, the Rogozhskoe Old Believers possessed one of the largest collections of ancient Russian manuscripts and icons in all of Russia.[88] These collections not only instilled a sense of pride among Rogozhskoe's Old Believers, but also inspired numerous Old Believers and Orthodox alike to flock to view the community's collection of traditional Russian icons and manuscripts held and displayed in Rogozhskoe's cathedrals.[89]

Collecting, maintaining, and displaying centuries-old icons became one of Rogozhskoe's key defining traits. Icons in particular served as a special medium to the community's understanding of the sacred. In the Old Rite mind, the Nikonian Reforms corrupted all aspects of Russian spirituality and spiritual expression, including icons and religious relics. In particular, late seventeenth-century and later Russian icons reflected the ritualistic changes Nikon introduced. The reformed spelling of "Jesus" from *Isus* in the pre-Nikonian Church to *Iisus* serves as an examaple of changes that were anathema in Rogozskoe. Responding to Nikon's changes, the iconographic abbreviation for Jesus Christ (formerly *IC XC*) changed to *IIC XC*, the depiction of blessing by subject of the icon changed from the two-fingered sign of the cross to three-fingers. Furthermore, Russian Orthodox icons adopted more "western" characteristics, particularly the use of specific hitherto proscribed details for the icons' subjects and greater variety and intensity of color.[90] To Old Believers, the new forms of iconography were nothing more than iconoclasm that not only depicted the new heresies, but Russia's spiritual loss of grace; iconography seemed now to focus on creating aesthetically pleasing images rather than employ symbols to lead worshipers to greater perceptions of the holy realms and deeper understanding of dogma.[91] As even Archpriest Avvakum noted in the immediate aftermath of the schism, "They paint the image of the Savior Emmanuel: the face is rounded, the mouth is bright red, the hair is curly, the arms and muscles are plump [...] and he is all big-bellied as a German [...] and all of it is painted in a fleshy way: for these sort of heretics have come to love fleshy corpulence and have rejected the value of tears."[92] Therefore, Old Believers across the Russian Empire held special reverence for icons painted before the schism.

Furthermore, during the period from the fourteenth to sixteenth centuries Russian icon painting distinguished itself as unique from its Byzantine and Greek-style heritage. Masters such as Andrei Rublev established a definitive Russian style of icon painting noted more for its use of gentle tones, an inner light, elongated figures, and emphasis on complex theological symbolism. For example, the overwhelmingly powerful and most renowned of Rublev's icons, *The Old Testament Trinity*, uses the story of the Hospitality of Abraham to three visiting angels to depict the mystery of the Holy Trinity.[93] The Old Rite upheld the old tradition as the *only* proper method of icon painting and rejected eighteenth and nineteenth-century changes to icon painting along with the Nikonian Reforms.

As the embodiment of Old Rite purity, many of Rogozhskoe's Old Believers made it their mission to obtain and protect these sacred icons and other antiquities from the "ignorant Orthodox."[94] Even though the Rogozhskoe Old Believers did commission new icons painted in pre-Nikonian styles for the iconostases of their new temples, icons from the fourteenth to the seventeenth century dominated the Rogozhskoe icon collection.[95] Relying on their wealth, the Rogozhskoe Old Believers obtained many of these icons from poorer Orthodox families who, in their minds neither appreciated nor understood the icons' true spiritual value as a sacred relic and a connection to Russia's history.[96] As Vladimir Makarov later claimed, many Orthodox "took their ancient icons and ignorantly discarded them as rubbish, or forgot them in the storerooms ever since Peter I picked up Western 'civilization,' preferring some external depiction of useless tinsel and glitter, with no internal content."[97]

Some of Rogozhskoe's earliest acquisitions in the years since their founding included a number of icons painted in the fourteenth century Novgorod School style and even an icon of Our Lady of Smolensk painted by Russia's most celebrated iconographer, Andrei Rublev.[98] Rogozhskoe's parishioners also regularly donated personal or family icon collections in commemoration of holidays, anniversaries, or, more commonly, in memorials of loved ones. One such example was the Gol'skii family, who made several of the initial icon donations before 1800, one a large icon of the Theotokos of Tikhvin, one of Orthodox Russia's most revered images of the Virgin Mary and Christ Child, in memory of Nazar Stefanovich and Peter Nazarovich Gol'skii.[99]

Rogozhskoe's cathedral icons and collections shared many of the same themes seen in churches throughout the Orthodox world, included depictions of Christ as Acheiropoietos (Not Made by Human Hands) and Pantocrator (Ruler of All); as well as the Theotokos (Mother of God) in her traditional Hodigitria (She who shows the Way) and Eleusa (Tenderness) depictions.[100] The Rogozhskoe Old Believers also collected many icons depicting the lives and works of many traditional saints such as Nicholas the Wonderworker, George the Warrior, and John the Baptist. In addition, the Rogozhskoe collections included icons of many celebrated Russian saints such as Dmitri Donskoi, the twin Martyrs Boris and Gleb, and Sergius of Radonezh, of whom Rogozhskoe's Intercession Cathedral displayed six icons.[101]

Rogozhskoe even possessed some icons that reflected their devotion to the Old Rite and their dissent against tsarist and church authorities.

Like many Old Rite churches, Rogozhskoe's cathedrals displayed a number of icons of archpriest Avvakum Petrov, Patriarch Nikon's most outspoken critic, viewed as a Father of and Saint in the Old Rite movement.[102] However, a more curious part of Rogozhskoe's collection included a pair of seventeenth century icons of Metropolitan Philip II of Moscow. While revered as a saint within all Russian Orthodoxy, Philip's legacy deserves attention in order to understand the significance of these icons to Rogozhskoe's efforts at building their sense of morality. Serving as Metropolitan of Moscow at the height of Ivan the Terrible's oppression under the *Oprichnina* in the mid-sixteenth century, Philip, once Ivan's close childhood friend, openly challenged the tsar's royal authority and proclaimed it subservient to the power God granted to the Orthodox Church and its offices. Directly challenging Ivan ultimately led to Philip's murder at the hands of the notorious *oprichnik*, Maliuta Skuratov.[103] Eventually recognized as a martyr for the Church, Philip posthumously received recognition as a Hierarch of Moscow. Ironically, Patriarch Nikon glorified Philip as a saint in 1652, making Philip one of the last mutual saints recognized by both the Old Ritualists and Orthodox Church.[104] However, to the Rogozhskoe Old Believers, one can see how the veneration of Philip's icons catered to the idea of the community's embodiment of Orthodox purity as one of the final, mutually recognized, pre-reform saints. In like manner, Philip's recognition as a Hierarch of Moscow reaffirmed Rogozhskoe's ties to the city of Moscow itself.

For the Rogozhskoe Old Believers, as well as to Old Believers and Orthodox visiting the settlement, their collection of ancient icons served as another display of the community's devotion to their sense of Old Rite spiritual purity. Furthermore, the use and collection of the ancient icons reaffirmed the community's understanding of Rogozhskoe's physical and spiritual boundaries in the community's efforts to preserve both historical and religious artifacts from outside corruption. Frescoes painted in pre-seventeenth century styles and ancient icons served as a means for Rogozhskoe's parishioners to transport themselves back to an idealized period and idealized reverence for the Old Rite. This presentation, in turn, would shape the Rogozhskoe community's own understanding of their faith in the Old Rite and how their devotion and piety could be used to reshape the external world around them.

The Rogozhskoe Old Believers and the Reimagining of Moscow, 1812–25

As the nineteenth century opened, Russia, like all European Great Powers, found itself embroiled in the Napoleonic Wars. While initially the battlefields of Europe seemed distant, events soon brought the war directly to Moscow with the city paying the ultimate price of near total destruction in the Great Fire following Napoleon's sack of Moscow in 1812. Yet in the aftermath of this calamity, both Moscow and the Rogozhskoe Old Believers entered into a new era. More specifically, the devastation of 1812 provided both tsarist authorities and the Rogozhskoe Old Believers with an opportunity to present their own models for a Moscow reimagined to their own ideologies.

After 1812 Moscow underwent a rebirth. Moscow represented much more to Russia and its people than its status as the Old Capital: it was Russia's city.[105] However, tsarist officials in Saint Petersburg and Moscow saw many opportunities rise from the city's destruction to introduce social reform efforts on the city and people of Moscow initially designed by Catherine the Great.[106] Since Catherine's reign, tsarist authorities attempted to find a means to turn Moscow into an "enlightened metropolis." Catherine and other officials hoped that by implementing a social project to reform the very city of Moscow in a tsarist vision of a more progressive society it would be effective because "Only Moscow could anchor European 'enlightenment' in the Russian interior."[107] Under the new project it meant to reimagine Moscow, and tsarist and city officials undertook numerous rebuilding and redesigning efforts throughout the city and completely renovated Moscow's layout through the creation of new roadways and the city's look through rebuilding countless structures in neoclassical styles.[108] For tsarist officials, then, Moscow was to become a symbol that reflected Imperial Russia's western cultural leanings.

For Rogozhskoe, however, not unlike the events of 1771, the devastation of 1812 provided new opportunities for the Rogozhskoe Old Believers to develop their ideal Holy Moscow. Following Napoleon's invasion of Russia, the French Occupation and the Moscow Fire left the old capital scarred both physically and psychologically.[109] The Moscow Fire left nearly three-quarters of the city destroyed with countless valuables either looted or lost in the blaze. Fortunately, Rogozhskoe

Cemetery remained unharmed and allowed the community to become an influential force in rebuilding Moscow. The catastrophes of 1812 allowed the Rogozhskoe Old Believers to actualize the ideals of their community and to serve as an example of true Orthodox piety and charity to all Muscovites.

While community legend held that Rogozhskoe was structurally unharmed during the French occupation, later accounts revealed that French troops destroyed the doors of Rogozhskoe's temples and other buildings while they searched for booty. However, Rogozhskoe's spiritual valuables remained unharmed and untouched.[110] Under the guidance of Rogozhskoe's spiritual leaders, particularly the priest Ivan Iastrebov who, "when all others left, remained behind in the cemetery,"[111] the community buried their valuable relics, icons, and other collections within the cemetery and the Church of the Nativity while the parishioners fled the city.

Rogozhskoe's survival in the destruction of 1812 buttressed the community's resolve and ideal that their community served a divine purpose. Community legends sprung up around the seemingly divine protection of Rogozhskoe while much of Moscow suffered. Accounts claimed that while Iastrebov and other members of the community removed or hid the vast majority of Rogozhskoe's icons and other antiquities, some relics were left behind to the mercy of the invading forces. One in particular, an icon of Saint Nicholas the Wonderworker, came to represent Rogozhskoe's perception of the events of 1812. This particular icon, housed in the Church of the Nativity, possessed a gilded silver frame, decorated with a number of gemstones. Miraculously, neither the icon nor its ornamental frame suffered at the hands of the French.[112] Upon their return, the Rogozhskoe Old Believers placed an inscription on the icon:

> In the Summer of 7320 [1812] during the disastrous invasion of the hordes of Napoleon, who forced his hand everywhere, designed to kidnap any items of value in this divine temple befitting God and this holy image of gilded silver was found constantly in the sight of the numerous villains as it was not stored by anyone and unprotected, and was mercifully kept intact by the most-illustrious Lord and his great saint of many miracles and blessings Saint Nicholas, from sacrilegious enemy hands.[113]

The fact that Rogozhskoe's structures and valuables survived allowed the Rogozhskoe Old Believers to turn away from the community's own needs and instead put all efforts into upholding their sense of Christian morality by providing charity and other aid to Moscow's rebuilding efforts.

Rebuilding Moscow in particular provided an opportunity for the Old Believers to offer their own model of communal purity to greater numbers of believers. Moscow's destruction left the city's economic foundations in tatters; however, many of the Rogozhskoe Old Believers' businesses remained unharmed. Since they required minimal financial aid, some of the Rogozhskoe Old Believers could establish some of Moscow's, and Imperial Russia's, future merchant and entrepreneurial dynasties. More established merchant families, such as the Rakhmanovs and Gol'skiis, found new opportunities to expand their businesses and industries. After 1812, Rogozhskoe and Moscow witnessed an influx of Old Believer migration as well. Among these newcomers were a number of entrepreneurial minded peasants, some of whom would found the most successful merchant and industrial dynasties in the Russian Empire.

The Morozovs, one of the most successful merchant families, arrived in Moscow after 1812. The progenitor of this dynasty, Savva Vasilievich, began his career as a serf in the silk-weaving factory of a merchant named Kononov in the Bogorodskoe District of the Moscow Province. Wanting his freedom and needing to repay Kononov a large amount for settling his army recruitment fee, Morozov and his family established their own weaving studio in the village of Zuyevo in 1797. Following Napoleon's destruction of most of Moscow's textile industry, along with an increased demand for silk and wool products, Savva profited significantly. Eventually Savva paid his debt and purchased his family's freedom from serfdom for 17,000 rubles.[114] Moving to Moscow, the Morozovs quickly became one of the wealthiest merchant families in Rogozhskoe and ultimately in all of the Russian Empire.

During this same time, other equally wealthy and influential merchant families, such as the Riabushinskiis and Soldatenkovs, came into prominence. The introduction of new families and wealth played a major role in Rogozhskoe and its idealization of Holy Moscow for the remainder of the nineteenth and early twentieth century. However, the aftermath of 1812 provided the Rogozhskoe Old Believers with a golden

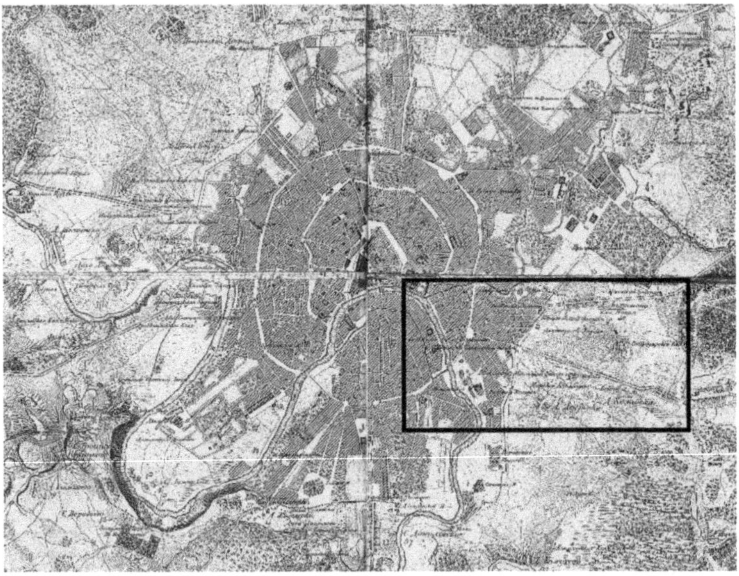

Figure 1.5 A portion of a map of Moscow in 1818 with highlighted box depicting Rogozhskoe Cemetery's location in relation to the rest of Moscow. From, "Topographical Map of the Suburbs of Moscow, recorded by the officers of the Quartermaster 1818." Military Topographic Depot, 1823.

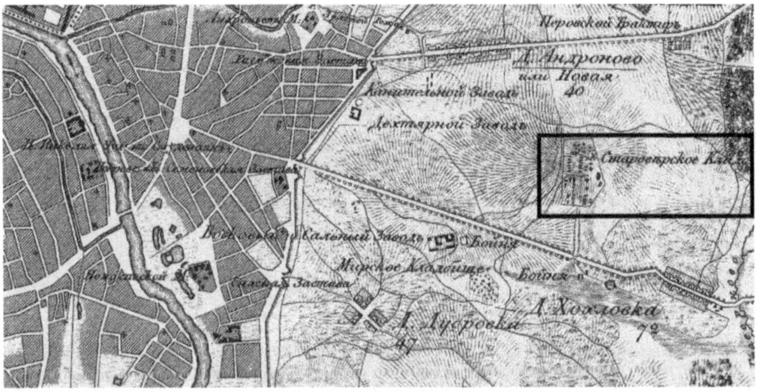

Figure 1.6 Detail highlighting Rogozhskoe Cemetery, listed only as "Old Believer (Staroverie) Cemetery."

opportunity to spread their moral ideals *outside* of their boundaries through extensive charity and patronage in Moscow. Their salutary efforts allowed the Rogozhskoe Old Believers to propogate Old Rite piety, to spread their economic influence and wealth, and to demonstrate their sense of duty and patriotism all as part of their reimagining of Moscow after 1812.

Rather than serving as an ideal for a single Old Rite community, the Rogozhskoe Old Believers now came to view their community as an ideal that needed to serve as a model for Moscow and the surrounding area. Consequently, the Rogozhskoe community's emphasis on charity became the *sine qua non* for all Christians. Particularly for Rogozhskoe's wealthy merchantry, charity evolved as the foundation of their shared identity and culture. The merchant Vladimir Riabushinskii wrote that "[t]he Lord hath sent three gifts. Yea, the first gift is the cross and prayer. The second gift is love and charity. The third gift is the night orison."[115] For the Rogozhskoe Old Believers, charity served as the beacon of morality that the Old Rite used to measure itself against the rest of Russian society. The Rogozhskoe Old Believers specifically emphasized use of wealth for philanthropy and charity not only as part of their Christian duty, but also as a means to set themselves apart from what they viewed as the greedy, "carefree and careless noble estate."[116] To Rogozhskoe's merchants, then, their ultimate challenge was to transform capital, something sinful, and use it for good.

The experience of the influential Prokhorov family best summarizes the Rogozhskoe merchants' approach to using their material assets. Although he was not born an Old Believer, Vasili Prokhorov, the founder of the eponymous manufacturing dynasty, like many of Rogozhskoe's wealthy merchants spent the early years of his life as a serf, who eventually paid for his freedom in 1764 and then founded a successful brewing business. Prokhorov emerged as one of the more fortunate victims of the 1771 plague. After Prokhorov contracted the plague, one of his business associates, an Old Believer, sent Prokhorov to Rogozhskoe Cemetery for medical care. During his time at Rogozhskoe, Prokhorov not only recovered, but took greater interest in and openly discussed issues of religion, spirituality, and use of capital with the Old Believers. He eventually converted to the Old Rite.[117] Soon after his conversion, Prokhorov gave up his brewing business as "inappropriate" for any pious man and transitioned to textiles; he eventually established the "Trimount" factory and one of Moscow's greatest cotton dynasties.[118]

The Prokhorov family best summarized the Rogozhskoe merchants' approach to wealth and use of capital after 1812 in essays written by Timofei Vasilievich to his brother, Konstantine Vasilievich: "On Acquisition of Wealth," and "On Poverty."

> Wealth is often acquired for vanity, luxury voluptuousness, etc. This wealth is bad and pure evil: it leads to the perdition of the soul [. . .] if wealth is acquired by work, its loss will preserve the man from downfall; he will resume working and can still acquire more than he had, for he lived in God.[119]

The historian Galina Ulanova described not only the Prokhorovs' but also all of the Old Believer merchants' strong emphasis on piety, patronage, and charity as practices central to their identity and more significant than their merchant status; thus they could create distance from "sinful" wealth.[120] For the Rogozhskoe merchantry in particular, charity and patronage not only provided a means for their own salvation but also to set themselves apart from the Orthodox Church and elite gentry whom the Rogozhskoe merchants viewed as both vile and corrupt for their use of wealth for self-glorification and self-gratification.[121]

Rogozhskoe's approach to financial capital and the need to use it for charity, then, played a major role in developing Rogozhskoe's communal ideals in the years following the events of 1812. Old Believers founded Rogozhskoe Cemetery itself in order to provide aid and charity to both victims and those seeking shelter from the plague. From that point on, Rogozhskoe never truly suffered from a lack of funds for pursuing more outlets for charity. The community received numerous generous donations from its wealthy merchants, from the body of the general parishioners, and from Old Believers throughout Russia.[122] Charity remained so firmly rooted in the very core of the Rogozhskoe Old Believers' sense of piety and identity that the formal duty of the Rogozhskoe Trustees required them to ensure that they would regularly meet the financial needs of Rogozhskoe's almshouse, and later its infirmaries, orphanage, and school.[123]

Charity remained so important to the Rogozhskoe Old Believers that even the duties expected of the community leadership, the Rogozhskoe

Trustees, stressed that "[t]his place is entrusted to you, and we offer our prayers to God [. . .] and ask that you serve as a kind and dear benefactor and remain vigilant, and we ask that you care and watch over all of those who do not possess shelter or refuge."[124] Rogozhskoe's almshouses became a central defining element of the community's self-identity, as well as the community's identity in Imperial Russia. Rogozhskoe's charities, in fact, gained so much renown that "Rogozhskoe Almshouse" became interchangeable with "Rogozhskoe Cemetery" throughout Russia over the course of the nineteenth century to identify the entire community.[125] Unfortunately, the make-up of the original almshouses and infirmaries remains unclear. A fire on June 13, 1840 destroyed the original construction plans and records for the first buildings. By that time, the original structures had been replaced with eight, two-story stone edifaces.[126] In Rogozhskoe's first decades, the almshouses alone required an annual 2,000-ruble fund simply for basic maintenance and decoration to create a more livable atmosphere for the various inhabitants; most often widows, the infirm, or elderly.[127]

Prior to 1812 Rogozhskoe never refused to admit non-Old Believers into their almshouses; after 1812 soldiers, the homeless, the impoverished, and all others found refuge at Rogozhskoe, which had by now become a model of charity in Moscow.[128] Furthermore, like the Morozovs and Prokhorovs, other Rogozhskoe owners of many of the surviving textile, candle, paper manufacturing, and other industries grew even more wealthy, and by extension the entire community. More wealth for Rogozhskoe's merchants ensured more funds for Rogozhskoe's charities.

After 1812, Rogozhskoe expanded its charitable outreach. One of Rogozhskoe's first projects included building additional facilities on its grounds, and renovating its existing structures such as the almshouses and medical facilities to provide greater space and the means to accommodate more people seeking aid. Rogozhskoe quickly gained fame throughout Moscow as its facilities rivaled, and even surpassed, almshouses, orphanages, and hospitals administered by the State and the Orthodox Church primarily in terms of the funding provided for the community's facilities and wards.[129] Rogozhskoe merchants also surpassed many Orthodox Church and state officials by privately donating funds for rebuilding Moscow and even in designing many new construction projects.[130]

Charity was not the only means the Rogozhskoe Old Believers used to champion their model of Christian piety after 1812. Patronage, whereby many merchants saw themselves as patrons and fathers to their workforce, also became a key element in Rogozhskoe's postwar identity. Workers became by far the most important resources that Moscow required after 1812. Moscow needed workers not only to serve as labor for construction, but also to work in factories to meet the increased demands placed on the surviving industries. The main source of labor came from the peasantry. In turn, the merchants provided numerous opportunities for Russian serfs, such as Savva Morozov, to find work in order to earn enough to purchase their freedom. However, Rogozhskoe merchants, too, saw opportunity in the need for labor, particularly because many of their factories needed more workers. To meet this need, many Rogozhskoe merchants sought out Old Believer serfs for their workforce.[131] Not only did such practices meet labor demands, it also served the purpose of strengthening the bond between merchant-industrialist and worker economically, socially, and even spiritually in the Old Rite.[132] Merchants commonly hired Old Rite serfs or purchased their freedom outright.[133] Through such practices, the Rogozhskoe merchants put into practice the community's model of Christian patronage and charity.

Initially, their influence provided even greater opportunities for the Rogozhskoe Old Believers. For example, the Rogozhskoe Old Believers regularly held well-attended religious services in its community. Even though Orthodox authorities regularly protested the Old Believer's services as violations of laws prohibiting such public displays of the Old Rite, tsarist authorities did not want to disrupt the aid Rogozhskoe's merchants provided to help rebuild the city or cut off charity to needy citizens.[134] Furthermore, during the years immediately following 1812, part of the garrison that helped to maintain order in Moscow and the area surrounding Rogozhskoe, was comprised of a regiment of Cossacks, a group historically noted for their devotion to the Old Rite.[135] Vladimir Makarov later claimed that the Cossacks ensured that the Rogozhskoe Old Believers and their property remained unharmed, thanks to the Cossacks' sympathy for their Old Rite brethren. Consequently, the community received special permission from the Moscow civil authorities to conduct religious services, including the Divine Liturgy, an allowance that directly contradicted the laws that forbade that the Divine Liturgy be said in any structure other than an official Russian Orthodox Church.[136] With seemingly more freedom to express their faith, other Old Rite communities turned to Rogozhskoe to meet their spiritual needs. Such a demand soon allowed Rogozhskoe's image as an Old Rite Holy Moscow to serve as a unifying idealization for priestly Old Believers throughout the Russian Empire.

Rogozhskoe as a Center of the Old Rite

In the decade after 1812, Rogozhskoe Cemetery's fame and success made it the center of the priestly Old Rite in the Russian Empire. Rogozhskoe saw to many spiritual needs of the priestly Old Rite; thus they contributed to the community's desired role as model of Old Rite purity. Pilgrims from throughout the Empire flocked to Rogozhskoe to participate in services held in the communities's grand temples.

> On the big holidays the large cathedrals could not hold all of the zealous pilgrims who travelled from all corners of Moscow; before the old icons glittering with gold and jewels and lit candles the service was decorous, the choir sang beautifully, and the processions to the cemetery and holy waters with the icons was especially solemn [...] Such a sight touched the hearts of all devout Old Believers![137]

Tourists, too, came from all over Moscow and Russia to view the grandeur of Rogozhskoe's temple decorations, frescos, and icons; their donations added to the wealth of Rogozhskoe's coffers.

Because many priestly Old Rite communities lacked priests or spiritual leaders, Rogozhskoe served as a center for any Old Believers to have access to baptism, marriage, communion, or confession–sacraments that Old Rite communities could not administer. At its peak of power in the 1820s, *twelve* priests and four deacons made Rogozhskoe their home. The numbers of Old Rite clergy served the community's rapidly growing population as Rogozhskoe's number of *registered* Old Believer parishioners exploded from 35,000 in 1822 to an estimated 68,000 members in 1825, as Old Rite peasants from the surrounding countryside flocked to Moscow.[138]

The services Rogozhskoe's priests offered created immeasurable spiritual and cultural influence for the community throughout the Russian Empire. Priestly Old Believer peasants from around Moscow and the rest of Russia turned to Rogozhskoe to fulfill some of their most basic spiritual needs. The demand for Rogozhskoe's priests proved both beneficial and strenuous for Rogozhskoe. On the one hand, the priests received substantial financial compensation for their services; consequently, the entire community benefited because the priests regularly donated at least half of their pay to the community funds.[139] Yet even with such a large number of clergy, the demands for Rogozhskoe's grew exponentially. For example, it was not uncommon that around major holidays Rogozhskoe's priests performed between ten to 15 weddings a day, one right after the other.[140] Ultimately, however, the fact that Rogozhskoe could provide such a service allowed the community not only to spread its influence, but also come to identify itself as a spiritual center to priestly Old Believers throughout the Russian Empire.

The establishment of a school at Rogozhskoe Cemetery not only strengthened the community, but also disseminated its teachings throughout the empire. Since the schism, educating future generations in their faith turned into a central priority of Old Rite culture. In many instances, their young people relied entirely on their parents and older generations for their formal secular and religious education. However, with the institution of schools, literacy among Old Believers reached extremely high levels since the Old Rite emphasized the need to protect ancient manuscripts, but also the ability to read them.[141]

By establishing a school for the children of Old Believers, Rogozhskoe came to serve as both a protector and transmitter of Old Rite education. In the rewriting of the duties of Rogozhskoe's Trustees in 1823, the community placed more of an emphasis on the need to formalize education for its younger members. With Rogozhskoe's increasing wealth, duties of the Trustees expanded to "ensure that care and training are given to the young by capable instructors in literacy and writing in Russian."[142] Rogozhskoe's school taught its students the skills of reading and writing in both contemporary and Church Russian, arithmetic, and church singing. Priests, deacons, and designated "book-readers" all participated in educating Rogozhskoe's youth and orphans.[143] These new educational efforts also allowed Rogozhskoe's older generations to instill morality and piety in their successors;

constantly emphasizing the community's importance as a spiritual ideal not only for the Old Rite, but also for Moscow and the Russian Empire. In particular, the Rogozhskoe trustees needed to ensure funding for the school so that "all of the youths are trained in reading and writing in Russian, so that they may establish themselves as notable members of a peaceful society."[144] Merchant dynasties such as the Morozovs and Riabushinskiis exemplified to successive generations the strong sense of duty they would need to maintain and spread the ideals of Rogozhskoe Cemetery.

Rogozhskoe's school provided instruction for the community but soon took on the identity of an instructional center for priestly Old Believers as well, a move that allowed Rogozhskoe to help to maintain the Old Rite.[145] Rogozhskoe also housed five convents and two monasteries constructed over the previous decade; therefore it could send instructors to Old Rite communities throughout the land.[146] Through instruction and teaching spiritual leaders of other church groups, Rogozhskoe gradually developed the image as the spiritual and educational center for the entire priestly Old Rite in the Russian Empire. This favorable position further allowed Rogozhskoe to extend its own moral values to influence the Old Rite world as a whole, since other communities sent their own priests or spiritual leaders to learn from the Rogozhskoe priests.[147]

Conclusion

The Rogozhskoe Old Believers found themselves in truly fortunate times in the first quarter of the nineteenth century when Rogozhskoe's self-identity as a moral and pious center of Old Rite Orthodoxy took shape. Gradual realization of their true sense of place in the larger Russian world, along with their considerable material assets, allowed the Rogozhskoe Old Believers to re-conceptualize their idealized Orthodox community in relation to a much larger Old Rite community outside of its walls, outside of Moscow, and outside of the Moscow District.

However, Rogozhskoe's good fortune did not last. As Rogozhskoe's influence and wealth increased, so did the animosity and jealousy of Orthodox and tsarist officials. Although Rogozhskoe Old Believers still presented themselves as ardent Russian patriots and a major participant in Moscow's economy, their ties to the Old Rite continued to brand them as outcasts in the eyes of the authorities. In spite of such open hostility, Rogozhskoe's ideal society appeared to be a success, albeit conditional on two counts: acceptance and usefulness. Major acceptance of the Rogozhskoe Old Believers derived from their ability to adapt their community to the changing social and cultural environment. And so they had to respond both to the religious policies of the time and catastrophic events such as the Moscow Fire in 1812. The ensuing necessary changes provided both opportunities for and restrictions to the Rogozhskoe Old Believers' ability to define themselves. However, their "usefulness" may have held more weight in the eyes of the tsarist authorities. Numerous studies on religious minorities in the Russian Empire describe how such groups received preferential treatment as long as they did not disrupt social stability; yet at the same time they had to be perceived as a benefit to the state, most often economically.[148] Such factors ultimately played a major role in the Rogozhskoe Old Believers' need to adapt their community and identity in response to the world around them during the community's early history.

CHAPTER 2

FAITH AND IDENTITY UNDER SIEGE, 1822–56

In the decade after the events of 1812, Rogozhskoe served as a beacon of a potential peaceful and prosperous relationship between the Old Rite community and Tsarist Russia. However, Rogozhskoe's success and renown throughout Moscow and the Russian Empire eventually created resentment among Orthodox tsarist officials and members of the Russian Orthodox Church. The gratitude and praise that Rogozhskoe once received from tsarist and Church officials, as well as the greater leniency extended to the community concerning their faith and ideals, eventually turned to suspicion, slander, and open hostility toward the Rogozhskoe Old Believers. Beginning in the mid-1820s, and then particularly during the reign of Nicholas I, the Rogozhskoe Old Believers faced an increasingly hostile and oppressive situation at the hands of both tsarist and Church authorities.

In the aftermath of 1812 and Russia's victory over France, the Empire witnessed an outpouring of Russian pride, which initially created the atmosphere for the Rogozhskoe Old Believers to flourish, especially because they presented themselves as staunch Russian patriots, contributing to Moscow's and Russia's postwar recovery and growth. However this same pride also inspired many tsarist and Orthodox officials, who hoped to find a way to unify the people of the Russian Empire under the guise of Russian patriotism, and even nationalism.[1] What developed, then, was a new breed of officials who adhered to Russian Orthodoxy with renewed vigor and a resurgent idea that

Russian Orthodoxy held a special destiny in Russia's and Europe's development. The Old Rite, as an alternative form of Russian Orthodoxy, then, challenged the national and cultural narrative of Orthodox Russia. To that point, officials quickly equated the Old Rite with not only a spiritual threat, but a political threat to the very unity of the Russian state.[2] Rogozhskoe's success soon made the community a primary target of the state's new efforts to combat the Old Rite.

In the mid-nineteenth century in particular, officials including the Minister of Internal Affairs Dmitri Bibikov, Metropolitan of Moscow Filaret, and even Nicholas I viewed state intervention and control of Rogozhskoe Cemetery as integral to ending the schism once and for all. For much of the nineteenth century, Rogozhskoe served as a critical focal point for the relationship between Russia and the Old Rite as a whole. The new hostility toward Rogozhskoe Cemetery by the state and church initially began as a process to weaken Rogozhskoe's influence as a priestly spiritual center. Eventually, tsarist oppression turned into a combined effort by both the government and church to gain total spiritual and social control of the community by directly attacking the community's Old Believers spiritual and financial identity.

The second quarter of the nineteenth century served as a particularly challenging period for the Rogozhskoe community once the State and the Church strategically used *Edinoverie*, the state-approved branch of the Old Rite against them. During Nicholas I's reign, *Edinoverie* lost its original purpose to attract Old Believers with promises of an officially recognized and sanctioned Old Rite that allowed for Old Believers to practice their religion freely. Instead, Nicholas, Filaret, and other officials turned *Edinoverie* into a state-sponsored weapon to combat the Old Rite, and use it to target Rogozhskoe. Using *Edinoverie*, the state now preferred coerced conversion as its primary tactic to attack Rogozhskoe's Holy Moscow, its symbolism, and its empire-wide influence, as well as the community's self-identity and faith.

Nicholas's reign introduced a new period of state efforts to challenge the Rogozhskoe Old Believers. In response to this new attack on their faith, the Rogozhskoe community resisted Nicholas's efforts by supporting the creation of a new Old Rite Hierarchy. These two distinctly different trends shaped the relationship between the Rogozhskoe Old Believers and Imperial Russia during this period and make up the focus of this chapter. First, it examines the combined efforts of state agencies such as the Ministry of Internal Affairs, the Ministry of Finance, the Holy Synod, and especially the Metropolitan of Moscow, Filaret, who was one of the Rogozhskoe Old Believers' greatest critics and enemies. A second focus shows how the Rogozhskoe Old Believers responded to renewed oppression by turning more to their spiritual needs. This critical change of direction ultimately established Rogozhskoe's vital role in restoring a Church hierarchy for the Old Rite through their efforts to help in founding the Belokrinitskaya Hierarchy. Finally, this chapter explores how tsarist and Orthodox officials directly attacked the Rogozhskoe Old Believers' community and challenged the community's own ideology and sense of sacredness by shutting structures within Rogozhskoe and confiscating other structures specifically for use by *edinovertsy.*

Since their founding, the Rogozhskoe Old Believers developed a unique image and perception of how their community could not only uphold the Old Rite but also interact with Imperial Russia and thus define their community as a model of Old Rite idealism. While Rogozhskoe's interaction with imperial authorities always played a major role in shaping and defining the community, Rogozhskoe's experience under Nicholas introduced new, extreme challenges. Rogozhskoe became a spiritual and cultural battleground between tsarist Russia and the Old Rite. The policies introduced under Nicholas's autocracy forced the Rogozhskoe Old Believers to fight not only for their physical and spiritual existence but also for their own identity as a community and as believers of the Old Rite.

Targeting the Old Rite

While Alexander I upheld his grandmother's and father's approach to the Old Rite, ultimately allowing communities like Rogozhskoe to flourish, by the early 1820s, specifically with the rise of Filaret to Metropolitan of Moscow in 1821, church officials and state agents in both Moscow and Saint Petersburg sought ways to interfere in Rogozhskoe's affairs. The Russian Orthodox Church criticized the seemingly arbitrary approach by secular authorities to uphold state and Holy Synod regulations against Rogozhskoe's harboring of runaway priests and their public displays of Old Rite faith. In particular, the Orthodox officials' greatest complaint concerned the authorities' apparent unwillingness to enforce restrictions placed on Old Rite services that prevented Old Believers to perform the Divine Liturgy in their chapels.

Under Nicholas, Filaret and other church and state officials found a ruler willing to curtail any lienency toward the Old Rite. Nicholas's policy toward the Old Rite could easily be reduced to an ultimatum to Old Believers everywhere: convert to Orthodoxy, adopt the terms of *Edinoverie*, or face punishment and religious restriction under the law. The Rogozhskoe Old Believers now expressly served as one of the primary targets for the new policies of tsarist oppression. The Rogozhskoe Old Believers found themselves besieged by oppressive polices introduced by the Tsar, the Ministry of Internal Affairs, Metropolitan Filaret, other church officials, and the Holy Synod itself. Rogozhskoe Cemetery became a battleground on which Tsarist Russia sought to combat the Old Rite throughout the Russian Empire by means of civil and religious oppression. The motive behind Nicholas and his allies' battle was the destruction of Rogozhskoe as a religious and ideological center of the Old Rite throughout the empire.[3] They ultimately wanted to end the *raskol* through the total conversion of Rogozhskoe and other Old Rite communities to *Edinoverie* or the Russian Orthodox Church.

The Old Rite particularly disgusted Nicholas because it remained outside the control of both the State and Church.[4] Likewise, accommodation of the Old Rite by Orthodox leaders such as Platon gave way to renewed animosity toward the movement with the rise of Filaret to the post of Metropolitan of Moscow. Born Vasili Drozdov in Kolomna in 1782, Filaret quickly established himself as a well-known theologian and minister in the early nineteenth century. Appointed to the Metropolitanate in 1821, Filaret saw tolerance of the Old Rite as preventing true national and spiritual unity in Russia after the events of 1812. To this point, Filaret viewed the Old Rite as divided between the loyal *edinovertsy* Old Believers and the disobedient and "dangerous" Old Believers, who refused to accept the authority of the Russian Orthodox Church and the Holy Synod.[5] Both Nicholas and Filaret, then, saw Old Rite communities such as Rogozhskoe as clear displays of disloyalty to the Russian Empire and directly challenged any definition of Russian identity and culture. An alternative approach to Russianness and Russian Orthodoxy deserved only extermination.

In addition to Filaret and Nicholas's personal inclinations toward the Old Rite, Rogozhskoe's growth as a religious center of the *popovtsy* Old Rite throughout Russia turned into a major concern for tsarist authorities. Not only did *popovtsy* from around the empire travel to Rogozhskoe to attend services in Rogozhskoe's extravagant cathedrals and chapels, but also went there to train as priests, attend the community's school, and even to hold wedding services. As Rogozhskoe's influence in Moscow grew, Moscovites, including non-Old Believers, turned to Rogozhskoe for its charities, hospital, orphanage and almshouses rather than their Orthodox Church counterparts. Rogozhskoe's immense wealth and influence in and outside of Moscow by the 1820s became more problematic and spurred on jealousy among church leaders and rival Orthodox merchants.

This atmosphere prompted the first government action against the Rogozhskoe Cemetery in 1823 when Jacob Ignatiev, a merchant of the third guild and a "Pious Orthodox who could not stand to witness such temptations,"[6] informed Metropolitan Filaret that the Rogozhskoe Old Believers openly conducted the Holy Liturgy in their cathedrals on January 13 and 14.[7] Even though Filaret admitted that no corroborating evidence existed to back Ignatiev's claims, he urged authorities to take action against Rogozhskoe for "it would be the triumph of the *raskol*, and terrible for the Orthodox" if the community went unpunished for even their assumed illegal actions.[8] Ultimately, authorities did temporally close Rogozhskoe's churches. However, without evidence to support Filaret's claims, Moscow authorities reopened the churches with a guarantee from the community that the churches would not conduct the Holy Liturgy.[9]

By 1825, for a number of state and church officials, Rogozhskoe represented not just one Old Rite community, but the hub of a much larger, Old Rite network that spanned the Russian Empire. Furthermore, the unknown size of the Old Rite made Rogozhskoe a potential religious, financial, and social threat to maintaining order throughout the empire. Ultimately then, under Nicholas's reign and Filaret's tenure as Metropolitan, Rogozhskoe Cemetery suffered under oppression of the Old Rite as a whole, as well as unique regulations solely designed to weaken the Rogozhskoe community itself.

Nicholas's earliest decrees against the Old Rite struck at the foundations and identity of the family and community: marriages and churches. First, Nicholas and his advisors redefined how the state recognized Old Rite marriages. Under the new marriage laws, only Orthodox priests could perform marriages between Old Believers, thereby invalidating any marriages performed by priests in the Old Rite. Furthermore, the new laws made marriage violations by Old Believers a civil crime rather than a religious matter. Therefore, those who refused to have their marriages performed according to Orthodox practices now became subject to civil authorities rather than the Holy Synod.[10]

The new legislation essentially criminalized Old Rite marriages.[11] By redefining the legality of Old Rite marriages, the state thereby challenged the very legality of Old Rite families. Of particular concern for Old Believers, and especially a fear among the wealthy Rogozhskoe merchant families, such legislation could call into question issues of familial legitimacy and the ability to pass wealth and property through wills.[12] By attacking the institution of marriage, Nicholas therefore challenged much more than an Old Believer's marital status, but the financial stability of wealthy families and the community as a whole. Furthermore, as Old Rite marriages now fell under the jurisdiction of civil authorities, the State therefore redefined its own understanding of the Old Rite predominately as a civil, rather than religious, threat.

Following on the heels of Old Rite marriage bans, Nicholas soon issued decrees directly attacking the very heart of any Old Believer community, their churches.[13] In 1826, and again in 1827, Nicholas approved legislation proposed by the Ministry of the Interior to prohibit Old Believers from repairing old churches or building new ones.[14] While not recognized by authorities as official churches, Old Believer chapels and churches still served as a foundation for Old Rite communities. For the Rogozhskoe Old Believers, their churches represented the physical embodiment of Old Rite sacredness in a world of corruption. For many Old Believers, not only Rogozhskoe, the interiors of their churches remained one of the few symbols and spaces of pre-Nikonian Russian Orthodoxy. Forbidding repairs or building new churches directly attacked the physical image of many Old Rite communities. Furthermore, tsarist authorities ordered the removal of all exterior crosses on Old Rite churches to diminish further the structures' physical symbolism by reserving crosses solely for sanctioned Orthodox and *edinovertsy* churches.[15]

For communities such as Rogozhskoe, their wealth allowed them to create some of the most beautiful and elaborate churches in Moscow, which inspired awe in even some of the community's greatest detractors, such as the nineteenth-century historian Nikolai Subbotin.[16] For church leaders like Filaret, Rogozhskoe's grand churches and elaborate priests' vestments spurred jealously and hatred for the community. Filaret and other leaders of the Holy Synod and Russian Orthodox clergy admittedly feared that Rogozhskoe Old Believers' visible wealth and the physical majesty of Rogozhskoe Cemetery would "confuse" and attract mainstream Orthodox to the Old Rite.[17] Therefore, the new laws ensured that without joining *Edinoverie* or the Russian Orthodox Church, Rogozhskoe's physical manifestations of their piety and wealth could not maintain the outward appearance of a holy site and eventually would crumble to ruins, rather than the grand representations of Rogozhskoe's success.

The Rogozhskoe Old Believers found themselves as targets of not only empire-wide legislation aimed at restricting the rights of Old Believers but also attempts by tsarist authorities to regulate their specific community. For example, a major concern for tsarist and Church officials focused on how to restrict Rogozhskoe's influence both in and outside of Moscow. In 1831, in an effort to establish a government presence and gather information on Rogozhskoe Cemetery (as well as the priestly community at Preobrazhenskoe Cemetery), Nicholas ordered the formation of the Moscow Secret Committee.[18] This organization represented the spearhead of direct government oversight of the Moscow Old Believers. The instructions to the committee on their objective went straight to the point: "to guide [the Old Believers] toward a rapprochement with the Church."[19] Furthermore, in 1836, the Secret Committee established the post of Superintendent of Rogozhskoe Cemetery. The superintendent's duties included keeping census figures on Rogozhskoe's population as well as providing monthly reports to the Secret Committee to ensure that Rogozhskoe remained within the laws, specifically ensuring that Rogozhskoe did not bring in any new priests or renovate their buildings.[20]

As described earlier, one of the most important community ideals that contributed to Rogozhskoe's success and widespread influence was its ties to charity. Particularly after 1812, Rogozhskoe's almshouse grew to become one of the largest charitable centers in all of Moscow.[21]

The almshouse generated much of the leniency the state authorities granted Rogozhskoe in the years that followed. Furthermore, Rogozhskoe's charitable outreach directly rivaled and surpassed many similar institutions overseen by the State and Church.[22] Furthermore, by the 1820s, the almshouses were not the only sources of charity provided by the Rogozhskoe Old Believers. For example, families such as the Morozovs funded the creation of a hospital within Rogozhskoe Cemetery grounds.[23] For the Rogozhskoe Old Believers, and other Old Rite merchants, charity enhanced their social and spiritual standing and allowed them to take on the role of a "*paterfamilias*."[24] The concern for tsarist authorities, and particularly the Russian Orthodox Church, was that Rogozhskoe not only provided charity to Old Believers, but also took in anyone who needed charity regardless of their faith.

The fact that the Orthodox turned to the Rogozhskoe Old Believers for aid clearly spoke poorly about the state of Orthodox charities. However, rather than direct their efforts to improve their own charities, church officials feared that the Rogozhskoe Old Believers used their charities to proselytize wards of their almshouses. In response, the Ministry of Internal Affairs and the Moscow Secret Committee enacted legislation throughout the 1830s and 1840s designed to regulate and restrict Old Rite charities. One of the first regulations placed on Rogozhskoe's charities required that local authorities regularly inspect the almshouses to ascertain that the wards of Old Rite almshouses and hospitals were genuinely ill or destitute. Such legislation introduced further regulations that restricted the ages of the wards and furthermore prohibited the Rogozhskoe almshouse from housing anyone younger than 50.[25] Age restrictions served two goals. First, introducing an age restriction on almshouse wards limited the ability of communities such as Rogozhskoe to potentially attract or cater to groups of people in need, thereby weakening their own ability to uphold their ideals on charity. Second, age restrictions also ensured that the wards, particularly men, did not escape other duties such as military conscription.[26]

Similarly, orphans at Rogozhskoe's almshouses created another concern for State and Church authorities. The primary issue regarding orphans also derived from the need to determine the age of any orphans living in Rogozhskoe, to ascertain the orphan's parentage (if possible, in order to determine if an orphan in question was born to Orthodox parents), and to formulated means to transfer all orphans to become wards of the State or the Russian Orthodox Church. In 1834, the Ministry of Internal Affairs passed new laws that forbade Rogozhskoe from housing orphans over the age of three. Authorities forcefully removed children over three and placed them in the Moscow Foundling Hospital; as a result, male orphans 16 or older faced immediate conscription into the military.[27]

Regulations restricting childrearing in Rogozhskoe did not end with orphans. In March 1835, under advice from Filaret and the Holy Synod, the Ministry of Internal Affairs ordered Rogozhskoe's school closed for "teaching in the schismatic way." The school's closure limited Rogozhskoe and Old Rite parents' options for their children's education. They either had to find a means to educate children themselves, or to enroll their children in an Orthodox-sponsored school or military schools.[28]

The thread connecting the regulations on the ages of Rogozhskoe's wards, orphans, and its schoolchildren all reflect similar concerns on the part of the tsarist government. Specifically, the Ministry of Internal Affairs drew particular note that Rogozhskoe's almshouse and orphanage served as a means of harboring boys who "were more or less adults" with the intent of hiding them from possible conscription.[29] The issue of childrearing, then, became yet another of the conflicts between the Rogozhskoe Old Believers and the tsarist state during this period. By regulating how Rogozhskoe's Old Believers interacted not only with impoverished or orphaned children, but also with their own children's education, tsarist and Church authorities sought to interfere directly with a cornerstone of Rogozhskoe's identity and influence.

On the surface, authorities presented their measures against Rogozhskoe as a means to prevent the community from circumventing laws that forbade Old Believers from taking in the children of Orthodox parents, or preventing able-bodied boys registering for conscription. In actuality, these new restrictions on Rogozhskoe's orphans and schools endangered Rogozhskoe's identity and its future. First, these regulations called into question the nature of Rogozhskoe's "charity," the very heart of Rogozhskoe's own Christian morality. The new laws openly challenged Rogozhskoe's ideological narrative and publically presented Rogozhskoe's charity as an ulterior motive to weaken and corrupt those faithful to the church through clandestine conversions of the sickly and orphaned. Second, the closure of Rogozhskoe's school ensured that all but the children of the wealthiest families would likely attend Orthodox or military schools. Such a goal then challenged the Rogozhskoe Old

Believers' ability to educate their community's next generation both in the Old Rite, and the community's own ideals.

A hallmark of Nicholas and Filaret's oppression of the Old Rite, and especially Rogozhskoe, came from more invasive legislation that intended to restrict the lives and spiritual experience for Old Believers. One of the most serious blows against the Rogozhskoe community came in the form of new state regulations regarding fugitive priests. Rogozhskoe, and the vast majority of priestly Old Rite communities, relied on priests ordained in the Orthodox Church, who later converted to the Old Rite, to serve as their clergy. Since the community's founding, Rogozhskoe regularly attracted or harbored runaway priests from authorities with little concern from Moscow's authorities. However, under Nicholas's new regulations, the Ministry of Internal Affairs passed legislation forbidding Rogozhskoe from taking in fugitive priests beginning in 1827.[30] Clearly the tsarist authorities assumed that without access to future priests, the Rogozhskoe Old Believers would have no choice but to join *Edinoverie* or convert to the Russian Orthodox Church upon the death of their last surviving priest.

Tsarist and church authorities correctly assumed that forbidding access to new priests directly affected Rogozhskoe's ability to maintain its community's ties to the Old Rite, and consequently its spiritual life. However, the desired outcome of the Rogozhskoe Old Believers' turning to the Orthodox Church never came to fruition. Instead, Rogozhskoe looked to a new means to ensure the spiritual survival of their community. Specifically, in 1846, the Rogozhskoe Old Believers soon found a new alternative to build their spiritual life with the founding of the Belokrinitskaya Hierarchy, a bishopric devoted entirely to the Old Rite in the Austrian Empire. Therefore, while facing increased tsarist and Church efforts to eradicate the Old Rite, the Rogozhskoe Old Believers found new opportunities to redefine their very understanding of their faith and their Holy Moscow through the creation of their own Old Rite Church Hierarchy.

The Rogozhskoe Old Believers and the Founding of the Belokrinitskaya Hierarchy

The early 1820s proved to be a period of momentary religious freedom as tsarist authorities often turned a blind eye toward regulating the community. While the Holy Synod and Church authorities in Moscow resented Rogozhskoe's religious success and its new status as a major social and economic influence within Moscow, secular authorities often saw little reason to disrupt the Rogozhskoe Old Believers. In the eyes of the Moscow authorities and police, any perceived threat linked to Rogozhskoe's ties to the Old Rite appeared negligible when compared to the community's significant economic influence.

Therefore, state interference in Rogozhskoe prior to Nicholas's reign often proved to be only a moderate inconvenience for the community. While authorities investigated claims made against Rogozhskoe in 1823 that the community illegally participated in the Divine Liturgy in the Church of the Nativity, with no evidence to support the accusation, tsarist authorities permitted the Rogozhskoe Old Believers to continue their normal activities.[31] However, in the same government statement, Tsar Alexander seemingly foretold of Rogozhskoe's coming tribulations, as he noted to the Rogozhskoe trustees: "If they want to preserve the churches at Rogozhskoe Cemetery, then their path is to join *Edinoverie*, but if [the Synod] does not agree – send in the Church."[32] The Rogozhskoe trustees, however, refused to join *Edinoverie*; instead they pledged not to perform the Divine Liturgy.[33]

Rogozhskoe's spiritual activities served as one of the key characteristics of the community. As priestly Old Believers, Rogozhskoe's community actively sought means to maintain any sense of a spiritual tie to a clergy. Such efforts then threatened the Orthodox Church as the Old Rite could potentially perform many spiritual duties and rituals expected of Orthodox Christians. Many of the restrictions placed on Old Rite spirituality, such as forbidding Old Believers from performing the Divine Liturgy, served the purpose of denying Old Believers a complete Orthodox spiritual experience and forcefully turn them toward the mainstream church. However, as many Old Believers practiced either in secret or in closed communities, upholding such restrictions proved nearly impossible. Therefore, for priestly Old Believers, such as the Rogozhskoe community, access to priests provided the potential, and likely reality, of access to the complete range of spiritual services performed by priests, including the Divine Liturgy. As a spiritual center for the priestly Old Rite, Rogozhskoe built much of its spiritual influence throughout the Russian Empire on the community's ability to attract, house, and provide its parishioners with access to priests. Rogozhskoe's priesthood, in fact, became one of the key forces that rallied the community to remain devoted to the Old Rite, and resist the advances of *Edinoverie* and the Orthodox Church under Nicholas and Filaret.[34]

While tsarist authorities implemented measures to punish priests for turning to the Old Rite, enforcing such laws proved difficult as most runaway priests maintained a mobile lifestyle by travelling between Old Rite communities. However, more prominent communities, such as Rogozhskoe and others in cities and regions with larger Old Rite populations such as Nizhni Novgorod, Saratov, Tula, and Orenberg, held some advantages. Most importantly one such advantage for more wealthy and established Old Rite communities became the ability to hide their priests among their larger populations as one of their congregation, or to move priests from household to household as needed. For affluent communities like Rogozhskoe, another method to protect these runaway priests from tsarist and Church authorities included using the financial backing of wealthier members to bribe officials to leave their priests in place.[35] Such circumstances, then, created a situation that allowed the Rogozhskoe Old Believers to attract and maintain a functioning priesthood to serve their spiritual ideals of their Holy Moscow.

In Rogozhskoe, the community's priests established themselves not only as spiritual officials, but as leaders of the community itself. Without question, Ivan Iastrebov established himself as Rogozhskoe's most influential spiritual leader of the first half of the nineteenth century. As stated by one parishioner, "Father Ivan remained the most strong and solid in the ancient faith [. . .] with just one word, or even with a single glance, everyone obeyed him without question."[36] Beginning his career as an Old Rite priest in the diocese of Vladimir, Iastrebov arrived in Rogozhskoe in 1803 at the age of 33 and soon became abbot of the entire community.[37] In this role, Iastrebov enjoyed an enormous amount of prestige in Rogozhskoe and throughout the Old Rite world. Of particular note is that the community credited Iastrebov with formulating the plans to save or bury Rogozhskoe's icons and relics when faced with the French capture of Moscow.[38] Throughout his career, Iastrebov served not only as a spiritual leader for Rogozhskoe, but came to embody the community's spiritual strength and devotion to the Old Rite and the ideal of their Holy Moscow in the face of the era of oppression under Nicholas and Filaret.

As Rogozhskoe's congregation grew rapidly into the 1820s, the community ultimately needed more priests to serve their spiritual needs

Figure 2.1 Father Ivan (Ioann) Iastrebov, Russian Orthodox Old Rite Church.

as well as maintain their new spiritual influence among priestly Old Believers. By 1822 Rogozhskoe served as the home for 12 priests and four deacons.[39] While Iastrebov became the most outspoken spiritual leader, the most senior priests at Rogozhskoe were Alexander Arseniev, Peter Rusanov, and Ivan Maximov.[40] Unfortunately for Rogozhskoe, many of the priests were elderly. Therefore, the community continuously needed new candidates to serve as their priests. Furthermore, Rogozhskoe's need for priests continually returned the community to the debates on possibly joining *Edinoverie*.[41]

The Rogozhskoe Old Believers essentially faced three scenarios for their spiritual future. The first option remained that Rogozhskoe could accept *Edinoverie*, and thereby gain official recognition of their churches as legal Orthodox churches, gain access to priests, but then fall under the authority of the Holy Synod. A potential second, but extremely unlikely, option for the Rogozhskoe Old Believers became to use their economic and spiritual influence as a bargaining tool. Perhaps their influence would allow the community to negotiate special terms for joining *Edinoverie*, such as renewing the effort to obtain an Old Rite Bishopric or for the community to select their own rather than appointed priests. Alternatively, as the final option, the Rogozhskoe Old Believers could continue to exist as before and seek out or provide shelter for Old Rite spiritual leaders or Orthodox priests willing to provide services in the Old Rites to their community.

While maintaining priests in Rogozhskoe which directly challenged tsarist and Holy Synod legislation, Rogozhskoe's prestige and identity as a spiritual center for the Old Rite hinged on maintaining an active clergy.[42] If Rogozhskoe truly embodied Old Rite piety, then one of the greatest needs for the community was to have access not only to a stable priesthood, but also to its own Church hierarchyin order to emulate pre-Nikonian Russian Orthodoxy. Not only would a hierarchy and steady priesthood strengthen Rogozhskoe's own ideals and morals, it would also legitimize the Old Rite and allow it to flourish throughout the Russian Empire since priests could be ordained for any Old Rite community who desired one.

Rogozhskoe's symbolic standing as a beacon of Old Rite success did not escape the interest of Filaret upon his appointment as Metropolitan of Moscow in 1821. Filaret fully understood that Rogozhskoe's prestige, influence, and presence in Moscow proved problematic.

> the first chapel at Rogozhskoe Cemetery, as it is known, was built with government permission along with the requested almshouses, but after time they opened a chapel with a large structure and dome, the church is there to this day [...], even though this capital has long been a strong hotbed for the *raskol*, consequently, the assumption of a pseudo-holy church of the *raskol* is in this place, a center near the old Orthodoxy, this would be the triumph of the *raskol* and more harmful to Orthodoxy than many of those churches created somewhere away from the capital at the whim of many *raskol'niki*.[43]

Filaret's attack against Rogozhskoe proves significant on a number of levels. First, Filaret reveals his concern with Rogozhskoe's seemingly unchallenged influence. Second, the Metropolitan understood and, more importantly, *feared* the spiritual link between the Old Rite and Moscow as "this capital has long been a strong hotbed for the *raskol*."[44] Most importantly, however, Filaret's letter reveals that the Rogozhskoe Old Believers *successfully* transmitted their identity as a bastion of Old Rite piety to non-Old Rite audiences. Filaret's concerns reveals that Rogozhskoe's Holy Moscow directly challenges the Russian Orthodox Church's ability to combat the Old Rite. By its existence, the Rogozhskoe Old Believers succeeded in presenting the community as a return to pre-Nikonian Orthodoxy which "would be the triumph of the *raskol* and more harmful to Orthodoxy than many of those churches created somewhere away from the capital at the whim of many *raskol'niki*."[45] Therefore, Filaret specifically feared that Rogozhskoe's Holy Moscow directly challenged the Russian Orthodox Church and its cultural influence more than any other Old Rite community throughout the empire.

Furthermore, Rogozhskoe's large number of priests attracted Filaret's increased animosity since the very existence of Rogozhskoe's clergy blatantly disregarded restrictions on Old Rite communities harboring runaway priests. In a letter to tsarist authorities in Moscow in the mid-1820s, Filaret referenced laws passed in 1817 targeting Old Believers in Saratov as precedent for illegalizing the priesthood within Rogozhskoe.[46] Ultimately, in Filaret's opinion, the greatest problem with Rogozhskoe's priests became that a strong priesthood in Rogozhskoe appeared to be the only influence preventing the community from going through a "natural" transition to *Edinoverie*.[47] For Filaret the objective became clear. By ending Rogozhskoe's ability to maintain a priesthood, the community would have no choice but to return to the Russian Orthodox Church and Holy Synod through conversion to *Edinoverie*.

Rogozhskoe's priesthood first came under attack in the early 1820s shortly after Filaret's ascension to the Metropolitanate. Under increased pressure from Filaret, the Holy Synod and the Ministry of the Interior passed legislation that targeted Old Rite communities harboring runaway Orthodox priests in 1822.[48] The new legislation designed to end Old Rite access to priests. First, the law did allow Old Rite communities to keep any "established" priests, as long as they had not left the Orthodox Church to escape criminal prosecution in another diocese. However, the law forbade any communities to take in new fugitive priests or continue to harbor "criminal" priests under the threat of penalties including fines, loss of property, the closure of chapels, or even imprisonment or exile for anyone harboring the runaway priests.[49] Without access to new priests, Filaret envisioned communities like Rogozhskoe leaving the Old Rite for the Orthodox Church or *Edinoverie en masse* as they would not be able to maintain their spiritual needs.

However, Filaret's initial salvo failed to inspire his desired mass exodus of Rogozhskoe Old Believers to *Edinioverie.* Instead, Father Iastrebov became the most unwavering voice in Rogozhskoe by rejecting any compromise with the Russian Orthodox Church. Filaret, and ultimately the Moscow Secret Committee, viewed Iastrebov's presence and influence as the greatest threat to efforts to drive the Rogozhskoe Old Believers to *Edinoverie.* As noted in 1837 by the Moscow Secret Committee:

> among the dissenters of Rogozhskoe cemetery there was an expressed desire to apply to join the Glorious Church, while others remained in their long-held evils and unconformity and invited them to pray before making their final decision. They held an all-night vigil, and in the morning held a service and procession of the icons around the chapel. At the end their priest, Ivan Matveev, stood before the entire congregation and insisted that they all stand firm in their faith until the last drop of blood, and then kissed the Gospel, which was soon followed by all in attendance.[50]

As revealed by this account, Iastrebov remained adamant that Rogozhskoe continue to reject *Edinoverie* in favor of maintaining their spiritual and community identity. For Rogozhskoe members such as Iastrebov, becoming *edinovertsy* and placing the community under Holy Synod's authority meant rejection of their idealized society in favor of compromise with their oppressors.

As the Rogozhskoe Old Believers faced increasing oppression under the combined assault of Nicholas and Filaret, the dwindling priesthood became a severe concern for the community. By 1841, primarily because of the deaths of elderly priests, only four priests remained in Rogozhskoe: Iastrebov, Alexander Arseniev, Peter Rusanov, and Ivan Maximov.[51] As the number of priests dwindled, Rogozhskoe's members debated over their future. For the Rogozhskoe Old Believers there appeared few options. The two most obvious choices available became for the community to petition the state to allow Rogozhskoe to take on

Orthodox priests who desired to leave the mainstream Church, or to seek new terms for Rogozhskoe's joining *Edinoverie*. Unlikely to receive permission for new priests given the political atmosphere under Nicholas's reign, and still seeing *Edinoverie* as outright rejection of their own ideals and the Old Rite, the Rogozhskoe Old Believers made a desperate decision. Rather than hope for new leniency from tsarist or Church officials, Rogozhskoe's parishioners and trustees made the fateful decision to send delegations to seek out an Orthodox bishop willing either to ordain Old Rite priests or convert to the Old Rite himself.[52]

Seeking out a Russian Orthodox bishop for their plans could not be an option, as it only risked further harassment and severe punishment at the hands of tsarist authorities. Ultimately the Rogozhskoe Old Believers supported a search for a bishop outside of the Russian Empire by funding the travels of two Old Rite monks, Pavel Velikodvorskii and Alimpii Milorad.[53] As much of the Orthodox world remained under the control of the Ottoman Empire, Pavel and Alimpii travelled throughout Ottoman territory in hopes of finding and convincing a bishop unhappy with life under Muslim domination to join the Old Rite's cause. Eventually, while travelling through Constantinople, the two monks found Ambrose Pappa-Georgopoli, the former Metropolitan of Bosnia-Sarajevo.

Greek by birth, Ambrose served as the Metropolitan of Bosnia-Sarajevo from 1835 until 1840. While popular among Serbs, and openly supporting Serb insurrection against the Ottomans, Anthimus IV, Patriarch of Constantinople, deposed Ambrose to appease the Ottoman Sultan.[54] Ambrose then moved to Constantinople to live with his son's family. In 1846, the monks Pavel and Alimpii arrived in Constantinople and found Ambrose. The monks began negotiations by explaining the history of the Old Rite and asking Ambrose to become their new Church Father and establish an Old Rite hierarchy at the newly established Belaia Krinitsa Monastery, founded in 1838 in the Austrian Empire by priestly Old Rite monks. While initially hesitant, Ambrose eventually consented, writing to the monks:

> Yesterday, after speaking with you, I was busy thinking, what would I have to offer to you. With this thought, I prayed to God, and I lay down. But before I could even fall asleep, when suddenly appeared before me in a great holy light and a voice said, "Why do

> you sweat with so much thinking. This is a great thing that God has destined you to fulfill and to aid those who suffer under the Russian Tsar." At the last word "suffer", I shuddered and looked around, but no one was visible and only light remained in the room, which gradually disappeared, just as if someone left a lighted candle. My heart turned, with fear and joy, so that in delight I spent the whole night without sleep in prayer to God, and decided to give you my full consent for if this is God's grace, and I am obliged to perform it with joy.[55]

The Old Rite now had its own Metropolitan. On October 28, 1846, shortly after his arrival at the Belaia Krinitsa Monastery, Ambrose ordained two bishops, five priests, and three deacons in the Old Rite, thereby establishing the Belokrinitskaya Old Rite Hierarchy.[56]

Ambrose's conversion seemingly provided a miracle to the Rogozhskoe Old Believers by founding an Old Rite Church. Following Ambrose's conversion, the Rogozhskoe Old Believers quickly accepted

Figure 2.2 Metropolitan Ambrose, Russian Orthodox Old Rite Church.

the Belokrinitskaya Hierarchy; thus they eliminated a glaring absence in their Old Rite identity, established their own Old Rite Orthodox Church, and thereby filled the void of a "pure" Orthodox Church since before the schism. The Rogozhskoe community's role in the founding and eventual acceptance of the Belokrinitskaya Hierarchy not only fulfilled the community's desire to establish an Old Rite Church hierarchy, it also ensured that the Rogozhskoe Old Believers could actively combat the increased pressure by tsarist and Russian Orthodox authorities for the community to join *Edinoverie.* Even under threat of punishment for harboring or housing priests, the Rogozhskoe Old Believers proved more than willing to aid Belokrinitskaya priests to serve the community and use their own resources to aid the priests' travels throughout the Empire.[57] Now serving as a "nerve center," the Rogozhskoe community proved determined to express their ties to the new hierarchy by reestablishment of what they saw as a legitimate Orthodox Church.[58] So much so that on June 19, 1850, willingly ignoring tsarist legislation, Sophroni, the newly ordained Belokrinitskaya Bishop for Old Believers in the Russian Empire, secretly celebrated the Divine Liturgy in Rogozhskoe Cemetery and cemented this glorious moment in the community's history.[59]

Divide and Conquer

Rogozhskoe's part in founding the Belokrinitskaya Hierarchy did not go unnoticed by tsarist authorities. Instead, Rogozhskoe's actions only sparked a new wave of fury amongst government and Church leaders, especially Nicholas and Filaret.[60] For Nicholas, Austria's allowing the formation of an Old Rite Metropolitanate on their territory meddled in Russia's domestic affairs. While Austria closed the Belo Krinitsa monastery and forced Metropolitan Ambrose into exile in 1848 under pressure from Nicholas, the monastery reopened in 1849.[61] To Filaret, Rogozhskoe's roll in funding, forming, adopting, and then supporting the Belokrinitskaya Hierarchy's spread through Russia only proved that the authorities needed to increase their pressure on Rogozhskoe to bring the community to *Edinoverie* or back into the Russian Orthodox Church.

The formation of the Belokrinitskaya Hierarchy on Austrian soil in the backdrop of the revolutions of 1848 spreading throughout Europe, clearly now made the Old Rite a more serious political threat as much as a purely spiritual one. That Old Believers supported a *foreign*-sponsored hierarchy added a new foreign element to Russian spiritual matters.[62] Therefore, such efforts by the Old Rite to support a foreign influence in Russian domestic issues changed the relationship between the State and the Old Rite. Specifically, the appearance of a foreign, Old Rite Metropolitanate made the Old Rite a matter of national security for now all supporters of the Belokrinitskaya Hierarchy could be targeted as foreign agents seeking to undermine Russia.[63]

Even with the new Belokrinitskaya Hierarchy, by 1850 government officials proclaimed Nicholas's policies against the Old Rite as a success. According to officials throughout Russia, they claimed that over one million Old Believers converted to either *Edinoverie* or the Orthodox Church.[64] Furthermore, these officials theorized that only 750,000 dissenters remained throughout the Russian Empire.[65] However, in 1852, the Ministry of Internal Affairs provided the more appropriate, yet likely still low, estimate of Old Believers living in the Russian Empire to be closer to nine to ten million.[66]

Regardless of Old Rite population estimates, tsarist authorities in the 1850s knew they still faced a significant challenge in combating the Old Rite. Furthermore, the many restrictions placed on Rogozhskoe and the Old Rite throughout Nicholas's reign did not at all result in a mass conversion to *Edinoverie*. In fact the Old Rite appeared more resilient than anticipated. The Rogozhskoe Old Believers, in particular, still prospered economically. Rogozhskoe also witnessed a new surge in spiritual influence throughout the priestly Old Rite with the adoption of the Belokrinitskaya Hierarchy as the Episcopal authority over Rogozhskoe Cemetery and began actively to transport priests into Moscow and throughout Russia.[67] Clearly then, efforts to force Rogozhskoe to adopt either *Edinoverie* or join the Russian Orthodox Church, failed. Rogozhskoe Cemetery still stood as an embodiment of an Old Rite Holy Moscow.

While Rogozhskoe families often housed and hid travelling Belokrinitskaya priests, the community still faced the challenge of maintaining a permanent priesthood.[68] Of the priests who served Rogozhskoe legally under the laws established in 1827, only two remained by the early 1850s; the situation became further complicatd with the death of Ivan Iastrebov in December 1853. With only one remaining priest, the Rogozhskoe Old Believers decided to place an effort into petitioning the Military Governor-General of Moscow, Count Arsenii Zakrevskii, for permission to bring in new priests. "The one remaining priest, who advanced in years, cannot perform all of the duties needed in Rogozhskoe [. . .] he may die, and end the service of all sacraments and rites of worship."[69] However, before Zakrevskii could respond, a series of unexpected events developed in 1854 that changed Rogozhskoe Cemetery as a community both culturally and spiritually.

Early in 1854, a Rogozhskoe merchant, Vladimir Sapelkin, approached Metropolitan Filaret with the offer that he convinced "a significant number" of Rogozhskoe Old Believers to accept *Edinoverie* without any additional conditions.[70] What spurred Sapelkin to reach out to Filaret remains unknown. But, Filaret seized on the opportunity and immediately sent word to Nicholas and the Holy Synod about Sapelkin's offer with a claim that this moment could bring the entire Rogozhskoe community under *Edinoverie*. Convinced that Sapelkin spoke for a large following in Rogozhskoe, Filaret believed that Rogozhskoe's conversion to *Edinoverie* would be a near seamless process once a portion of the community converted.[71]

Determining "compromise" as the most effective means for introducing *Edinoverie* to Rogozhskoe, Filaret decided that government confiscation of one of Rogozhskoe's three churches for the new Rogozhskoe *edinovertsy* congregation provided the most strategic means of conversion. "To avoid any animosity or resentment toward *Edinoverie* or the *edinovertsy*," and as a show of his "compromise" Filaret concluded that the confiscated new *Edinoverie* church in Rogozhskoe should be the "smaller of the three" churches, St. Nicholas, rather than the larger, and more richly decorated churches.[72] On September 23, 1854, St. Nicholas became an *Edinoverie* church. The Holy Synod, and by extension Metropolitan Filaret, now established a foothold in the physical boundaries of the Rogozhskoe community and would use this opportunity to place even greater pressure on the remaining Rogozhskoe Old Believers.

Unfortunately for the authorities, *Edinoverie* in Rogozhskoe Cemetery never produced the success that Filaret anticipated. Rather, the new *Edinoverie* congregation numbered only about 100 individuals, a small fraction of Rogozhskoe's registered congregation of nearly 2,000.[73] Filaret refused to accept the fact that the vast majority of the Rogozhskoe Old Believers did not join *Edinoverie*. Furthermore, Filaret claimed that the Rogozhskoe Old Believers chose to "abuse" and to "harass" Sapelkin and the other *edinovertsy*. To Filaret the open mockery by Rogozhskoe's Old Believers proved that the state needed to take even more drastic action to ensure that *Edinoverie* had "the chance to sow good seeds in the ground of Rogozhskoe Cemetery, in which so many bad weeds have grown."[74]

Even without the expected success, *Edinoverie* remained as only one of the state's weapons against Rogozhskoe. In August of 1854, immediately prior to St. Nicholas's consecration as an *Edinoverie* church, the Moscow Secret Committee appointed State Counselor Nikita Mozzhakov to serve as superintendent over Rogozhskoe Cemetery. Under direct orders from and only reporting to the Minister of Internal Affairs, Dimitri Bibikov, and Metropolitan Filaret, Mozzhakov's objective stopped nothing short of pressuring the remaining Rogozhskoe Old Believers to join *Edinoverie*.[75] Mozzhakov used his new position to wield unquestioned authority as he relentlessly investigated and persecuted anyone believed to be harboring priests.[76] While the Rogozhskoe Old Believers came to despise Mozzhakov, the community's hostile critic, Nikolai Subbotin, later praised Mozzhakov as a man of "incorruptible probity, an energetic and skilled performer of any police duties entrusted to him [. . .] and fulfilled his duties to the government with honesty and energy."[77] To that end, under Mozzhakov's extreme harassment, Peter Yermilov, the last remaining priest in Rogozhskoe, turned to *Edinoverie* and left the larger Rogozhskoe Old Believer community without any legal priests.[78]

Rogozhskoe's Old Rite ideals appeared to suffer a near fatal blow. As Subbotin argued, "Deprived of the last permissible priest, and the loss of access to new priests [from the Belokrinitskaya Metropolitans], Rogozhskoe Cemetery completely lost its religious character and its significance in the Belokrinitskaya Hierarchy."[79] With Yermilov's defection, the Rogozhskoe Old Believers faced two choices: adopt *Edinoverie* or illegally bring in new priests and risk Mozzhakov's harsh persecution. In any case, losing their last priest to the *edinovertsy* directly challenged Rogozhskoe's religious life as well as the community's efforts to maintain their self-identity.

Not only did the *Edinoverie*'s forced introduction into the community split the Rogozhskoe Old Believers spiritually, as intended, but also physically. The *edinovertsy* specifically demanded equal use and access to Rogozhskoe's institutions such as the almshouses and hospital; they even disputed the ownership of some private buildings and houses. By demanding either ownership or equal use of the community's buildings, the *edinovertsy* directly challenged the Rogozhskoe Old Believers' sense of sacred spaces. Therefore, in this new trial of their faith, the Rogozhskoe Old Believers' greatest focus became a need to protect their sacred boundaries; essentially any structure, icon, and other items owned by the community as a whole. Unfortunately, for the Rogozhskoe Old Believers, the dispute between the community and the *edinovertsy* provided the opportunity for tsarist authorities to take even greater control of Rogozhskoe's affairs.

Looking to establish their own community within Rogozhskoe Cemetery, the *edinovertsy* demanded access to roughly 50 buildings built in the early nineteenth century. The structures in question were all located in the southern areas of Rogozhskoe Cemetery, directly adjacent to the Church complexes.[80] Thanks to the ban on the Old Rite's ability to maintain their buildings, many of the structures badly needed repair.

Figure 2.3 Nikolai Ivanovich Subbotin.

However, since the buildings in question housed wards of the almshouse and other Rogozhskoe charities, this fight between the Rogozhskoe Old Believers and the *edinovertsy* drew the attention of superintendent Mozzhakov. Under Mozzhakov's guidance, tsarist authorities intervened in the dispute primarily for two purposes: support for the *edinovertsy* in Rogozhskoe and a show of power over Rogozhskoe.[81] The issue focused on whether the structures in question fell under communal property or private property. As the state did not recognize private property as part of Rogozhskoe Cemetery, if members of the Rogozhskoe Old Believers provided evidence of private ownership, then the *edinovertsy* had no grounds to demand use of the properties.[82]

Unfortunately, the Rogozhskoe Old Believers could not prove that the structures were not communal property because in the decades since their construction, many of their original owners left the buildings to Rogozhskoe Cemetery. Two years after the disputes over the property began, the Moscow Secret Committee recognized all of the structures in question as public property and transfered 22 of the buildings to the *edinovertsy* congregation and ordered the remaining structures destroyed.[83] For the Rogozhskoe Old Believers, losing control of these structures to the *edinovertsy* proved that the State and Church could forcefully challenge the community's sense of boundaries within Rogozhskoe. The issue of these structures became only the first stage in tsarist Russia's direct attack on Rogozhskoe's boundaries and self-identity.

The dispute over property in Rogozhskoe paled in comparison to one of Nicholas's greatest efforts to quash the Old Rite. For generations, Rogozhskoe Cemetery's renown and successful charities rested on the fact that many wealthy merchants belonged to the community. Rogozhskoe's merchants proudly wore their beards and traditional garments in public as a visible sign of their adherence to the Old Rite. For tsarist authorities, however, Rogozhskoe's merchants became emblematic of the Old Rite's infiltration into the Russian merchantry as a whole. Therefore, targeting Old Rite merchants would not only limit the financial success for many Old Believers, but also directly attack Rogozhskoe Cemetery's financial foundations. In October 1854, Nicholas instituted new restrictions requiring that all merchants must register either as Orthodox or as part of *Edinoverie* by early 1855.[84] The law therefore directly attacked the Rogozhskoe merchants' ties to their faith, and thereby requiried them to choose between their livelihoods or their faith.[85] Rogozhskoe's merchants then needed to redefine their own self-identity as part of Rogozhskoe's Holy Moscow or as a part of Imperial Russia.

In a letter to the Holy Synod in March 1855, Filaret gleefully proclaimed the victory of *Edinoverie* over Rogozhskoe. According to Filaret, in the months since the introduction of the law targeting merchants, and most notably in the last days of December, a grand total of 1,451 Rogozhskoe Old Believers joined *Edinoverie*.[86] However, even in his hasty declaration of victory, Filaret acknowledged that the number of converts quickly overwhelmed the Rogozhskoe *edinovertsy* priests. In turn, the high demand placed on them prevented the proper rebaptism or registration of many of the new converts.[87] Undeterred, Filaret still believed that his campaign to crush Rogozhskoe, and by extension the Old Rite, neared completion. Following the "conversions" and Mozzhakov's oppressive hunts for the "Austrian priests", he believed that the remaining Rogozhskoe Old Believers surely would soon join the Russian Orthodox Church or *Edinoverie*.

Yet Nicholas's death in March 1855 spurred new life into the Rogozhskoe Old Believers who looked to the new Tsar, Alexander II, with hope that the reign of oppression against their community might end. Wishing to draw attention to the abuses the community faced, the Rogozhskoe Old Believers petitioned both Alexander and Count Zakrevskii with a renewal of their request to lift the ban against finding new priests; they also detailed the many abuses Mozzhakov had inflicted on the community.[88] Filaret quickly sent his own letter to the Holy Synod, and with visible disgust, argued that Rogozhskoe Old Believers fraudulently sent their petition.

> It is an exaggeration to say that the written petition of the dissenters is not only false, but also unconscionable [...] To collect these signatures, there had to be a great gathering of dissenters from the city and country, or they sent agents to the villages to get fellow dissenters to sign the petition. No good can come from such a rally by the schismatics, but to a similar effect, is it any less troubling that such a gathering was concealed from the government?[89]

However, Filaret's protests did not convince the Secret Committee. Citing Mozzhakov's hostility toward the Rogozhskoe Old Believers, Zakrevskii denounced Mozzhakov and ordered his removal due to his "suspicious nature, restless bile, and proving to be not only incapable, but even a harmful demon [. . .] creating ceaseless claims and insults to put the schismatics against themselves and against the government."[90] Zakrevskii then appointed Mikhail Longinov as the new Superintendent for Rogozhskoe Cemetery. Longinov proved to be far more lenient toward the Rogozhskoe Old Believers than his predecessor; often he even sided with the Rogozhskoe Old Believers against the *edinovertsy* in their efforts to maintain their property.

Sergei Lanskoi's appointment as Minister of Internal Affairs also introduced a more soft-handed approach toward Rogozhskoe Cemetery. The tsarist authorities also granted permission to Rogozhskoe in 1856 to once again begin worshiping in their churches with visiting priests. In celebration, on January 21 and 22 Rogozhskoe held services, that saw upwards of 3,000 attendees at each service.[91] Witnesses to the services specially noted in their reports that the Rogozhskoe Old Believers only celebrated Matins, Hours, and Vespers with no special celebration or other disturbances.[92] In that moment, it appeared that the Rogozhskoe Old Believers might see their Holy Moscow survive for a return to its former glory.

Unfortunately, many enemies still sought Rogozhskoe's downfall. In a letter dated January 30, 1856 a monk by the name of Parfeni, contradicting even government witnesses, denounced the Rogozhskoe Old Believers publically.

> We here in Moscow, the children of the One Holy Apostolic Greco-Russian Church of Christ, suffered a great, barely survivable anguish, as the Rogozhskoe schismatics offered up their great service in their chapel on 22 January, some simple peasants, and all the worshiping congregation, openly and brazenly mocked the Orthodox, especially those *edinovertsy*, who last year acceded to the Holy Church.[93]

While later it was proven that Parfeni falsified his claims and never witnessed the events at Rogozhskoe, his denunciation achieved its goals.[94] Using Parfeni's claims, Filaret and other church leaders demanded action against the Rogozhskoe Old Believers. Eventually the original claims against Rogozhskoe grew to include a report of a violent riot against the *edinovertsy*, allegations of brazen disregard for the laws, and assertions that Rogozhskoe performed the Divine Liturgy.[95] Filaret pounced at the opportunity to strike a fatal blow to the Rogozhskoe Old Believers. In a letter to the Holy Synod dated February 16, 1856, Filaret argued that all toleration toward Rogozhskoe must end: "Supporting the schism in Rogozhskoe Cemetery – is to support it even to the remotest parts of Russia, and, conversely, to weaken it in Rogozhskoe Cemetery – means to weaken it everywhere."[96] While initial investigations by authorities in Moscow revealed that the Rogozhskoe Old Believers neither rioted nor violated any laws, the community felt the effects of these claims for the remainder of the nineteenth century.[97] Forced to act, Alexander called for the formation of the Saint Petersburg Secret Committee to investigate the claims against Rogozhskoe and to "curb any possible criminal activities of the Rogozhskoe schismatics."[98] Nine members, six of them clergy, voted for immediate closure of Rogozhskoe's chapels. The only dissenters, Minister of State Property Count Pavel Kiselev, Minister of Internal Affairs Lanskoi, and Secretary of State Count Victor Panin, all demanded more time for a proper investigation into the claims against Rogozhskoe. Overruled, the dissenters convinced the majority to compromise by only sealing Rogozhskoe's altars.[99] Alexander held the ultimate decision in his hands. Siding with the clergy, Alexander ordered Rogozhskoe's altars sealed and all services stopped in their cathedrals: "priests at Rogozhskoe Cemetery are not and will not be tolerated; if they will not join the Orthodox Church or *Edinoverie* then they do not need altars or services."[100]

On July 7, 1856, the Moscow police sealed the Intercession and the Nativity cathedral altars, thereby preventing their use for any religious services.[101] Eventually, the Saint Petersburg Secret Committee undertook a more in-depth investigation and found no evidence to support the claims against Rogozhskoe. In addition, the committee even chastised Metropolitan Filaret for falsifying his claims and creating unnecessary conflict.[102] Nevertheless, in spite of the committee's condemnation of Filaret's false statements and adament calls for action, the closure of Rogozhskoe's sacred spaces dealt a major blow to the community's self-identity and understanding of their Old Rite morality and purity. For the Rogozhskoe Old Believers to move forward, they would need to redefine themselves, their ideals, and their community without a proper physical embodiment of their faith.

Conclusion

The Rogozhskoe Old Believers' experience under Nicholas I challenged the very notions of their community, its ideals, their self-identity in their faith, and their very livelihoods. This period witnessed direct conflict between Rogozhskoe and tsarist Russia over not only the definition and identity of Old Believers, but also the very notions of public, private, and sacred spaces. Nicholas himself and Metropolitan Filaret became Rogozhskoe's greatest adversaries as they deliberately intruded and forcibly challenged the Rogozhskoe Old Believers' sense of communal purity.

Even under such extreme persecution, the Rogozhskoe Old Believers found ways to preserve their identity as an ideal, priestly Old Believer community. Needing to redefine themselves and maintain their connection to spiritual rites, the Rogozhskoe Old Believers took desperate measures. With no options available, the Rogozhskoe Old Believers ensured the survival of their priesthood by creating an entirely new, Old Rite Orthodox Church by aiding in the creation of the Belokrinitskaya Hierarchy.

However, despite Nicholas's death and a seemingly new era of hope under the early years of Alexander II's reign, Rogozhskoe faced its greatest challenge yet with the closure of the spiritual heart of their community. Even with such a blow, many Rogozhskoe Old Believers did not give in to state demands for their conversion to Orthodoxy or *Edinoverie*. Instead, the loss of their churches served as yet another moment in which the Rogozhskoe Old Believers needed to redefine themselves and to determine how their community could still embody their sense of Old Rite purity.

CHAPTER 3

ROGOZHSKOE IN THE REFORM ERA, 1856–1905

The mid-nineteenth century witnessed the greatest ideological, spiritual, cultural, and even physical challenges that the Rogozhskoe Old Believers faced in maintaining their idealized community. Spiritually and physically divided with the forced invasion of *Edinoverie* and prevented from using their sacred spaces by the state closure of their cathedrals, the Rogozhskoe Old Believers now needed to redefine their understanding and representation of their communal ideals and piety. With the onset of the Great Reforms, the Rogozhskoe Old Believers, like the rest of Russia, struggled to definine its own self-identity during this period.

Even with such uncertainty, through the second half of the nineteenth century, the Rogozhskoe Old Believers found a means to strengthen their community's representation of Old Rite piety. In fact, by the end of the nineteenth century, the Rogozhskoe Old Believers completely redefined themselves not only as the center for the priestly Old Rite, but also established themselves as a force of loyalty to the tsarist state. During this critical period in the community's history, the Rogozhskoe Old Believers redefined themselves in the face of Russia's social, political and cultural turmoil of the Reform Era. To that end, the Rogozhskoe Believers presented their community as a model of Old Rite devotion, but also as a community loyal to tsarist autocracy. The Rogozhskoe Old Believers, then, sought to utilize their Old Rite morals to guide their actions to present themselves as examples of patriotic and loyal stability in light of the chaos brought on by the introduction of the Great Reforms, emancipation of the serfs, and Russia's drive to industrialization.

While Russia faced many uncertainties during the Reform Era, the Rogozhskoe Old Believers used their entrepreneurial skills, capital, and charity as a means not to flaunt their success, but in order to present their ideal of a greater Christian and Orthodox society to stand against the corruptions of Western capitalism and Western industrialization. With these guiding principles, the Rogozhskoe Old Believers made use of their community to stand as a beacon of Orthodox piety in a corrupt world. Most importantly, the story of Rogozhskoe Cemetery in the late-nineteenth century mirrors the many concerns and challenges faced by all of Russian society during this same period as now the Russian Empire struggled to redefine itself in the face of rapid changes to make Russia a modern state.

The second half of the nineteenth century, then, witnessed the Rogozhskoe Old Believers adapt their community not only in response to the closure of their churches, but also to the social, cultural, and political turmoil of late-nineteenth century Russia. First, because Rogozhskoe needed to adapt to the loss of their sacred spaces, the Rogozhskoe Old Believers reinforced their spiritual identity through greater ties to the Belokrinitskaya Hierarchy. This period also witnessed a series of debates within Rogozhskoe, as well as in the Old Rite itself, over the spiritual or dogmatic validity of the Belokrinitskaya Hierarchy. However, the most critical debate that Rogozhskoe undertook during this period centered on the community's own understanding of the Old Rite and demands for greater autonomy within the Belokrinitskaya Hierarchy itself.

Second, the Rogozhskoe Old Believers needed to respond to the many changes introduced by the Great Reforms, particularly, how the Rogozhskoe Old Believers attempted to adapt their community to the reforms. On the one hand, a number of Rogozhskoe's more influential individuals attempted to encourage tsarist authorities to include reforms regarding the Old Rite as part of the social, political, and religious changes throughout the empire. Yet, on the other hand, seeing the many challenges Russia faced in the aftermath of reform, the Rogozhskoe Old Believers increased their public presence through patronage and philanthropy while going to new lengths to proclaim the community's loyalty to tsarist autocracy.

In the Reform Era, the greatest challenge for the Rogozhskoe Old Believers became the need to maintain their self-identity as defenders of Old Rite Orthodox purity, but also to redefine themselves in response to the many new opportunities provided by tsarist reform efforts. Ultimately then, like Moscow and the Russian Empire around them, the Rogozhskoe Old Believers confronted the period of the Great Reforms as a new and uncertain era. Like the rest of Imperial Russia, the Rogozhskoe Old Believers needed to try to adapt rapidly to the changes around them.

Redefining the Old Rite in Rogozhskoe Cemetery

Sealing Rogozhskoe's altars by tsarist authorities directly challenged the very spiritual identity of the Rogozhskoe Old Believers. First, sealing the altars prevented the Rogozhskoe Old Believers from practicing their faith as a community. While families had the option to pray privately in their homes, religion is a shared experience, and as seen, shaped the very people who built Rogozhskoe Cemetery. Removing services from the cathedrals prevented that shared experience. Furthermore, the Rogozhskoe Old Believers could no longer use their sacred spaces as Orthodox Christians. By losing the ability to use their churches for religious services, the Rogozhskoe Old Believers seemingly lost the very symbols of their ties to Orthodoxy and their communal experience.

Therefore, maintaining their spiritual identity became one of the greatest challenges for the Rogozhskoe Old Believers in the second half of the nineteenth century. First, the Rogozhskoe Old Believers now needed to find a means to maintain their identity as an Old Rite community without the use of their sacred spaces. Furthermore, loss of their schools, death of their priests, inability to bring in new clergymen, the presence of *edinovertsy*, along with unfriendly tsarist authorities severely limited Rogozhskoe's ability to maintain the same influence that the community once held in the Old Rite and throughout the Russian Empire. The challenge for the Rogozhskoe Old Believers in the mid to late-nineteenth century, then, became the very need to redefine themselves and their faith within the Old Rite. Most importantly, the Rogozhskoe Old Believers needed to find a means to reaffirm themselves as a restored Third Rome in the face of these new trials and tribulations.

Rogozhskoe Cemetery's ties to the Belokrinitskaya Hierarchy provided such an opportunity for the community to redefine their understanding of their faith as well as reinforce their communal values and sense of Old Rite piety. As a major influence in the hierarchy's founding, as well as a major patron for the Belaia Krinitsa monastery, the Rogozhskoe Old Believers quickly turned to this relationship as a means to reaffirm their ties to the Old Rite. The relationship between Rogozhskoe and the Belokrinitskaya Hierarchy served as the grounds for Rogozhskoe to influence how the hierarchy functioned for all Old Believers in the Russian Empire, thereby maintaining Rogozhskoe's symbolic position among priestly Old Believers throughout Russia. During the second half of the nineteenth century, then, Rogozhskoe capitalized on their relationship with the Belokrinitskaya Hierarchy to reaffirm the ideals and values of their community.

Rogozhskoe and the Belokrinitskaya Hierarchy maintained a vitally important symbiotic relationship. For example, priests ordained at the Belaia Krinitsa monastery, outside of the jurisdiction of the Russian Empire, provided access to a clergy for the Rogozhskoe Old Believers. Equally important, the Rogozhskoe Old Believers clandestinely imported and housed priests among the community's wealthier members who used their social influence, or their financial wealth, to bribe officials or the police to avoid detection by tsarist authorities.[1] While the Belokrinitskaya Hierarchy provided the community with some access to priests, the hierarchy and Belaia Krinitsa monastery relied heavily on Rogozhskoe's continued financial and spiritual support as well as the community's role in maintaining the new hierarchy in the Russian Empire, because Rogozhskoe Cemetery served as a stopover for Old Rite priests travelling from one community to the next.[2]

However, in the second half of the nineteenth century, the Rogozhskoe Old Believers themselves questioned their place within the Belokrinitskaya Hierarchy. This internal debate reflected the very concerns that the Rogozhskoe Old Believers held about their own self-identity as members of the Old Rite and as a community. Specifically, when the presence of *edinovertsy* hindered use of their own churches, Rogozhskoe as a community found itself debating the very essence of their faith.

The Rogozhskoe Old Believers faced two major concerns. The first centered on the Belokrinitskaya Hierarchy's very existence as a Church.

Specifically, the Rogozhskoe community found themselves in a much larger debate within the Old Rite itself, among both priestly and priestless communities, about the Hierarchy's ordaining new priests as well as the Hierarchy's legitimacy within Orthodoxy and Christendom. Second, the Rogozhskoe Old Believers now questioned their place in relationship to the Belokrinitskaya Hierarchy; namely, Rogozhskoe now pondered why their community continued to rely on a foreign Metropolitan as their spiritual leader, rather than receive their own Russian Old Rite bishop. Ultimately then, these very issues forced the Rogozhskoe Old Believers into a series of internal spiritual debates concerning not only their relationship with the Belokrinitskaya Hierarchy, but their identity as an Old Rite spiritual center and its place within Christendom.

Since the Belokrinitskaya Hierarchy's founding, the Old Rite Church faced its own challenges both inside and outside of Russia. For example, shortly after Belokrinitskaya's founding, the Old Rite Church faced a number of risks concerning its existence. As described earlier, Austria's initial refusal to shut down the Old Rite monastery at Belaia Krinitsa infuriated Nicholas I and Metropolitan Filaret. However, in order to appease Nicholas and solicit his aid against the Revolutions of 1848, Austrian authorities initially closed the Belaia Krinitsa Monastery and forced Metropolitan Ambrose into exile. Fortunately for the Old Rite, the monastery reopened in 1849 and Bishop Kirill Timofeev became the new Metropolitan of the Belokrinitskaya Hierarchy. With the seat of the Belokrinitskaya Hierarchy restored, Kirill served as Metropolitan while Ambrose maintained his role as a Church Father and a spiritual adviser for the Belokrinitskaya Hierarchy until his death in 1863.[3]

Under Metropolitan Kirill, the Belokrinitskaya Hierarchy expanded throughout Russia when in 1853 Kirill consecrated three Russian archdioceses in Vladimir, Kazan, and Moscow, the last housed in Rogozhskoe Cemetery. However, due to the increased tsarist oversight of Rogozhskoe Cemetery in the 1850s, the Old Rite Archdiocese of Moscow remained vacant while under Metropolitan Kirill's personal authority. To remedy his geographic distance from Moscow and the Russian Old Believers, Kirill appointed the newly ordained Antonii Shutov as Archbishop of Vladimir and the hierarchical authority over all Old Believers in Russia.[4]

Born Andrey Shutov and raised in Kolomna in the Orthodox Church, Antonii joined the priestless Old Rite Norskii Monastery in Starodub in 1828 following his father's death. However, needing to support his elderly mother, Antonii traveled to Moscow, ultimately working for and befriending the Guchkov merchant family, members of the Preobrazhenskoe Cemetery community. After serving as Preobrazhenskoe's community treasurer for seven years, Antonii eventually returned to the Norskii Monastery and took his monastic vows. However, with increased persecution of the Old Rite, Antonii left Russia for the Klimoutskii Monastery in Austria, very near Belaia Krinitsa. The close proximity to the Belaia Krinitsa monastery brought Antonii into contact with one of Belaia Krinitsa's most influential monks, Pavel Velikodvorskii. Pavel played a critical role in convincing Metropolitan Ambrose to leave the Greek Orthodox Church for the Old Rite. Antonii soon found himself debating with Pavel over perceived errors the priestless Old Rite held about the clergy. After months of spirited debates, Pavel convinced Antonii to join the Belaia Krinitsa monastery in 1852. The following year, Kirill selected Antonii to serve as Archbishop of Vladimir. Following his appointment, Antonii immediately returned to Russia in order to ordain enough priests to meet the spiritual needs of Old Believers throughout the Empire.[5]

Antonii's appointment and actions did not escape notice of tsarist authorities, particularly during the height of repression against the Old Rite in the 1850s; consequently authorities issued a 12,000-ruble reward for his capture and arrest. Coming to Antonii's aid, the Rogozhskoe Old Believers took on their usual role to protect Belokrinitskaya clergy. Making connections with and hiding among many of Rogozhskoe's wealthy merchant families, Antonii spent most of his time in or near Moscow disguised as a failed businessman staying in Moscow to work off his debts.[6] However, Antonii's difficulties appeared to be a godsend for the Rogozhskoe Old Believers for not only did he become a spiritual leader for the community but he also ordained priests and held services for the community in secret.[7]

In reality then, Antonii maintained his position as Archbishop and also conducted religious services expected of a bishop; his ties to Rogozhskoe and Moscow made Rogozhskoe Cemetery the *de facto* center of the Belokrinitskaya Hierarchy in the Russian Empire. Yet, Antonii's spiritual authority and Rogozhskoe's potential claims as seat of the

Belokrinitskaya Hierarchy in Russia, remained limited in two key factors. First, while the Old Rite Archbishopric of Moscow remained vacant, Metropolitan Kirill officially retained direct spiritual control over Moscow and thereby Rogozhskoe Cemetery–control he would not give up easily.[8] Second, as Metropolitan, Kirill's decisions could supersede Antonii's, particularly in appointing or ordaining clergy along with other spiritual matters concerning the Belokrinitskaya Hierarchy. Therefore, both Antonii and the Rogozhskoe Old Believers remained under the authority exerted by Kirill from the Belaia Krinitsa Monastery in Austria.

Soon, however, a series of events intensified Rogozhskoe's debates about their place within the Belokrinitskaya Hierarchy and the means to guide their own spiritual destiny. In step with the mood of this period in Russian history, many Rogozhskoe Old Believers firmly believed that not only did Rogozhskoe need greater spiritual autonomy to meet their immediate needs but also desired public expressions of greater loyalty to the Russian Empire, part of the community questioned their spiritual subjugation to a foreign Metropolitan.[9] On the other hand, not oblivious to Rogozhskoe's efforts to weaken his direct control, Kirill appointed his own deputy and closest advisor, Onuphrius Parusov, to serve as Archbishop of Moscow in 1861. Directly at odds with the Rogozhskoe Old Believers' expressed wishes, Kirill's decision only angered the community who requested to elect their own, Russian bishop, rather than continue to rely on Kirill in Austria.[10] Given the situation in which they found themselves, the congregation feared for their own existence as Old Believers, especially because both the tsarist authorities and their own heirarchy challenged their unique spirituality. As a result the Rogozhskoe Old Believers soon found themselves debating their own understanding of their new Church hierarchy within the Old Rite and Russian Orthodoxy as a whole.

In questioning their own faith, and in particular their place within the Belokrinitskaya Hierarchy, the Rogozhskoe Old Believers realized that they needed to resolve two major issues in order to determine how their ties to the hierarchy fulfilled the expectations of their Holy Moscow. The Rogozhskoe Old Believers needed to legitimize the very existence of the Belokrinitskaya Hierarchy at once. Such action required them to respond to numerous criticisms by both the Russian Orthodox Church and other Old Believers, specifically the *bespopovtsy*, who questioned and attacked the new hierarchy's spiritual legitimacy. At the forefront of counter-Rogozhskoe attacks, the priestless Old Believers argued that any formal Church hierarchy ceased to exist following the schism, mainly because the State and Church imprisoned or killed many of the clergy who rejected the Nikonian reforms; such tactics thereby brought to an end the last, and legitimate Christian hierarchy.

Along with such criticism, priestless Old Believers in particular saw how the Belokrinitskaya Hierarchy's creation mirrored the events of the schism. Namely, the hierarchy itself found its origins in a foreign influence in Russian Orthodoxy: its founder, Ambrose, was Greek, and the Belaia Krinitsa monastery was located in the Austrian Empire.[11] Priestless criticism toward the Belokrinitskaya Hierarchy reached new heights in the 1850s when a number of apocalyptical writings spread throughout priestless Old Rite communities in central and southern Russia. These works attacked the Belokrinitskaya Hierarchy and their clergy as proof of the impending End Times along with the Antichrist's attempt to corrupt the Old Rite as a disguised attempt to restore an Old Rite Church.[12]

Another major issue for Rogozhskoe concerned the community's position in the Belokrinitskaya Hierarchy. Specifically, in the eyes of the Rogozhskoe Old Believers, their community's role in founding, funding, and aiding the Belokrinitskaya Hierarchy required that the Archdiocese of Moscow finally receive its own bishop. More important to the Rogozhskoe Old Believers, this bishop should have equal clerical authority with the Metropolitan of Belaia Krinitsa, including the ability to ordain bishops and establish new bishoprics within the Russian Empire. Therefore, as the primary patrons for the Belokrinitskaya Hierarchy, the Rogozhskoe Old Believers needed to legitimize their new hierarchy by insisting that Rogozhskoe Cemetery serve as the unquestioned spiritual authority of the hierarchy in Russia.

This series of events and concerns culminated in the Rogozhskoe Old Believers' establishing a community-led Rogozhskoe Spiritual Council. At their first gathering, the community decided to address many of the criticisms of the Belokrinitskaya Hierarchy, as well as the growing number of grievances against Metropolitan Kirill and the seeming lack of spiritual autonomy for Rogozhskoe Cemetery. The debates within the Spiritual Council resulted in a major turning point in the history of Rogozhskoe Cemetery, the Old Rite, and the Belokrinitskaya Hierarchy.

On February 24, 1862, shortly after the first meeting of the Rogozhskoe Spiritual Council, an open letter entitled the "*Okruzhnoe poslanie Rossiiskikh arkhipastirei Belokrinitskoi ierarkhii*" (*The Encyclical of Russian Archbishops of the Belokrinitskaya Hierarchy*) appeared in the community. Authored by Ilarion Kabanov, using the pseudonym "Xenos" one of Rogozhskoe's librarians and most celebrated dogmatists, the *Okruzhnoe poslanie* directly responded to the many criticisms questioning the legitimacy and sanctity of the Belokrinitskaya Hierarchy. The first half of the *Okruzhnoe poslanie* strongly disputed the slanders against the Hierarchy by priestless Old Believers. The *Okruzhnoe poslanie* denounced all critical written attacks as "false and fabulous works [. . .] dangerous corruptions of scripture" serving to "stumble gentle and guileless children of the Church."[13] "Xenos" noted in particular that the priestless Old Believers did not base their criticisms of the Belokrinitskaya Hierarchy on scripture, but rather on their own contempt for the clergy. "Such obscure and ridiculous sophistry is maliciously planted in the darkened conscience of the priestless and inconspicuously painted the minds of these Christian

Figure 3.1 Ilarion Kabanov, "Xenos." *Okruzhnoe poslanie*, Moscow: E. Lissner and Iu. Roman, 1893.

Figure 3.2 Antonii (Shutov), Archbishop of Moscow and All Rus', 1870s. *Tserkov'*, 1908.

people, in their simplicity, to where they cannot distinguish the truth from falsehood."[14]

The second half of the *Okruzhnoe poslanie* became the most important, but also most controversial, effort by the Rogozhskoe Old Believers to define their faith in the greater history of Christianity. Specifically, "Xenos" provided ten detailed explanations of the Belokrinitskaya Hierarchy's spiritual and dogmatic legitimacy by connecting the Church's creation to the spiritual foundations of the universality and eternity of the priesthood, thereby placing the Old Rite in the *universal* dogmas of Orthodoxy and Christianity.

> The Holy Orthodox-Catholic Church and the priesthood will continue to the end of time and until the Judgment of the Lord [. . .] The current dominant Russian Church, as well as the Greek one, do not believe in a different God, but are in communion with us: "The

> Maker of Heaven and Earth, of all things visible and invisible" [The Creed]. They believe in the Holy Trinity, consubstantial and undivided: the Eternal Father, the Eternal Son and Holy Spirit. [Their priests] take confession and teach about Christ's redemption for the deeds of mankind. They honor and celebrate the same holidays as we do on the same old calendar: Christmas, the Epiphany, the Crucifixion, the Burial, the Resurrection, and the Lord's glorious ascension into heaven, and the other holidays of the Immaculate Virgin and the holy saints. They honor and pray to the holy icons of images of Christ with the writing of his names: IC XC. They kiss the holy and miraculous icons, saints' relics. And these all clearly prove that they believe in the one, same, and true God as do we, and with us confess Christ [. . .] So while schism and discord came into being, we are still children of the one holy, catholic, apostolic, ancient Orthodox Catholic Church.[15]

What sparked the greatest controversy within the Old Rite as a whole, as well as the Belokrinitskaya Hierarchy in particular, was Kabanov's apparent attempt to reconcile the Old Rite to the Russian and Greek Orthodox Churches. In his effort to legitimize the Belokrinitskaya Hierarchy's founding by former Greek and Russian bishops, "Xenos" seems to dismiss many of the Old Rite's core rituals and symbols, such as the use of two fingers to make the sign of the cross, the use of pre-Nikonian spelling in liturgy and scripture, and the use of eight-pointed crosses. However, "Xenos" presented them as secondary concerns when compared to maintaining Orthodox dogma and spirituality, yet another part of the universality of the Christian Church. For example, the *Okruzhnoe poslanie* explored the history of the different spellings for names and terms in Orthodox scripture; "Xenos" demonstrated that by 1646 Russian spiritual texts regularly used the Old Rite spelling of Jesus (*Isus'*) and the "Greek" spelling (*Iisus'*) interchangeably. As another example of the universalities of the churches, "Xenos" pointed out that all Orthodox Churches still used the same abbreviated spelling for Jesus (*IC XC*) in their icons, and that "Thou name Iisus' carries the name of God and there is no given name of the enemy of Christ."[16]

The *Okruzhnoe poslanie* also attempted to explain the debates concerning the use of two or three fingers in the sign of the cross. "Xenos" in particular argued that both practices appeared throughout

Christian tradition since ancient Christian texts varied on the use of one form over the other.[17] The *Okruzhnoe poslanie* also dismissed Old Rite issues with the use of non-Byzantine Crosses.

> The image of the Cross is not the image of the Antichrist and is not a godless idol, and is not an abomination by standing in the holy places, as noted in the evil notebooks, but the image of the Cross is the image of Christ, from the days of the Apostles to the present day the Cross is acceptable to the Orthodox-Catholic-Church.[18]

With such arguments, the *Okruzhnoe poslanie* clearly attempted to place the Rogozhskoe Old Believers' own understanding of the Old Rite into a larger relationship with all of Christendom, thereby legitimizing the Old Rite as part of the universality of Christianity.

Furthermore, it becomes clear that as stated in the *Okruzhnoe poslanie*, "Xenos" viewed the creation of the Belokrinitskaya Hierarchy as mirroring the original Baptism of Rus'. Just as Vladimir borrowed and introduced Orthodoxy to the Russian people with the aid of Greek priests, the Belokrinitskaya Hierarchy "borrowed" Ambrose from the Greek Church to reestablish a legitimate Orthodox hierarchy for the Old Rite. The Rogozhskoe Old Believers defined their faith thus, and sought to establish their community as the seat of the restored Russian Old Rite Orthodox Church in Russia. Throwing his own support behind the *Okruzhnoe poslanie*, Archbishop Antonii signed and fully endorsed the ideology presented in the document; numerous Belokrinitskaya priests in Moscow shortly followed his lead.[19]

However, the *Okruzhnoe poslanie*, and Antonii's endorsement, initially caused confusion and division within Rogozhskoe Cemetery and the Belokrinitskaya Hierarchy, as well as within the Orthodox Church itself. Antonii's supporters, the *okruzhniki*, viewed the *Okruzhnoe poslanie* as a manifesto of Rogozhskoe's spiritual autonomy and authority in defining dogma for the Belokrinitskaya Hierarchy in Russia.[20] Caught off guard by such a proclamation of seeming reconciliatory beliefs, Russian Orthodox theologians such as the historians Subbotin, and Popov, openly debated at the time whether the *Okruzhnoe poslanie* represented Rogozhskoe's true desire to return to the Russian Orthodox Church.[21]

Conversely, the *Okruzhnoe poslanie*'s opponents, the *neokruzhniki*, led by Archbishop Onuphrius, saw the document as heresy against both the Old Rite and the Belokrinitskaya Hierarchy. The *neokruzhniki*'s primary disagreement hinged on the fact that they believed that the *Okruzhnoe poslanie* disregarded many of the central tenants of Old Rite identity, such as the issues over the sign of the cross and spelling in liturgical books. Furthermore, the *neokruzhniki* argued that "Xenos" appeared as a Russian Orthodox apologist who too easily dismissed the nearly two centuries of persecution against the Old Rite at the hands of the Russian Orthodox Church.[22] With no end to the debate over the *Okruzhnoe poslanie* in sight and little spiritual support within the community, the *neokruzhniki* appealed directly to Metropolitan Kirill to intervene on their behalf.[23]

Hoping to restore spiritual and hierarchical order in Rogozhskoe Cemetery, as well as reaffirm his authority over the community, Kirill arrived in Moscow in January 1863 and openly denounced the *Okruzhnoe poslanie*. However, empire-wide events forced a series of immediate reactions that placed Rogozhskoe on the path toward spiritual autonomy. In particular, shortly after Kirill's arrival, the January Uprising in Poland put both the *okruzhniki* and *neokruzhniki* into action to see Kirill dismissed from Moscow quickly. More critical for the situation, both *okruzhniki* and *neokruzhniki* demanded that Kirill relinquish his authority in Moscow and Russia. All of Rogozhskoe feared that Kirill's presence in Moscow might draw the attention of tsarist authorities who viewed him as a foreign, "heretical" bishop.[24]

Kirill's effort to reassert his authority over Rogozhkoe Cemetery failed. Even though it appeared that the *neokruzhniki* held a small majority among the Rogozhskoe Old Believers, with such pressure from his supporters and opponents alike, Kirill had no choice but to oversee the selection of an Archbishop of Moscow and then return to Austria. Furthermore, in order to restore spiritual harmony, Kirill realized that he must meet Rogozhskoe's demands for a new Rogozhskoe Spiritual Council to elect their own bishop.[25] As a final concession, Kirill guaranteed that the elected Archbishop would hold authority over all Belokrinitskaya Old Believers throughout the Russian Empire, and have the ability to ordain and consecrate new bishops and dioceses.[26] However, rather than serve as a sign of his contrition, Kirill secretly believed that his concessions, combined with the influence of the *neokruzhniki*, guaranteed Onuphrius's election as Archbishop of Moscow.

Rogozhskoe's debates concerning the *Okruzhnoe poslanie* and the community's identity within Russia and the Belokrinitskaya Hierarchy remained far from solved. In a surprise decision, in order to show support for Kirill's authority and "desire to restore peace in the Church," Antonii withdrew his support for the *Okruzhnoe poslanie*.[27] At the same time, Antonii urged that the Rogozhskoe Old Believers as well as the Belokrinitskaya Hierarchy in Russia, needed to establish closer ties with the Russian state.[28] Antonii's established relationship with the Rogozhskoe Old Believers, combined with his new stance on the *Okruzhnoe poslanie* and his grasp of the political and social situation of the Old Rite in Russia, ultimately undermined Kirill's intended outcome. By a significant majority, the Rogozhskoe Spiritual Council elected Antonii, not Onuphrius, as the new Archbishop of Moscow and All Russia in 1863.[29]

While the majority of the Rogozhskoe Old Believers celebrated Antonii's election as a step toward spiritual autonomy, the conflict between the *okruzhniki* and *neokruzhniki* reignited. Infuriated by Antonii's election, some of Rogozhskoe's most vocal *neokruzhniki* appealed directly to Metropolitan Kirill to intercede, throwing both Rogozhskoe and the Belokrinitskaya Hierarchy into further turmoil. Kirill rejected Antonii's victory and instead reclaimed his authority over the Moscow diocese, reinstating Onuphrius as Archbishop while threatening to excommunicate Antonii and all of Rogozhskoe's *okruzhniki* as heretics.[30] Yet, as Antonii's election revealed, Kirill enjoyed minimal support in Rogozhskoe. Additionally Kirill's continued meddling in Russian affairs finally alienated him from the Russian Belokrinitskaya bishops. In the end, Kirill's efforts and threats backfired: the unanimous vote by a council of the Russian Belokrinitskaya bishops decided to expel Kirill from Moscow, and ordered him to return to Austria, and forever cease his interference in the affairs "of all foreign bishops."[31]

With his seeming victory and overwhelming support, Antonii openly agreed not to enact any of the tenets of the *Okruzhnoe poslanie* as dogma. Yet Rogozhskoe's new Archdiocese and the spiritual unity of their Holy Moscow remained in turmoil. Undeterred by his expulsion from Moscow, Kirill, Ornuphrius, and their *neokruzhniki* supporters continued to demand Antonii's removal and to refuse to acknowledge his authority.

Following through with his initial threats, Kirill excommunicated Antonii and his supporters and thus removed them from the faith they so ardently defended for generations.[32] With a new dispute questioning the very legitimacy of the Archbishop of Moscow, Kirill's acts of defiance, and the authority of the ideas presented in the *Okruzhnoe poslanie*, Antonii and Kirill took their cases to the exiled Metropolitan Ambrose for a fateful final decision in October 1863.

While on his deathbed, Metropolitan Ambrose still commanded respect as the Belokrinitskaya Hierarchy's Church Father. Ambrose's council and decision would determine the rightful spiritual and hierarchical authority in Rogozhskoe–Antonii and the *okruzhniki* or Kirill and the *neokruzhniki*. Initially, however, Ambrose only added to the state of confusion as on October 25, 1863, after hearing arguments from Kirill's delegation, Ambrose proclaimed his decision to side with the *neokruzhniki* and insisted that Antonii give up his office.[33]

However, after hearing the case as presented by Antonii's delegation two days later, in what became his last, but most fateful decision to shape the Belokrinitskaya Hierarchy in Russia, Ambrose reversed his decision. In a letter dated October 28, 1863, two days before his death, Ambrose fully acknowledged Antonii as Archbishop of Moscow and All Russia. But in a surprising move, Ambrose announced his own support for the *Okruzhnoe poslanie* and denounced Kirill for his "deceptions" of the document.[34] Ambrose's letter to Antonii defends his position.

> I gave all my consideration of the rules and teachings of the Holy Fathers and do not find [the *Okruzhnoe poslanie*] against doctrine [. . .] I beseech that all of you responsible for the message through the admission of your pen, will not overturn it. I agree with all the humility of our fraternity and fasten you all to act bound by your signatures. And that you teach this as a blessing [. . .] I, the humble, Metropolitan Ambrose, ask all of the Sanctified church for forgiveness for wrongfully giving my approval for Metropolitan Kirill's message, as I am at such a great distance, I did not hear or know about this case [. . .] But upon arrival of your ambassadors to me, who personally and verbally explained all of your actions and I could see that that he (Kirill) deceived me [. . .] And by this, I destroy and renounce all of my signatures to Kirill And as for the *Okruzhnoe poslanie*, [. . .] every Christian can

> understand and should be convinced that it is nothing harmful to the Holy Church. And for my part I acknowledge the *poslanie* as it is very helpful, and thank all of those who labored on it and the unity and shared opinion of the bishops. Please continue to remain in agreement and abide by these sacred canons unquestionably and unshakable.[35]

With his final act, Metropolitan Ambrose established an autonomous Russian Old Rite Church with Rogozhskoe Cemetery as the seat of the Archbishop of Moscow and All Russia. Furthermore, Ambrose's declaration in favor of the *Okruzhnoe poslanie* encouraged the vast majority of the Rogozhskoe Old Believers now to support the *Okruzhnoe poslanie* as well as Antonii as Archbishop, thereby providing a dogmatic and spiritual foundation for their community and new Church.

Ambrose's decision did not mean an end to the Belokrinitskaya Hierarchy's spiritual divide, particularly between Metropolitan Kirill and Moscow. Dismissing Ambrose's final letter as a forgery, Kirill hoped to rally what remained of the *neokruzhniki* and reaffirm his authority in Rogozhskoe Cemetery. In July 1864, Kirill upheld his excommunication of Antonii and the *okruzhniki* and ultimately ordained a Belaia Krinitsa monk, Antonii Klimov, as bishop of Moscow for the *neokruzhniki*.[36] However, Klimov failed to combat the *okruzhniki*'s growing popularity, forcing Kirill to rescind his excommunications in 1869. The following year, Kirill dismissed Klimov, and openly declared his own adoption of the *Okruzhnoe poslanie* in order to restore peace within the Belokrinitskaya Hierarchy.[37]

Even in the end, Metropolitan Kirill's support for the *Okruzhnoe poslanie* did not completely heal the spiritual divide in Rogozhskoe. Some *neokruzhniki* refused to accept either the *Okruzhnoe poslanie* or Antonii's authority, left Rogozhskoe, and joined the ranks of the *beglopopovtsy* Old Believers who continued to accept runaway priests from the dominant Russian Orthodox Church. However, the debates over the *Okruzhnoe poslanie* significantly reinforced the Rogozhskoe Old Believers' understanding of their faith, as well as their community's embodiment of their devotion to Old Rite purity. After nearly a century of only maintaining a resemblance of a church hierarchy by bringing in runaway Orthodox priests, Rogozhskoe Cemetery was now the seat of the Old Rite Archbishop of Moscow and All Russia.

Community and Order in Rogozhskoe's Holy Moscow, 1856–1905

Just as the Rogozhskoe Old Believers made efforts to redefine their place within the Old Rite, the community also needed to reaffirm and maintain their commitment to their sense of morality and piety. Learning from the debates over the Belokrinitskaya Hierarchy and the *Okruzhnoe poslanie*, the Rogozhskoe Old Believers realized they needed to adapt their community to the realities the community faced from an increased state and *edinovertsy* presence within Rogozhskoe Cemetery. The civil, social, religious, political, and economic changes introduced by the Great Reforms presented new opportunities for the Rogozhskoe Old Believers to redefine their own understanding and presentation of their community's commitment to their sense of Old Rite piety.

As with other Old Rite communities, Rogozhskoe's laity played the dominate role in shaping not only the community's organization, but its spiritual affairs as well. Especially in Rogozhskoe, because the Old Rite clergy and the Belokrinitskaya Hierarchy remained illegitimate under civil and spiritual law, Rogozhskoe's laity were required to make all official organizational and spiritual decisions for the community in order to function within the Russian Empire.[38] Under such organization, Rogozhskoe's laity ensured that their community complied with all laws concerning the Old Rite to the satisfaction of both tsarist and Russian Orthodox authorities.

Organization and order became a major necessity for a community of Rogozhskoe's size. Furthermore, direct election of community leaders, the Rogozhskoe Trustees, remained an important part of the Rogozhskoe Old Believer's sense of community. The trustees served as the community's most important elected officials for they embodied the community's core ideals: devotion to the Old Rite, devotion to Rogozhskoe Cemetery, success in their personal lives through business and state contacts, and their ability to uphold the community's ideals of Christian charity and Christian community. Through their election, then, the trustees took on the obligation to serve as models of the community's ideals.

Rogozhskoe's trustees established themselves as primary representatives in interactions with tsarist authorities. Therefore, the community relied on their trustees to protect Rogozhskoe's worldly and spiritual interests. During the selection of the trustees, parishioners initially voted for members of an election committee. However in 1869, the Minister of the Interior, Alexander Timashev, instituted a change to Rogozhskoe's election process, restricting voting to Rogozhskoe members who owned property in Moscow. The eligible voters then elected a committee of 30 members of the community to elect two trustees to serve three-year terms.[39] By 1870, with Rogozhskoe's spiritual matters now resolved, the community restricted their trustees' authority "exclusively and purely to economic actions" with their primary duty to maintain Rogozhskoe's remaining physical symbols of their Holy Moscow, their sacred spaces and almshouses.[40]

Nevertheless, more critical to the community was the expectation that Rogozhskoe's trustees not only set themselves apart through their own business acumen, but that they also strictly observed their very ideals of Christian charity.[41] While the Rogozhskoe trustees ensured allocation of community funds to maintain structures and equip facilities, many of them often used their own private wealth for restoration projects in gratitude for their election.[42] For example, the merchants Dmitri Milovanov and Peter Mel'nikov, serving as trustees for the periods from 1873–6 and 1882–5, personally financed extensive restoration projects for the Intercession Cathedral and its icons.[43] For their part in restoring some of Rogozhskoe's most important sacred spaces and sacramentals, Milovanov and Mel'nikov became two of the community's most celebrated trustees, even receiving special recognition.

> Elected by the parishioners of Rogozhskoe Almshouse, your services as trustees will always be remembered. For your selfless work for the benefit of our community, your care for the beautification of the Church of God and the beautification of the cemetery, and for your high respect for your true Christian love of peace we thank you for your pious care for the public good.[44]

The community then awarded Milovanov and Mel'nikov icons of St. Peter and St. Dmitri Donskoy, as well as commemorative plaques placed in the Intercession Cathedral in their honor.[45]

Rogozhskoe's trustees also commanded the favor and respect of Moscow and tsarist authorities because the trustees dictated how Rogozhskoe utilized their charities. For example, one of Rogozhskoe's most outspoken supporters in Moscow, Prince Vladimir Dolgorukov, often boasted of Rogozhskoe's charitable efforts for Moscow and Russia because of the trustees' guidance. In one such case, when Ivan Butikov decided not to seek reelection as a trustee in 1878, choosing instead to work with his son in the family textile empire, both the community and Dolgorukov urged him to reconsider.

> You have great influence with the people [. . .] You have done much good for the [Rogozhskoe] community, you have ensured that the people remained safe, and when I confided in you, you always spoke to me sympathetically. You sacrificed for the Serbs, for the wounded, and for the fleet in the last war. No Sir, I beg you to stay and continue to serve your community and society.[46]

Such an appeal by a public figure as Dolgorukov reveals how influential Rogozhskoe's trustees became throughout Moscow and the Empire.

In the aftermath of the state's sealing of their churches, Rogozhskoe's charities became the community's primary means of presenting their sense of Christian morality. Therefore, Rogozhskoe's trustees made great efforts to ensure that the Rogozhskoe almshouse and sacred spaces remained proud physical and ideological examples of their community. Reflecting this sentiment, the instructions for Rogozhskoe's trustees emphasized that their position's primary concern was maintaining the almshouses and ensuring that all of the wards' needs remained met. Seeing that many of these structures dated back to the early nineteenth century, in the Reform Era maintaining Rogozhskoe's almshouses and medical facilities took special precedence, inasmuch as they required extensive restoration.[47]

Fortunately for Rogozhskoe's trustees, as well as the community's efforts to uphold their values, the community itself often embodied their very ideals of Christian charity and regularly fulfilled the financial needs of the almshouse through their own charitable donations. As Rogozhskoe's accounting reveals, throughout the end of the nineteenth century, the Rogozhskoe Old Believers regularly donated more than enough money to meet the annual needs of the almshouse, but also contributed additional funding to update the facilities regularly. For example, in 1873, community donations for "the construction and improvement of the cemetery's almshouse" totaled 20,808 rubles and 89 kopeks, of which the community spent 14,784 rubles and 31 kopeks.[48]

The Rogozhskoe trustees regularly invested any remaining funds into banks, bonds, and deeds to ensure the financial foundations of the community remained strong.[49]

The almshouse, then, now served as the very heart of Rogozhskoe's Holy Moscow. In the late-nineteenth century, Rogozhskoe's almshouse remained the largest in Moscow. In 1872 Rogozhskoe's almshouse housed 558 people (83 men and 475 women), ultimately growing to 730 people (114 men and 616 women) by 1877, the majority of the wards made up of the elderly and infirm.[50] Fifty-eight buildings made up the entirety of Rogozhskoe's almshouse. As only four stone buildings made up the almshouse complex, the remaining structures required regular maintenance due to normal usage as well as age.[51] However, an even more important feature of the almshouses was that they could double as sacred spaces. Specifically, as almshouses did not fall under the same legal and religious restrictions as Old Believer chapels, each building of the almshouse contained its own iconostasis as well as the capacity to offer specific church services such as Matins and Vespers. Furthermore, the almshouse chapels remained open and usable even after the sealing of the Nativity and Intercession Cathedrals.[52] Therefore, the almshouse now played as much of a significant role in defining the Rogozhskoe Old Believers' public and spiritual identity since the chapels could meet some of their needs as sacred spaces.

The almshouse represented Rogozhskoe's very ideals of Christian piety; therefore the entire community mainly focused on the integrity of the buildings through repair, total rebuilding, or updating the structures. However, as an Old Rite community, Rogozhskoe still required permission from tsarist authorities to complete any major construction projects. Thanks to Rogozhskoe almshouse's sterling reputation their petitions to state authorities met with little or no resistance. For example, in response to a petition in 1881, Rogozhskoe received permission to replace a number of the almshouse's more dilapidated buildings with a single, stone building, complete with running indoor plumbing and a built-in hot water supply.[53] The renovations to the almshouse, in turn, allowed the community to care for even more wards. The Rogozhskoe almshouse housed 726 registered dependents in 1880, 828 in 1882, 882 in 1885, peaked at 934 in 1888, and remained steady around 900 dependents until the end of the century.[54]

With the emphasis on charity embodied in their almshouse, the Rogozhskoe Old Believers continued to channel funds and charity to it and thus ensured that it remained one of the most well-funded institutions in Moscow. By 1889 the almshouse's accounts totaled 173,498 rubles, of which charitable donations from the Rogozhskoe community accounted for 74,005 rubles.[55] By 1904, the estimated total of its assets and donations equaled 626,462 rubles.[56] In the end, financial success provided both the opportunity and a sense of duty among the Rogozhskoe Old Believers to use their gains to spread their ideals and to build their Holy Moscow as a bastion of Christian spirituality and Christian charity.

The Rogozhskoe Old Believers, particularly its number of wealthy merchant families, did not limit the expression of their Christian charity only toward Rogozhskoe Cemetery. Rather, many of Rogozhskoe's wealthiest members used their finances to reflect their morals in two primary ways. First, many Rogozhskoe families used their capital as an investment. However, in a manner that resonated with their Old Rite ideology, the Rogozhskoe merchants and businessmen used their investments to expand their businesses in order to provide jobs for those who needed them, or to grant loans to their fellow Old Believers wishing to start new businesses.[57] Rogozhskoe's merchants and entrepreneurs distributed their wealth mainly through donations or almsgiving to other charitable institutions throughout Moscow and Russia.[58]

Rogozhskoe's wealthiest families long viewed such investments and donations as emblematic of their Old Rite understanding of using wealth for the betterment of society rather merely for personal gain. Yet the Great Reforms and their resulting social changes, particularly the growth in peasants arriving in Moscow following emancipation, provided new opportunities for the Rogozhskoe Old Believers. Primarily, the influx of peasants into Moscow, allowed Rogozhskoe's wealthy families to share their Christian ideals regarding the use of capital by opening larger, or new factories, thereby providing jobs and wages for those who could work; or donating to almshouses and hospitals to tend to the needy.[59] Ultimately, the Rogozhskoe Old Believers use of their capital reflected their ideal goal–that they champion the embodiment of Christian charity by placing greater emphasis on "living not for wealth, but for God."[60]

Furthermore, the introduction of a series of administrative reforms for Moscow allowed the Rogozhskoe Old Believers to take an even more active role in shaping the city in the late-nineteenth century. For example, the Municipal Statute of 1862 and Municipal Reform of 1870 allowed the merchantry to play a more active role in Moscow's administrative bodies. However, non-*ednioverts*y Old Believers still could not hold public office, thereby preventing Rogozhskoe's merchants from running for any of the new governing positions. Alexander III's *ukaz* of May 3, 1883, discussed in detail later in this chapter, changed such issues as it granted the right for all Old Believers to hold minor public offices in city and parish administrations; at last Rogozhskoe's merchantry were granted the opportunity to participate in city administration and politics.[61] However, while a number of *edinovertsy* Old Believer families such as the Khludovs and Guchkovs saw politics as the best means to advance their personal interests,[62] most of Rogozhskoe's wealthy families rather saw such positions of power as opportunities to share their ideals of Christian charity and community.

The municipal reforms of 1862 and 1870 created greater opportunity, and increased demand, for Moscow's merchants to donate funds to new Moscow administrative bodies which meant to allocate monies to numerous charitable projects, including social welfare, medical facilities, and public education.[63] Displaying their sense of Christian charity, many of Rogozhskoe's wealthiest families donated millions of rubles to various Moscow charities. For example, Kozma Soldatenkov, one of Rogozhskoe's most prominent individuals, embodied Rogozhskoe's charitable efforts for the good of Moscow. Upon his death in 1901, Soldatenkov left 2,081,581 rubles to the city of Moscow to build a free hospital for Moscow's poor.[64] Soldatenkov also bequeathed 20,000 rubles to the Arnoldo-Tretyakov School for the Deaf, and donated over 67,500 books, an estimated value of 51,000 rubles, to Moscow schools and libraries.[65]

Another driving force behind the increased effort by Rogozhskoe's wealthiest members to interact more with Moscow, and by extension the Russian Empire, came from the families themselves. By the 1890s, Rogozhskoe, as well as many of Moscow's merchants, witnessed a generational change as the older generation of merchants, who made their fortunes and maintained their livelihoods in the pre-Reform Era, made way for their sons to take over management of their wealth and family businesses.[66] This younger generation matured during the Great Reforms, and often obtained their educations from European tutors or even studied at the premiere universities in Europe.[67] While direct exposure to European culture influenced a number of these young men to trim their beards and adopt Western dress, even some of the Old Rite's critics, such as Prince Vladimir Meshcherskii, begrudgingly admitted that this next generation of merchants had little trouble combining their European educations and values with their religious and cultural ideals of their faith. "[They] sent their sons to be educated in Bremen or Liverpool [. . .] these sons returned to the family nest with the faith of their fathers unshaken and brought back with them from England together with a superb knowledge of how to run a factory"[68] These sons not only took over their family businesses, but soon introduced new ideas on how to use their family wealth in order to advance their own influence, but also to maintain and champion their ideals as Old Believers.

The younger Moscow merchants, and particularly Old Believer merchants, combined their new European values and educations to become better businessmen without compromising their faith and ideals.[69] As Alfred Rieber states, "Unlike the bulk of the merchantry, [the Old Believers] were morally armed to resist interference by the bureaucracy and the police [. . .] they did not abandon their ethical norms and cultural identity but rather transferred them from [their] religious communities to the Great Russian people."[70] Like their parents, the next generation of Old Rite merchants found themselves not only armed with new ideas on business, but they also maintained a strong desire to use their wealth to express the ideals of their faith and Christian charity.

The Rogozhskoe Old Believers and the Era of Reform

Tsarist oppression against the Old Rite and the specific targeting of the Rogozhskoe Old Believers in the 1850s greatly strained the community's unity and self-identity. However, as the Russian Empire entered the Reform Era, the Rogozhskoe Old Believers hoped that they and the Old Rite too might benefit from reform. In particular the Rogozhskoe Old Believers hoped that many of the restrictions introduced under Nicholas and Filaret might meet their end in the reforms.

While holding out for any possible reforms, the Rogozhskoe Old Believers still needed to find a means to be able to practice their faith without any cathedrals. In an initial attempt to maintain some semblance of a communal religious experience, the Rogozhskoe Old Believers used private homes as temporary chapels. The merchants Ivan Shibaev and Kozma Soldatenkov opened up their homes for small groups from the community to come together for religious services. However, this trend shifted the religious experience for the Rogozhskoe Old Believers as now expressions of their faith, and thereby their spiritual connection to their Holy Moscow, became a private experience. For the Old Rite in particular, group expression and the ability to share in their spiritual experience maintained strong communal bonds and preserved the very self-identity of the Rogozhskoe Old Believers.[71] Therefore, while certainly serving as a temporary solution following the closure of Rogozhskoe's cathedrals, overreliance on using private homes for religious services threatened not only Rogozhskoe's spiritual unity, but also the very fabric that held Rogozhskoe together.

The fact that the spiritual heart of Rogozhskoe remained sealed in the late 1850s became one of the most important aspects in the relationship between the Rogozhskoe Old Believers and Tsarist Russia for the next 50 years. As long as their altars remained sealed, the Rogozhskoe Old Believers could not fully participate in their shared faith as a community. Therefore, throughout the second half of the nineteenth century, Rogozhskoe's most outspoken leaders and members made reopening, or at least preserving, the altars and their treasures the ultimate goal of their interactions and relations with tsarist officials during the Reform Era.

Along with the community's debates regarding their place within the Old Rite and Belokrinitskaya Hierarchy in the 1850s and 1860s, the Rogozhskoe Old Believers deliberated upon their very understanding of the physical manifestations of their faith as a community. With the inability to express their faith in public, or to use their cathedrals to hold communal religious services, Rogozhskoe's leaders faced the challenge of maintaining the very bonds of the community. Specifically, when faced with the fact that the *edinovertsy* in Rogozhskoe Cemetery could freely participate in a complete spiritual experience with all religious services, Rogozhskoe's leadership needed to find a means to prevent conversions to *Edinoverie.*[72]

More problematic to Rogozhskoe, tsarist authorities showed no inclination to practice greater toleration of the Old Rite as part of the Great Reforms. The Rogozhskoe Old Believers therefore remained at the mercy of the many oppressive entities and legislation left in effect from

Nicholas's persecutions. For example, Metropolitan Filaret continued his relentless harassment and persecution of Rogozhskoe and still urged the police and tsarist authorities to exile any priests, and the families harboring them, in order to prevent any spiritual expression by the Old Believers.[73] Furthermore, even though the Saint Petersburg Secret Committee completed their investigation in 1857, determining that the claims against the Rogozhskoe Old Believers that led to the authorities sealing the altars in the Intercession and the Nativity Cathedrals proved to be slanderous and false, the committee refused to unseal the altars for fear of "confusing the Orthodox."[74] In the face of such opposition, Rogozhskoe's leaders needed to find a way to maintain the unity and identity of the greater community.

Rogozhskoe's trustees and community leaders soon came to a single realization: just as they had during Rogozhskoe's early years under Catherine the Great, yet again the community needed to redefine its place and self-identity as a part of the Old Rite and the Russian Empire. The Rogozhskoe Old Believers therefore needed to come to some understanding of how their community still represented their ideals of a pure, Old Rite Orthodox community while facing Russia's rapidly changing society, economy, and politics. Even during this tumultuous period for the community, the Rogozhskoe Old Believers used the changes introduced by the Reform Era to redefine their community's place as a model society for all of Russia.

Rogozhskoe's top priority during the Reform Era focused on receiving permission to reopen their cathedrals' altars in order to restore the integrity of their entire community. The crux of Rogozhskoe's problem remained the community's need to obtain the proper permissions to function fully from both tsarist *and* Orthodox authorities. Ultimately, some of the Rogozhskoe Old Believers firmly believed that their situation would alleviate itself once the Tsar became aware of the falsehoods that made up the accusations about their community. As claimed in anonymous pamphlets distributed throughout the community in the late 1850s and early 1860s, Alexander II's decision to seal and subsequent refusal to reopen the altars stemmed from misinformation passed on by dishonest tsarist authorities and the Church officials.

> In January 1856, the highest command allowed us to arrive in our churches to worship again. But in February of the same year, the

> missionary hieromonk Parfeni made up false slander against us, claiming that the occurrence of a public service in the temples made the Rogozhskoe cemetery and the *raskol* tempting for the Orthodox, even though there was no conflict with the Orthodox. And Filaret, the Metropolitan of Moscow, was not ashamed by this obviously false libel and provided it on his own behalf in the Synod and to the emperor, and so deceived the good king and father of the Russian people. And at his highest command before the investigation on July 7 in 1856 our altars were sealed. In March 1857, when by imperial order an investigation was assigned to look into the accusation, then as a result the missionary Parfenni appeared and positively renounced his shameful slander, and other witnesses confirmed and denounced the injustice that the altars still remain sealed. It can be assumed that the results of the investigation were not submitted to the superior view [of the Emperor]. We believe that if the good Emperor Alexander II, learned of this trick that he would not fail to remove these seals.[75]

As the Rogozhskoe Old Believers sought any outlet to appeal to the Tsar and other authorities, such pamphlets served as a key instrument to galvanize the community's resolve to obtain greater social and spiritual freedom.

The Rogozhskoe Old Believers, then, placed greater emphasis on the community establishing a direct relationship with the Tsar and therefore the Russian Empire as a whole. Under Nicholas the State and Church equated Rogozhskoe Cemetery with disloyalty for Rogozhskoe's role in supporting and spreading what tsarist and Church authorities viewed as the *Austrian* Belaia Krinitsa Old Rite Hierarchy.[76]

Some of Rogozhskoe's leading individuals, such as Ivan Shibaev, Peter Mel'nikov, Timofei Morozov, and Kozma Soldatinkov, realized that the community's predicament not only stemmed from religious intolerance and jealousy over Rogozhskoe's economic and social influence, but also from misconstrued notions about Rogozhskoe and the Old Rite by their Orthodox counterparts. One such notion that Shibaev in particular sought to change became the long held notion among tsarist and Orthodox officials that all Old Believers viewed the Tsar as the Antichrist.[77] Under the influence of leaders such as Shibaev, the Rogozhskoe Old Believers now emphasized that as their history revealed, they never viewed the Tsar as Antichrist; but as Russia's benevolent ruler who, like the Rogozhskoe Old Believers, remained a regular victim of lies and other misinformation at the hands of corrupt civil and church officials.[78]

Since the community's founding, the Rogozhskoe Old Believers regularly expressed their gratitude for the favor of the Tsar, entirely realizing that the very existence of their community and influence relied entirely on maintaining a positive relationship with tsarist and civil authorities. However, the Saint Petersburg Secret Committee's refusal to conduct a complete investigation into the claims against the Rogozhskoe Old Believers in 1856, culminating in Alexander's decision to close their altars, seemingly revealed to the Rogozhskoe Old Believers that the inaction and intolerance of intermediaries did more to shape the Tsar's decisions and not his own prejudices. Therefore, the fact that the Rogozhskoe altars remained sealed derived more from the malice of civil and Orthodox authorities who intentionally deceived the Tsar, solely to portray Rogozhskoe as a danger to Russian religious life.

In this regard, such an attitude among the Rogozhskoe Old Believers falls within the greater context of the "tsar-*batiushka*" phenomenon that the Russian populace expressed during the Reform Era. Better described as "naïve" or "popular monarchism," the idea that the Tsar existed as the *batiushka*, or "benevolent father," of the people maintained that the Tsar always remained sympathetic to the sufferings of the oppressed. However, the Tsar remained at the mercy of his immediate subordinates, the nobles and other authorities, who corrupted any of the Tsar's attempts to alleviate the peoples' suffering. This attitude, in fact, occasionally led to civil disobedience and popular uprisings not *against* the tsar's policies, but to enact *the tsar's true will* against the true oppressors of the people, the nobility and civil authorities.[79]

Following a similar pattern, as a contrast to the growing social and political challenges to Russian autocracy in the Reform Era, the Rogozhskoe Old Believers actively sought to prove their loyalty to the Tsar, in the hopes of portraying themselves as grateful subjects in a time of turmoil. Guided by influential leaders such as Shibaev and Soldatenkov, the Rogozhskoe Old Believers took on a new understanding of their relationship with Imperial Russia and sense of shared victimization with the Tsar. Therefore Alexander II and his successors all became part of Rogozhskoe's new understanding of their community's place in Reform Era Russia. Unlike their counterparts in the peasantry and working class, the Rogozhskoe Old Believers realized that civil disobedience only aided Rogozhskoe's enemies. To Shibaev and others, Rogozhskoe needed to find a means to circumvent the malice of their critics and attract the attention of the Tsar and the highest government officials in order to present their "truths" concerning Rogozhskoe Cemetery and its community. Primarily under Shibaev's direction, the Rogozhskoe Old Believers attempted to find common ground with the Tsars and their closest advisors in Saint Petersburg and Moscow through direct petitions.

Rogozhskoe's success with petitions remained mixed throughout the community's history. The most notable successes were the very permissions for founding the community, as well as the right to build stone cathedrals in the late-eighteenth century. However, following the waves of increased oppression in the previous decades, Rogozhskoe's trustees and other leaders insisted on the need to petition the Tsar, his family, and closest advisers directly to circumvent the likes of Metropolitan Filaret and other hostile entities.[80] Fortunately for Rogozhskoe, while a direct dialogue with Alexander seemed impossible, the Rogozhskoe Old Believers, beginning in the 1850s, often did find rare support among few influential government individuals such as State Censor Mikhail Longinov and the Minister of Internal Affairs, Sergei Lanskoi.

While Imperial Russia experienced the first stages of the Great Reforms, the Rogozhskoe Old Believers remained encouraged that it was only a matter of time before the reforms reached their community and the Old Rite as a whole. In a glimmer of hope, Alexander gave his "highest approval" in 1863 to the new Minister of Internal Affairs, Peter Valuev, to consider revisions to all statutes concerning Old Believers. However, it appeared that the Ministry of the Interior harbored little concern for reform for the Old Rite within the Russian Empire.

The Rogozhskoe Old Believers made no progress with tsarist authorities concerning Rogozhskoe's altars. Nearing the twentieth anniversary of the altars' closure in 1874, some Rogozhskoe members' concerns shifted away from regaining full control of their cathedrals, simply to preservation of the cathedrals and their treasures. Realizing that time and Moscow's climate, not religious intolerance, proved to be the greatest enemy of their sacred spaces, the Rogozhskoe Old Believers petitioned Alexander directly to allow them to rescue their sacred icons and other relics.

> On the orders of the local administration the altars at the chapels were sealed with all of their sacred treasures, icons, gold and silver utensils, the Gospels in their rich coverings and vestments stored inside. One of the altars, is the altar of [the Nativity Cathedral], heated from inside by two furnaces, now left without heating for the duration of 18 years, the temple and its holy, rare, and ancient icons and other items have been subjected to dampness and damage– and the Old Believers, gather in their chapels for prayers, condemned with a serious sense of inexpressible grief with the daily contemplation of the gradual destruction of their cherished shrines [...] without reopening the temples, we can neither save our churches, nor escape the ruin and damage of the temple's accumulated treasures and relics of ancient Russian piety.[81]

This petition clearly reveals both the frustration and urgency with which the Rogozhskoe Old Believers viewed the Great Reform's lack of concern for the Old Rite. While tsarist Russia underwent sweeping reforms, the Rogozhskoe Old Believers felt that the reforms did little to alleviate the injustices against the community. Furthermore, as no signs of greater reforms for the Old Rite that would allow Rogozhskoe to reopen their altars appeared on the horizon, the community now viewed the issue as a race against time. The longer authorities delayed reform the more Rogozhskoe Old Believers feared that little would remain of their cathedrals.

As reform for the Old Rite stalled, a major concern for Rogozhskoe came from legislation still in place since 1826 that forbade any repairs to any Old Believer religious structures. Therefore, the Intercession and Nativity Cathedrals went nearly 50 years without any significant maintenance. Without any empire-wide reform for the Old Rite, by the 1870s the Rogozhskoe Old Believers fortunately established close relationships with some Moscow officials who occasionally allowed the community to obtain special permission to undertake restoration projects for the cathedrals. As described above, the restoration projects led by the trustees Dmitri Milovanov and Peter Mel'nikov from 1873 to 1874 serve as one example. After having received permission, Milovanov and Mel'nikov personally funded the restoration for the Intercession Cathedral's roof and floor; as well as the cleaning, "correcting" and varnishing of the cathedral's crosses, and 363 icons and their covers.[82]

Even in spite of such temporary victories, the Rogozhskoe Old Believers continued their petitions for greater reform to tsarist authorities. Under increased pressure from many Old Rite communities, the Ministry of Internal Affairs finally decided to act. In 1875 the Ministry of Internal Affairs established a committee to discuss reforms for the Old Rite, chaired by the Deputy Minister of Internal Affairs, Prince Aleķsei Lobanov-Rostovskii. The committee formed to discuss the many issues facing the Old Rite, among them freedom of worship, civil rights, education, and community status. Specifically, the committee needed to determine how to include, or justify exclusion, of Old Rite reform as part of the Great Reforms. However, under his own initiative, Lobanov-Rostovskii directly reached out to the Rogozhskoe Old Believers through his contact with Ivan Shibaev; he invited Rogozhskoe to elect a commission to participate in direct discussions with the Saint Petersburg Committee in their efforts to introduce reforms for the Old Rite.

The Saint Petersburg Committee's request for Rogozhskoe's participation resulted from the efforts of Ivan Shibaev who served as one of Rogozhskoe's most prominent leaders in the Reform Era. Born in 1830 into a wealthy Rogozhskoe merchant family, Shibaev became one of the most influential champions for Old Rite reform and toleration beginning in the 1860s until his death in 1908.[83] Described as having a "keen intellect and knowledge" of history, politics, and law, Shibaev often attempted to serve as intermediary between Rogozhskoe and the Tsar; he regularly traveled to or resided in Saint Petersburg for months at a time in order to gain an audience with government agents. While a Rogozhskoe Old Believer, Shibaev gained recognition throughout the Old Rite in the early 1860s for his attempts to seek the liberation of imprisoned Old Rite monks from the Evfimiev Monastery in Suzdal'. However, Shibaev's efforts ultimately aggravated the Ministry of Internal Affairs, who ordered his arrest and imprisoned Shibaev in the Peter and Paul Fortress for two years.[84]

Undeterred, Shibaev spent his time after his release building close relationships among Rogozhskoe's leading families as well as throughout the Ministry of Internal Affairs and Moscow authorities. Shibaev even established a close, personal relationship with Prince Vladimir

Dolgorukov, the Governor-General of Moscow (1865–1891), which proved to be beneficial for Rogozhskoe because Dolgorukov allowed the community to renovate the Intercession Cathedral in 1873. Furthermore, after discussions with Shibaev, Dolgorukov even took it upon himself to beseech the Tsar and Ministry of Internal Affairs to replace the term "*raskol'niki*" which returned to popularity under Nicholas I, in favor of *staroobriadtsy* in all government documents and correspondence.[85]

In addition, Moscow authorities ignored the fact that Shibaev's private home and chapel served as a *de facto* church for the Rogozhskoe Old Believers, one of the benefits of his relationship with Dolgorukov. Shibaev's privileges only antagonized Rogozhskoe's contemporary critics such as Nikolai Subbotin, who wrote in 1889: "In the chapel, Shibaev put a new carved iconostasis and hung an expensive chandelier; they held the feast for the Nativity of the Virgin as a solemn consecration for this schismatic church. All of this happened, of course, in front of the police, who did not even think to ask their good friend Ivan Ivanovich, what kind of work he produced and why he needed such a magnificent iconostasis and huge chandelier."[86] Making use of his relationship with

Figure 3.3 Ivan Shibaev, late nineteenth century *Tserkov'*, 1908.

tsarist authorities, Shibaev hoped to serve as an example of the potential for Rogozhskoe to achieve similar favors by building a similarly strong relationship with the Tsar and his agents.

The opportunity presented by the Saint Petersburg Committee, then, proved to be a golden opportunity for Rogozhskoe and Shibaev. First, Rogozhskoe's participation guaranteed that they could bring their requests for greater spiritual freedom and unsealing their altars directly to the Committee. More importantly, however, Rogozhskoe's participation held greater significance to the issue of reform for the Old Rite throughout the Russian Empire. This responsibility did not at all escape Shibaev and the Rogozhskoe Old Believers, who openly accepted the mantle of intercessor for all of the Old Rite.

> [The invitation to elect a commission] which grants the right to care "about the benefits and needs of the public" and work together with the committee to this subject as to the cumulative effects on other Old Believers, and it would not even hurt to consider the *bespopovtsy* in this subject. And in this order, we call upon God to help, start the process now as the time is convenient, so we do not repent later.[87]

Owing to his prior experience in Saint Petersburg, as well as the extent of his relationship with members of the Committee, Shibaev quickly established himself as one of Rogozhskoe's most outspoken representatives.

In particular, Shibaev believed that the primary obstacle preventing reform for the Old Rite and the failure of Old Believer petitions came from misunderstandings based on the state's long-held fears about Old Rite, particularly mistaken notions of disloyalty and conversion of gullible Orthodox. Regarding such attitudes toward Rogozhskoe Cemetery, Shibaev placed full blame for such sentiments on the Holy Synod and the Russian Orthodox Church. Shibaev, then, believed that this obstacle required that the Rogozhskoe Old Believers establish a direct dialogue with the Lobanov-Rostovskii commission.[88] Seeing a need for strength in numbers, in his report on the commission proceedings from May 17 to May 20, 1875, Shibaev appealed to the Rogozhskoe Trustees to elect representatives to travel to Saint Petersburg to present their case directly.

> They tell us that we need to take care of ourselves in the situation of our affairs and seriously. First of all, we must rely on God, but let us take care of ourselves and our serious work. As I tell you that from this it will depend a great deal to a successful completion of our business [. . .] It is positively and morally impossible for one or two [petitioners] to take this matter upon themselves, and I personally consider that I have become a burden in this important and serious case.[89]

In order to fulfill Shibaev's request, the Rogozhskoe Old Believers realized that their representatives needed to reflect the dual nature of Rogozhskoe's ties to both the Old Rite as well as to the economic and social development of Moscow and the Empire.

Therefore on June 17, 1875, the Rogozhskoe Old Believers elected a commission to serve as their voice in Saint Petersburg. Rogozhskoe's representatives came from some of the community's most influential leaders, merchants, and industrialists: Kozma Soldatenkov, Timofei Morozov, Rodion Martinov, Timofei Nazarov, Ivan Butikov, Dmitri Milovanov, Peter Mel'nikov; and, as recognition for his role in previously representing Rogozhskoe, Ivan Shibaev.[90]

At the very first meeting of Rogozhskoe's representatives on July 24, 1875, Shibaev welcomed his fellow members by reminding them of their duty to both the Old Rite and Rogozhskoe's significance to the Old Rite movement:

> We have assumed so serious a case involving everyone in the Russian Old Ritualist faith, we must by all means, with all of our forces and capabilities perform the mission entrusted to us, this performance must be regarded as a sacred duty, and in particular (although unfortunately) all Old Ritualists in Russia, look to and nourish their hope on Moscow. They say: "In Moscow there is a great community and there are people that can make and do." They are convinced of this. I say this on the basis of letters from many parts of Russia.[91]

The community's influence and relationship with Moscow and tsarist authorities led Rogozhskoe's representatives to see themselves as political intercessors for an entire faith.

The Rogozhskoe petitioners and the Lobanov-Rostovskii commission seemingly worked diligently together to incorporate the Old Rite into the Great Reforms. However, outside pressure from the Holy Synod urged the commission to severely restrict, or abandon Old Rite reform entirely. Pressured to produce something by the Ministry of Internal Affairs, and forced to appease the Holy Synod, the commission issued a draft of reforms on August 1, 1875. Under the proposed reforms, Old Believers could use their homes for religious services, but could not build new structures or designate buildings as "churches." Furthermore, buildings used for worship could not have permanent icons or crosses. However, Old Rite communities could establish and maintain their own primary schools.[92]

Rogozhskoe's representatives quickly deemed the drafted "reforms" as insufficient. Yet after many years of experience with tsarist officials and agencies, Shibaev urged Rogozhskoe that the drafted reforms served as a step in the right direction.

> We have something, which is good, because it is better to have something than nothing, as we did not have anything before the law. We do not pursue it. But as I said, it is good to have not only a little freedom, but freedom authorized by the law, and for this initial recognition by the law of our rights, we should be thankful to the government. It is our sacred duty to achieve gradually more and more satisfactory outcomes, and not only for us, in Moscow, but for the whole of Russia.[93]

Shibaev's approach ultimately underscores the Rogozhskoe Old Believers' efforts to forge a working relationship with the tsarist government. Rogozhskoe's leadership could prove their loyalty to the state, and therefore the community's loyalty, by showing that they accepted gradual, rather than immediate and radical reform. As Shibaev argued, Rogozhskoe's greatest hope for further reform in matters such as freedom of worship, which would guarantee the reopening of Rogozhskoe's altars and full control of their sacred spaces, remained gradual efforts to work with the state, not against it.

In an effort to build on the positive decisions of the Lobanov-Rostovskii commission, on August 3, 1875 two days after they received the reform draft, Shibaev suggested that the Rogozhskoe commission petition tsarist and Moscow authorities to allow the community to photograph the interiors of their cathedrals. Shibaev reasoned that "[if we] have photographs from our churches in the cemetery they would serve as a visual reference for the commission members, who will discuss the issue of worship."[94] Shibaev and the Rogozhskoe Old Believers hoped that actual images of what Rogozhskoe sought to restore would help make their case for greater freedom of worship.

> If we take [photographs] from both the outside and interior of the temples at Rogozhskoe Cemetery and present them to the same senior government persons so to familiarize them of the temples which were built with the permission of the government in the old days and our Old Rite churches that exist to the present day for their consideration for granting freedom of worship for the Old Rite. With this purpose and photographs [. . .] will be a benefit in discussing the issue of freedom of worship, as well as inspire greater interest in the issue and community for many years.[95]

Inspired by the idea, Rogozhskoe's petitioners received offers from 39 prominent Rogozhskoe families and individuals, and additional parishioners, willing to fund the photography project.[96] The Rogozhskoe Old Believers hoped that photographs of their cathedrals' interiors might aid their efforts to convince the tsarist authorities to consider freedom of worship, or at the very least, unsealing their altars and restoring spiritual services to Rogozhskoe.

Photographing Rogozhskoe's cathedrals, particularly their interiors, served as an extremely significant moment in the Rogozhskoe Old Believers' self-identity, maintenance, and restoration of their community. The effort to have the cathedrals photographed introduced changes in terms of the community's relationship with the state, as well as their own understanding of their spirituality. First, the idea that Rogozhskoe should present photographs of their cathedrals to tsarist authorities reveals a new approach in Rogozhskoe's petitions. Essentially, Rogozhskoe's goal behind the photography project focused on making Rogozhskoe Cemetery a much more real community to tsarist agents living and working in Saint Petersburg. Many tsarist agents only knew about Rogozhskoe though their superiors, or the biased agendas of anti-Old Rite statesmen and Church officials, simply because they were unfamiliar with the capital city. The photographs then put Rogozhskoe on full display: the size of the community and the grandeur of their cathedrals and buildings; but most importantly, the photographs shared their sacred spaces with the outside world. The photographs of Rogozhskoe's cathedrals revealed the very heart of their community and spiritual identity. However, instead of revealing spaces used for pious worship, Rogozhskoe's photographs instead revealed elaborate sacred spaces that could not fulfill their true purpose owing to the injustice of the spiritual and legal restrictions against the community and Old Rite throughout the Russian Empire. Rather than reveal a holy space, where Old Believers gathered to sing praises and prayers for the Tsar and Russia, the photographs emphasized the emptiness and despair of a law-abiding, and genuinely loyal community of Old Believers who invested time, effort, and capital into charities, the economy, and other social projects throughout Moscow and the Russian Empire.

In March 1876, the Rogozhskoe Old Believers hired the firm Sherer, Nabgolts, and Company for the photography project consisting of ten photographs of the elaborate interiors of the Intercession and Nativity cathedrals.[97] The photographs also represented a point of pride among the Rogozhskoe Old Believers. First, Rogozhskoe's leaders realized that prominent families and other parishioners would donate for the costs of the project, or purchase their own copies of the photos. As Ivan Shibaev even noted, this income would most likely cover any costs for the photographs.

> Except for the 22 copies for senior government officials it is assumed other elected, as well as honorable parishioners would ask to be invited to aid the completion of this project's costs, and meet any additional prices at least [...] for instance [...] the parishioners' donations could cover the cost of this project.[98]

Knowing that the petitioners intended to use the photographs to raise the issue of freedom of worship for the Old Rite, the Rogozhskoe Old Believers met the financial requirements for the project.

Second, the photographs also represented a means to share and visualize Rogozhskoe's sacred spaces outside of the cathedrals. Even though the Lobanov-Rostovskii commission disbanded on December 26, 1875, the Rogozhskoe Old Believers firmly believed greater reforms for the Old Rite remained on the horizon. As a sign of their thanks, the Rogozhskoe community gifted copies of the photograph albums to each of the members of the Lobanov-Rostovskii commission, as well as to other government officials, "in memory of and as signs of deep gratitude for their supporters and benefactors."[99]

To the Rogozhskoe Old Believers' joy, it appeared that their hopes for greater reform might bear fruit. In response to numerous letters of thanks, as well a copy of Rogozhskoe's photo album, the Minister of Internal Affairs, Alexander Timashev, assured the Rogozhskoe petitioners that the Lobanov-Rostovskii commission's suggestions received his full support. Furthermore, in a letter sent to the community on New Years Day, 1876, Timashev assured the Rogozhskoe Old Believers that the commission's efforts ensured future reforms, adding in his letter, "I have and will do all that I can for you and hope that you will not take any offense or remember any evil against me."[100]

However, Rogozhskoe's hopes of further reform for the Old Rite remained unfulfilled; even worse, by March 1878, the Ministry of

Figure 3.4 Interior of Intercession Cathedral, Sherer, Nabgol'ts and Co., 1876.

Figure 3.5 Intercession Cathedral, Sherer, Nabgol'ts and Co., 1876.

Internal Affairs still had not submitted the Lobanov-Rostovskii commission's reforms to the State Council. Certainly direct blocking of the reforms came from the Holy Synod and the Director of the Department of General Affairs, Nikolai Mansurov who argued that

> my friends, [the suggested reforms] at present cannot get through, as it may bring great harm to Orthodoxy, and therefore they must be decided under the general question of freedom of

Figure 3.6 A View of Rogozhskoe Cemetery, Sherer, Nabgol'ts and Co., 1876.

> worship [. . .] [the Old Believers] are a danger if given broad freedom of worship in particular temples such as those at Rogozhskoe cemetery where there would be flocks not only thousands of Old Believers, but the sons of the dominant church, and then we can assume that the Old Believers will increase at the expense of the Orthodox Church.[101]

The old criticisms toward the Old Rite and Rogozhskoe led to the Lobanov-Rostovskii commission's eventual failure. The Rogozhskoe Old Believers remained at the mercy of many of the laws put in place under Nicholas decades before. The Rogozhskoe Old Believers understood that they could not wait for another commission to debate reform for the Old Rite. Rather, as the state continually refused to issue reforms, the Rogozhskoe Old Believers took it upon themselves to disprove the criticisms against their community by emphasizing their devotion and loyalty to the state as part of their community's identity.

A Community of Loyal Old Believers

Russia's Reform Era instilled a level of hope not only for the Old Rite, but for religious minorities throughout the Empire. Subjects throughout Russia petitioned the tsarist government for the opportunity to express their true faith more freely, often fearful of the encroachment of the Russifying forces of the late tsarist period.[102] Yet, in the bigger picture of religious reform throughout the Empire, tsarist agencies found themselves, as Paul Werth describes, "paralyzed." Like the issue of reform for the Old Rite, the tsarist state could not find an effective means to implement blanket religious reform without the risk of losing control over religious minority groups, disappointing minority groups; or weakening or antagonizing the Orthodox Church.[103] Religious reform, then, continued to stagnate for many groups for various reasons, particularly for those religions with a "nationalizing" character to them such as Catholicism among Russia's Poles.[104]

In this larger picture of religious toleration, the Rogozhskoe Old Believers fully understood that many of the tsarist and Church criticisms and oppression of their community stemmed from many long-held misconceptions about the Old Rite itself: namely, claims of their disloyalty, allegations of their refusal to acknowledge the Tsar's legitimacy, or even assertions that the Old Rite actively weakened the Russian Orthodox Church. On the contrary, communities such as Rogozhskoe remained more interested in simply existing as a model Christian community predominately for their own members while actively engaging with contemporary Russia. Rogozhskoe's emphasis on charity for Moscow's needy and the growing hard-pressed working class merely reflected their efforts to uphold their own sense of Christian duty and morality.

Rogozhskoe in particular faced specific challenges and criticisms questioning the community's loyalty to the Tsar and Russia. Rogozhskoe's successes and their refusal to renounce the Old Rite spurred enemies in the Russian Orthodox Church and other devout Orthodox government officials to view Rogozhskoe as a threat to Russian identity itself. Critics openly questioned Rogozhskoe's loyalty to the Tsar and the Russian Empire, the Orthodox Sovereign, and the Orthodox state because of Rogozhskoe's recognition as a spiritual center of the Old Rite movement.

After the sealing of their altars, the Rogozhskoe Old Believers realized that they still needed to combat the many misconstrued opinions against the Old Rite. In the Reform Era, Rogozhskoe directly challenged the misconception that Old Believers refused to pledge their loyalty to the Tsar and the Empire. Their overt displays of loyalty ultimately became part of the Rogozhskoe Old Believers' new method of presentating their community's deep ties to the Russian Empire. Leading by example through public displays of loyalty to the Tsar and other government officials, openly supporting tsarist policies against political and national enemies, continuing their charitable efforts, and contributing to Russia's economic growth all represented Rogozhskoe's attempt to challenge the notions of Old Rite disloyalty.

In the face of the growing turmoil of the late nineteenth century, the Rogozhskoe Old Believers exhibited their loyalty to the Tsar and Russian autocracy at every opportunity. Although offering congratulations to the imperial family and other high officials was by no means a new practice, by the second half of the nineteenth century, offers of congratulations and other public displays of loyalty took on greater meaning and purpose for the Rogozhskoe Old Believers. Even small gestures of congratulations to tsarist officials and the imperial family reaffirmed Rogozhskoe's loyalty to the state, and now reaffirmed that the Tsar, as an Orthodox ruler, maintained a place within their Holy Moscow. Throughout the remainder of the tsarist period, Rogozhskoe's trustees publically offered congratulations to the Tsar, members of the imperial family, and other key officials for weddings, coronation anniversaries, births, awards, promotions, and other events on a regular basis.[105] For example, the Rogozhskoe's trustees and other influential members participated in each of the jubilee festivals for Governor-General Vladimir Dolgorukov, one of the community's strongest supporters, in 1879, 1885, and 1890 – all at Dolgorukov's personal invitation.[106]

Religious holidays also played a defining role in Rogozhskoe's open displays of loyalty to the Romanovs and other officials. For example, gifting Easter eggs to the Tsar and other high-ranking officials became one of the most popular traditions in Rogozhskoe. Beginning in 1874, 26 of Rogozhskoe's leading families distributed Easter eggs to the imperial family, as well as high-ranking tsarist and Orthodox Church officials as "displays of our congratulations and reverent allegiance to Russia and the traditional Holy Easter greetings."[107] In this first effort, the Rogozhskoe Old Believers gave eggs to the Emperor, Empress, Tsesarevich Alexander Alexandrovich, and other officials who often interceded on the community's behalf, such as Dolgorukov and Alexander Abramovich Suvorov, the grandson of Russia's celebrated General Alexander Suvorov.[108] The Rogozhskoe Old Believers also sent Easter eggs to high-ranking clergy in the Orthodox Church including the Metropolitan of Saint Petersburg Isidore, the Archbishop of Vilnius and Lithuania Makary, and Metropolitan Innocent of Moscow, the successor of Rogozhskoe's nemesis, Filaret.[109]

Hoping not only to show their loyalty through the traditional Orthodox practice of exchanging Easter eggs, the Rogozhskoe Old Believers' choice to exchange eggs with both tsarist and Orthodox authorities emphasized the community's ties to the Russian Empire through the dogmatic unity of Orthodoxy. In each successive year, more of Rogozhskoe's families sent Easter eggs to the imperial family and Russia's high-ranking officials.[110] The wooden eggs varied in size and depicted images of the Resurrection of Christ and images of other saints as well.[111] Thanks to the tradition's success, in 1888 the Rogozhskoe Trustees commissioned the well-known nineteenth century icon painters, the brothers Yakov and Aleksei Tyulin, to personally design and paint their Easter eggs.[112]

Yet even as the Rogozhskoe Old Believers made overt efforts to display their loyalty, the Old Rite's opponents continued to delay the Lobanov-Rostovskii commission's reforms from reaching the State Council. Still serving as Rogozhskoe's most prominent spokesman, Ivan Shibaev regularly travelled to Saint Petersburg to urge that the Lobanov-Rostovskii reforms move forward. Unexpectedly, Shibaev happened to be in Saint Petersburg on March 1, 1881, the fateful day of Alexander II's assassination and quickly learned of the Tsar's demise. Shibaev's quick mind realized both the horror and significance of the moment. Specifically, Shibaev saw an opportunity for Rogozhskoe finally to prove their loyalty to the tsarist state beyond doubt. Shibaev quickly dispatched a telegram to his close friend, Ivan Butikov, at Rogozhskoe: "I will arrive there tomorrow, after breakfast, and gather you all to discuss [the election of] representative deputies. They will arrange for our oath of loyalty this very moment by our clergy in our churches, and ask Prince Dolgorukov to report and request it."[113] Simply put, Shibaev saw in the aftermath of Alexander II's assassination a critical moment for the Rogozhskoe Old Believers. By publically pledging their loyalty to the new Tsar, Alexander III, the Rogozhskoe Old Believers could prove, once-and-for-all, their loyalty to both the Tsar and the Russian Empire, as well as distance themselves and the Old Rite from the many more socially and politically radical groups that appeared in Russia in the aftermath of the Great Reforms.[114]

The idea of officially pledging their loyalty to and offering prayers for the Tsar completely changed Rogozhskoe's relationship with the state. While Rogozhskoe regularly saw the Tsar as their potential benefactor or oppressor in the civic sphere, the community's ties to the Old Rite inherently questioned the Tsar's spiritual authority. One of the defining traits of the Old Rite, and similarly a long held criticism by its opponents, questioned the place of the Tsar in Orthodox Christianity following the schism. Since Alexis not only supported, but also enacted the Nikonian Reforms,[115] the first Old Believers viewed the very idea of the Tsar as tainted, even possibly now the very embodiment, or even an agent for the Antichrist.[116] Furthermore, Peter the Great's rejection of traditional Russian culture and Westernization efforts only solidified the Old Rite's perception that the Tsar no longer represented the ideals expected of an Orthodox sovereign. Ultimately the Old Believers notably refused, *en masse*, to pledge oaths of loyalty to the Tsars for much of Russia's history after the schism.[117]

In response to such blatant disregard expected of loyal Russian subjects, tsarist authorities issued legislation throughout the eighteenth and nineteenth centuries specifically targeting Old Believers for such questionable loyalty.[118] One such example comes from the conflict between Vasili Tatishchev, one of the most influential statesmen in the mid-eighteenth century, and his direct targeting of the highly successful Demidov family and their metallurgical empire in the Urals because of their ties to the Old Rite. Tatishchev and other officials over the centuries regularly rejected any opinions of the Old Rite that did not conform to their narrative that portrayed all Old Believers as disloyal owing to their refusal to join the Orthodox Church as well as pledge their loyalty to the Tsar.[119] The Old Rite's tradition of not taking an oath of loyalty for each new Tsar therefore continually shaped many preconceptions about the Old Rite well into the early twentieth century.

Therefore, Rogozhskoe's offer to take the official oath of loyalty to Alexander III, became both a revolutionary and controversial idea for a community of Old Believers. By taking the oath, Rogozhskoe could restore their connection to the Orthodox sovereign and thereby recognize an official role for the Tsar in their community's existence. Rogozhskoe's offer to take the pledge of loyalty, then, served as a major adaptation of their ideals. They now hoped to regain full use of the community's sacred spaces, and obtain the freedom to practice Old Rite religious services as they had many times before; yet now they recognized secular Orthodox authority in the Tsar.

Furthermore, and even more significant, Rogozhskoe now represented the first non-*edinovertsy* Old Rite community to take the oath of allegiance. Throughout their shared history, the Old Rite and the tsarist state remained in a relationship in which tsarist policies provided the opportunities that ignored such conflicts as oaths of loyalty in exchange for productivity that benefited the goals of the Russian state. For example, Peter the Great's war efforts required a strong military, which in-turn required tax revenue and a stable supply of resources and supplies, particularly iron. Fortunately, for Old Rite communities such as those located in Vyg and entrepreneurial families such as the Demidovs and their iron producing empire in the Urals, Peter understood the potential for such groups to contribute to his goals, while still existing as Old Believers.[120] Rogozhskoe fit the pattern because of their ties to the merchantry with their economic influence. Old Rite communities received some protection as long as they performed all duties expected of them such as meeting their tax obligations and maintaining their economic niches.

Yet even with this symbiotic relationship, the most successful of Old Believers refused to make the oath of allegiance to the Tsar; especially because they had to take their oath of loyalty under supervision of Orthodox Priests. By sanctioning such practices, Old Believers feared that they opened themselves up to registration as Old Believers (and military conscription), collection of any back taxes, or possibly even forced conversion to the Orthodox Church.[121] Therefore, Rogozhskoe's offer to take an oath of allegiance served as a means of establishing a new level in their relationship with the state.

Understanding the significance of Rogozhskoe's offer to take an oath of loyalty, Governor-General Dolgorukov immediately granted his permission for the community to petition the Ministry of Internal Affairs to construct temporary altars in the Rogozhskoe cathedrals.

Likewise, the Minister of Internal Affairs, Mikhail Loris-Melikov, approved Rogozhskoe's request to erect portable altars and use Old Rite priests to administer the community's oath of allegiance to the Tsar.[122] With permission from the highest authorities, the Rogozhskoe trustees installed a temporary altar and folding iconostasis, both donated by Kozma Soldatenkov, in the Intercession Cathedral.[123] In a letter to Dolgorukov and Loris-Melikov, the community proffered the following report:

> In our church we positioned a collapsible altar and iconostasis, and performed the Divine Liturgy and a prayer service of Thanksgiving to God for the health and welfare of the Emperor, Empress and all the royal family in the presence of the nominated police officials, local police chief and others, and before the holy altar our clergy officially administered our oath of allegiance to the Emperor.[124]

Rogozhskoe's official declaration of loyalty went far to negate long-held negative perceptions of their community. Rogozhskoe's efforts achieved a somewhat minor, albeit welcome, victory; following Alexander III's coronation on May 15, 1883 Rogozhskoe received permission to keep their portable altars in place. They ultimately continued to use the altars to perform services until November 1885.[125]

Not only did Rogozhskoe make great strides to take the oath of loyalty, but also offered its services to aid and protect the Tsar and imperial family during Alexander III's official coronation in Moscow. Wishing to ensure the safety of Alexander III and the imperial family, tsarist authorities reached out to prominent citizens in Moscow to organize squads of "volunteer protectors" to patrol the streets and squares in their districts to demonstrate loyalty to the new Tsar and to deter anyone wishing harm to the ruler. As drafted by the Moscow Chief of Police, Alexander Kozlov, in January 1882, "the voluntary protectors [. . .] will be made up of the greatest number of people devoted to the throne and committed to make its every effort to prevent any attacks by any villainous person against the sacred person of His Majesty and his August family, and to prevent anything that might disturb the peace of the sovereign at His appearance among his people."[126]

Seeing yet another opportunity for the Rogozhskoe to demonstrate its loyalty as a community, in the presence of the Tsar, Ivan Shibaev insisted on Rogozhskoe's participation. Furthermore, Shibaev's close relationship with Dolgorukov and Kozlov allowed him to serve as one of the heads for the entire volunteer force.[127] Using his position, Shibaev selected a number of Rogozhskoe's prominent leaders to serve as his captains: Ivan Butikov, Peter Mel'nikov, Feodor Sveshnikov, Grigori Kleimenov, Kozma Soldatenkov, Timofei Morozov, and Nikolai Olenev.[128] Under the Rogozhskoe captains, volunteers from Rogozhskoe patrolled the Lefortovo and Nizhegorodskii (Karacharovo) districts of Moscow, just south-east of the city center.[129] Showing his personal thanks for Rogozhskoe's roll in the volunteer force, Alexander III issued commemoration medals for Rogozhskoe's Intercession Cathedral engraved with a message of special thanks to the volunteers for their efforts to protect the safety of the imperial family.[130]

Yet in the background of the preparations for Alexander's coronation, Shibaev and the former Rogozhskoe commission never abandoned the issue of Old Rite reform, as well as the reopening of their cathedrals' altars. Turning to their recent oath in hopes of gaining such favors, Rogozhskoe's trustees preceded their first petition following their oath with the following: "We, the Moscow Old Believers, of the priestly denomination, not only lived by the ancient faith and the ancient traditions, but also kept a deep loyalty and devotion to the ancient Russian throne and ancient Russian monarchy for centuries."[131] While initially blocked once again by the Holy Synod, the Rogozhskoe Old Believers petitioned directly to Minister Loris-Melikov in January 1883, urging him "to consider granting the long-awaited civil and religious liberties."[132] In a glimmer of hope, Loris-Melikov responded to Rogozhskoe on February 9, 1883, guaranteeing that the State Council and Alexander would now consider the issue of reform for the Old Rite.

Rogozhskoe's wait appeared to be over with Alexander's *ukaz* of May 3, 1883. The proposed law represented a sweeping attempt at civil and spiritual reform for the Old Rite. First, the reform ended many bans placed on the Old Rite since the schism, including the ban on building restoration. The *ukaz* included recognition of Old Rite parishes, which would thereby legalize the Belokrinitskaya Hierarchy. The *ukaz* also granted significant religious prerogatives such as the right for Old Believers to worship their faith freely, the freedom to perform all religious services including the Divine Liturgy; and significantly for Rogozhskoe, the oppportunity for all Old Rite communities to seek the reopening of any sealed temples or altars.[133] The *ukaz* also provided for greater political expression by allowing Old Believers to run for public office.[134] The Rogozhskoe Old Believers celebrated and welcomed the *ukaz* as the reform that the Old Rite awaited all along, and put the community in high spirits for their contribution to Alexander's coronation only days later.[135] It finally appeared that the Rogozhskoe Old Believers might finally obtain the rights to express themselves and their faith freely.

Unfortunately, while the Old Rite welcomed Alexander's reform efforts, the *ukaz* remained hollow as oppression of the Old Rite continued at the hands of the Holy Synod and some immovable Orthodox government officials. First, many of the reforms required Old Rite communities to petition the Ministry of Internal Affairs, the Holy Synod, local authorities, or all of these departments in order to restore any buildings, or reopen any sealed churches.[136] Under such stipulations, Old Rite communities found it nearly impossible to utilize their new "rights." The Rogozhskoe Old Believers now faced even greater challenges. With Rogozhskoe recognized as the center of the Belokrinitskaya Hierarchy in Russia, and the right for Old Believers to establish their own parishes, the Holy Synod in particular, now under the control of notorious reactionary Konstantin Pobedonostsev, approached Rogozhskoe with renewed animosity. Pobedonostsev, Alexander's former tutor and closest advisor, himself became a thorn in Rogozhskoe's side as he personally interfered in Rogozhskoe's affairs whenever possible to prevent the community from many reforms until Nicholas II later granted full religious freedom to the Old Rite in April 1905.

Furthermore, while granting extraordinary new freedoms that allowed the Old Rite to express their faith more freely, stipulations in the new laws prohibited any outward display of the Old Rite. Specifically, the new laws restricted Old Rite religious services to the privacy of properly designated religious buildings and private homes. Adding to the problems Rogozhskoe faced, while the *ukaz* did recognize the legality of their community as an Old Rite parish with the right to practice their faith, it did not recognize the Belokrinitskaya Hierarchy as a legitimate branch of Orthodoxy and expressly forbade any *Belokrinitsy* clergy to use titles such as "priest" or "bishop." Additionally, Rogozhskoe faced two major roadblocks in their efforts to restore their buildings or reopen their altars. First, any restored or renovated religious structures could not "imitate" Orthodox Churches. Although their cathedrals predated the original ban on restoration of Old Rite structures, Rogozhskoe Cemetery could never receive permission to restore the bells or crosses on their cathedrals. Second, all requests for restoration, construction, or reopening of Old Believer structures needed to receive approval from local civil and religious authorities, the Ministry of Internal Affairs, and the Holy Synod.[137] This stipulation often led to many Old Rite petitions regarding communal sacred spaces to face significant delays in receiving any response. Furthermore, any authority could modify, reject, or ignore the petition entirely at any stage in the process, thereby requiring Old Rite communities re-petition from the beginning.

However, on occasion, petitions for restoration efforts did meet with some positive results through the intervention of various local or state authorities. Rogozhskoe in particular successfully petitioned to continue restoration efforts on their cathedrals. For example, the Nativity Cathedral underwent extensive interior renovations from 1887 to 1890. During this time, the efforts focused on washing and restoring all of the Cathedral's frescoes and walls as well as the cathedral's iconostases, gilding, and crosses.[138] In total, the cathedral's 438 icons and images alone amounted to 3,530 rubles for restoration and 2,365 rubles for renovation of the cathedral's wall murals.[139] Eventually beginning in 1897, the Intercession Cathedral also undertook extensive restoration of its interior frescoes and murals as well as major repair to some structural damage. Ultimately, the restoration of the Intercession's icons, walls, its iconostases, other decorations, and structural repair totaled nearly 60,000 rubles.[140]

The aftermath of the *ukaz* of 1883 only confirmed Rogozhskoe's perception that they remained at the mercy of nefarious government officials who corrupted the Tsar's true intentions. In particular, old animosities still overshadowed Rogozhskoe's ability to uphold their communal values and ideals, as reactionary politics took hold over Russia at the end of the nineteenth century. Specifically, the Holy Synod and the Russian Orthodox Church still feared Rogozhskoe Cemetery and its influence within the Old Rite as a direct spiritual threat to the

Church and the Empire as a whole. More problematically for the Rogozhskoe Old Believers, their community and ties to the Belokrinitskaya Hierarchy made them the personal target of Konstantin Pobedonostsev, the Ober-Procurator of the Holy Synod.[141]

Like Metropolitan Filaret decades before, Pobedonostsev saw the Old Rite, and particularly Rogozhskoe Cemetery, as a threat to the very being of Russian Orthodoxy and Russian identity. For example, in 1884, Pobedonostsev argued that the "blatant indulgence of the raskol threatens state security [. . . and] it humiliates the Orthodox Church." Rogozhskoe, then, served as the embodiment of this threat and soon felt Pobedonostsev's meddling in 1885 when he used his authority as Ober-Procurator to pressure then Ministry of the Interior, Dmitri Tolstoi, to force the Rogozhskoe Old Believers to remove the temporary altars, thereby again ending the community's access to their sacred spaces.[142] Pobedonostsev once more interfered against Rogozhskoe in 1896. As they did with Alexander III's ascension to the throne, the Rogozhskoe

Figure 3.7 Old Rite Rogozhskoe Cemetery, 1886. Nikolai Naydenov, Album, *Pictures of Views of Locations, Buildings and Other Structures*, Vol. 3, 1886.

Old Believers wished to give their oath of loyalty to the new Tsar, Nicholas II upon his coronation; to that end they requested to use temporary altars to complete their oath. However, Pobedonostsev quickly issued a demand to the Ministry of Internal Affairs to refuse even to consider the community's petition either to unseal their altars or to erect temporary ones for their oath; he argued that any measure in favor of the Rogozhskoe Old Believers guaranteed near collapse of the entire Russian state.[143] Unfortunately then, while Rogozhskoe could overtly defy the preconceptions of the Old Rite as disloyal to the Tsar, as long as individuals such as Pobedonostsev remained in authority, Rogozhskoe's idealistic community remained incomplete.

Conclusion

The Great Reforms provided a number of new opportunities for the Rogozhskoe Old Believers to establish themselves as a communal and spiritual authority within the Belokrinitskaya Hierarchy and to define their Church within the greater Orthodox and Christian worlds. Concurrently, the Rogozhskoe Old Believers also sought to define their place within the Russian Empire more clearly. The Rogozhskoe Old Believers reaffirmed their identity through more traditional means such as charity, but actively sought to challenge many preconceived notions about the Old Rite and its "disloyalty" to both the Russian Tsar and Russian state. Rogozhskoe instead established a new relationship with the tsarist state by incorporating the Tsar into their understanding of how their community maintained Old Rite Orthodox purity. Yet even after responding to such critical moments, the Rogozhskoe Old Believers still found themselves as an oppressed religious minority yearning for greater opportunities to build and realize their community ideals.

CHAPTER 4

A NEW BEGINNING, 1905–17

Russia entered the twentieth century facing an uncertain future as the Empire strained under the weight of political, social, economic, and soon, military challenges. The Revolutions of 1905, in the aftermath of the Bloody Sunday massacre on January 9, left the Russian Empire reeling and tsarist autocracy fighting for its very existence.[1] In the end, 1905 culminated in a new era of political and social expression for the people of the Russian Empire, including the Rogozhskoe Old Believers and their Holy Moscow. Specifically, in one of the earliest efforts to calm Russian society following the onset of revolution, Nicholas II introduced his *ukaz* "On Beginning the Improvement of Religious Toleration," providing the greatest opportunity for the Rogozhskoe Old Believers to take full control of their own community.[2]

For the Rogozhskoe Old Believers, the aftermath of 1905 represented the first opportunities for the community to define a sense of morality and piety freely. Unfettered by restrictive legislation, Rogozhskoe's community and ideals now represented the triumph of their society. Ultimately, following the *ukaz* on toleration in April and the October Manifesto, Rogozhskoe's community adapted in two major ways. First, the Rogozhskoe Old Believers needed to determine how full religious freedom would, and should, shape the community and its ideals. Although Rogozhskoe still recognized its community as the spiritual center for the entire priestly Old Rite, after 1905 they needed to define how best to express their place within the greater context of the Old Rite and Russian Orthodoxy. Second, after 1905 the Rogozhskoe Old Believers found even greater opportunities to contribute to the Russian

Empire economically and now politically. Rogozhskoe's merchant and business dynasties experienced a major generational transition in which younger, dynamic leaders took control of their family businesses and introduced new ideas to both their own professions as well as to Rogozhskoe. For example, the extremely successful and highly ambitious Riabushinskii brothers introduced new efforts to use their wealth, economic influence, and sense of Christian duty to shape both Rogozhskoe Cemetery and the Russian Empire.

This chapter explores how the Rogozhskoe Old Believers upheld and adapted their community following the time of religious toleration and events of 1905 until the Bolshevik Revolution. Rogozhskoe experienced an unprecedented, albeit brief, period in which they fully expressed their community's ideals physically, ideologically, and spiritually. First, religious toleration directly affected Rogozhskoe Cemetery and its community physically and spiritually. With the new freedom for their faith, the Rogozhskoe Old Believers legally reopened their altars and thereby fully restored the community's spiritual functions within their community. More important, toleration allowed Rogozhskoe to physically restore their cathedrals, as well as expand the physical appearance of their community through new construction projects. Second, toleration also raised the issue of defining the Old Rite itself. One of the most critical aspects of toleration was now the Old Rite could display and debate their faith in public; in a crucial move, Rogozhskoe and some of its members took the issue of defining the Old Rite into the public sphere with Orthodox officials as well as other Old Believers. The introduction of toleration would finally allow for Old Rite communities such as Rogozhskoe to look back through history in order to affirm the very origins and major theological ideas that made their faith unique in the history of Orthodoxy. Religious toleration also influenced the Rogozhskoe Old Believers' efforts to organize their spiritual and community life. Because members of Rogozhskoe's community soon used the new political reforms in Russia to enter into politics themselves, a major issue for Rogozhskoe's future centered on questions concerning the best organizational leadership within Rogozhskoe Cemetery between the laity and the Belokrinitskaya Hierarchy. Finally, this period allowed the Rogozhskoe Old Believers to spread their community's ideals to the rest of Moscow as well as the Russian Empire. Some of the Rogozhskoe Old Believers participated in the broader world both through traditional means such as charity and industry, and through new opportunities such as legally publishing in the mass media and Old Rite newspapers. The period from 1905 to 1918, then, witnessed a brief moment in which the Rogozhskoe Old Believers found numerous outlets to express their ideals in response to the many opportunities created in post-1905 Russia.

"Now we have a Church!"

In Tsarist Russia's final decades, Rogozhskoe's prominence as an Old Rite spiritual and economic center continued to make the community a target of selective persecution. In the eyes of some powerful officials, such as Konstantin Pobedonostsev, Rogozhskoe Cemetery remained the crucial battleground in which they fought to maintain both civil and spiritual authority over the Old Rite to ensure that it could not challenge the Orthodox Church in the battle for the Russian soul. Even as Rogozhskoe found allies among local and state authorities, the likes of Pobedonostsev successfully blocked any of the community's spiritual and civil gains; he went so far as to make outlandish claims that oppression of the Old Rite would prevent the Empire's downfall. For example, following Nicholas II's coronation in 1896, State Comptroller Terty Filippov approved Rogozhskoe's petition to reopen their cathedrals' altars, forwarding it to Nicholas for his approval. However, once learning of the petition, Pobedonostsev intervened and rejected the petition while claiming that "indulgence of these schismatics threatens state security [. . .] and would potentially contribute to the collapse of the Russian state."[3]

However by the early twentieth century, the Russian Empire teetered on the edge of revolution as tensions rose between the autocracy and the Russian people. Russia's struggles with industrialization and the economic and social strains of the Russo-Japanese War finally pushed Russia's society to the breaking point. Tsarist authorities first considered reformist legislation aimed at appeasing an increasingly disgruntled populace in response to the outbreak of workers' strikes in December 1904. Drafted on December 12, one of the earliest possible reforms provided complete religious freedom for all Christian denominations throughout Russia, particularly the Old Rite.[4] The purpose of such a reform meant to appeal to the often traditionalist and conservative leanings for many of Russia's Christian communities to counterbalance the forces of revolution and liberalism. However, seeing the move as dangerous to Russian Orthodoxy, Konstantin Pobedonostsev urged Nicholas to reconsider; he reminded Nicholas of his earlier conviction that any gains for the Old Rite surely meant the end of Russia.[5] Pobedonostsev feared that full religious toleration of the Old Rite and other denominations only weakened the Orthodox Church, possibly the strongest pro-autocracy force throughout the Russian Empire. Pobedonostsev maintained that Old Rite freedom directly threatened the Orthodox Church through conversion to minority religions or through any loss in the Russian Orthodox Church's privilege and prestige as the only legal form of Orthodoxy in the Empire.[6] Therefore, thanks to continued protests from Pobedonostsev and other advisors, Nicholas chose to delay his considerations on religious toleration.

Only weeks later, Russian society boiled over in the aftermath of Bloody Sunday on January 9, 1905. As the Russian Empire spiraled into anarchy, Nicholas and his ministers desperately debated reform designed to quell the growing number of strikes and protests throughout the Empire.[7] Hoping to avoid reform that compromised autocratic authority, debate focused on issuing greater civil rights in the hope of appeasing the populace. Once again, discussion turned to the issue of religious toleration. However, tsarist authorities realized that they could not just issue religious freedom. Instead, any effort at religious reform required that several questions needed answering before such reform could take place. First, tsarist officials needed to determine what "religious toleration" actually looked like in Russia. Second, authorities need to determine who can receive religious freedom. Third, tsarist officials needed to determine how to best "protect" the Russian Orthodox Church following religious toleration. Finally, and most important, religious toleration required that the very definition of "Russian Orthodoxy" would change once the state allowed for the existence of Orthodox pluralism.

On April 17, 1905, Nicholas released his *ukaz* "On the Strengthening of Religious Toleration." Hoping that such an offering might quell some of the unrest by granting concessions to its people, the *ukaz* introduced religious toleration into the Russian Empire by allowing for the people of the Russian Empire to choose their religion. Specifically, the *ukaz* ended the prohibition on Orthodox members leaving the Russian Orthodox Church. Furthermore, the *ukaz* allowed "schismatic sects" to build their own temples and hold all religious services and allowed religious minorities to practice their faith openly, rather than register as Orthodox while practicing their true faith only in private.[8]

Released on Easter, the *ukaz* not only granted the Old Rite their long-awaited reform, but it legally recognized the Old Rite's historical and spiritual ties to both the Russian Empire and Russian Orthodoxy. First and foremost, the *ukaz* granted Old Believers the right to practice their faith freely and without harassment from Orthodox or state officials.[9] The Old Rite also gained many new rights that provided a more complete religious experience. For example, the *ukaz* granted Old Rite communities the freedom to elect their own clergy; to build Old Rite monasteries, convents, and hermitages; to repair or build churches and religious structures; it also ordered the unsealing of all closed Old Believer religious structures.[10]

In addition to the new religious freedoms, the Old Rite gained several civil rights previously excluded to them. The *ukaz* now granted Old Believers the prerogative to publish their own literature and religious books. Another significant part of the reform lifted the long-standing bans on individuals converting to the Old Rite from the Russian Orthodox Church and now allowed the children of mixed-faith marriages to adopt the Old Rite if they wished. Old Rite communities also received permission to build their own primary schools that taught a curriculum that allowed for education on the Old Rite. Communities also gained the right to keep their own records on births, marriages, and deaths rather than register them with the Orthodox Church; it also restored control over such vital records to the Old Rite itself.[11]

Furthermore, Nicholas's *ukaz* acknowledged the Old Rite's unique historical legacy, distinguishing the movement from other sectarians. More significantly, the *ukaz* acknowledged the Old Rite's distinction as a part of Russian Orthodox.

> The name of *staroobriadtsy*, now used instead of *raskol'niki*, recognizes the followers of all persuasions and consents who accept the basic tenants of the Orthodox Church, but do not acknowledge the adoption of specific practices into their worship and continue to use the original spelling of early Russian books.[12]

While a momentous achievement in the Old Rite's search for toleration, the *ukaz*'s significance did not end there; they now received complete recognition of their legitimate ties to the Orthodox world and Russian history.

The Rogozhskoe Old Believers, in particular, received special notice about the *ukaz*, a move that ensured that the community could prepare for this great moment. On Holy Saturday, April 16, Nicholas himself directly issued telegrams to the Rogozhskoe trustees and Moscow Police.

> Today, prior to the upcoming holiday, I give my order to unseal the altars at the Old Believer chapels at Rogozhskoe Cemetery and grant permission to the Old Believer clergy to resume performing their church services. This will achieve their long desired removal of the long-term ban against the Old Believers and be a new expression of my confidence, goodwill, and love for the Old Believers and their community.[13]

Nicholas's order to unseal Rogozhskoe's altars on Holy Saturday, provided an opportunity for the Rogozhskoe Old Believers to prepare for one of the most important events in their history and in the community's understanding of their Holy Moscow.

By the afternoon of Holy Saturday, hundreds of Old Believers gathered in Rogozhskoe Cemetery as word spread of the *ukaz* and opening of the cathedrals' altars. Three-hundred of the Rogozhskoe Old Believers crammed into the Intercession Cathedral to hear Prince Dmitri Golitsyn read Nicholas's *ukaz* granting religious toleration for the Old Rite. Once Golitsyn finished, the crowd remained in dead silence as the authorities unlocked and removed the remaining barriers on the altars. As the altars opened for the first time in nearly 49 years, one of the witnesses, Count de Shamborant, noted that, "[t]he Old Believers' hearts trembled with the first ray of light rushing [into the altars]. Their emotions gave way, and sobs were heard from excessive joy on all sides."[14] Golitsyn then moved on to the Nativity Cathedral and once again read the decree to another large crowd of Rogozhskoe's community.

The reopening of Rogozhskoe's altars became a monumental moment in the community's identity and collective memory. One of the most detailed eyewitness accounts from that Easter weekend came from one of Moscow's most famous poets, journalist, and essayist, Vladimir Giliarovskii. Known throughout Russia for his poems and stories based on his interactions with people in Moscow and his travels, including one of the most detailed eyewitness accounts of the Khodynka Field disaster during Nicholas's coronation in 1896,[15] Giliarovskii's depiction of the Rogozhskoe Old Believers beautifully captures the community's emotions at the reopening of their altars. In his work "Reopening the Altars at Rogozhskoe Cemetery," Giliarovskii described the community's reactions to the events in great detail.

> And so it happened. By two o'clock in the afternoon, the 16th of April, the Moscow Cemetery gathered to hear the good news that all four altars would be opened [. . .] All of the clergy and over three hundred people crammed to the end of the temple, and when those present heard the first sounds of a hammer on the locks of the altar's door – the keys had been lost – tears of joy welled up and gleamed in the eyes of the worshipers.[16]

Giliarovskii's essay continues with a vivid description of the Intercession Cathedral's altars immediately after their opening, highlighting, and in ways, symbolizing the devastation tsarist oppression of Rogozhskoe Cemetery had on not only the altars themselves, but also on the whole community and its very identity.

> The doors opened.
>
> There was a smell of dampness, even though [the interior] was lit, as the windows were not boarded over. Forty-nine years took their toll.
>
> Here and there icons had fallen, on the floor, covered with dust, littered with the skeletons of pigeons and jackdaws, who forced their way in here through the broken glass and missing frames. The walls are moldy.
>
> [. . .] Many, many icons were spoiled, and the wall paintings disappeared under the mold. Only two Gospels remained on their thrones, shining with gold and silver. One Gospel in particular

> was well-preserved, large, and according to tradition, donated by Catherine II.[17]

Giliarovskii's account revealed similar devastation found within the Nativity Cathedral's altar.

> Again, they banged their hammers, they chiseled, gnashed, and the doors creaked under the pressure of their shoulders – and when the door opened after great difficulty, all eyes present only appeared gaping darkness. With candles, they could barely make their way through the rubble. At the risk of falling into one of the many holes or the floor failing, the commission removed the seals and opened the gates of the royal and the southern doors.[18]

Giliarovskii's artistic flair soon revealed a supremely vivid description of the scene as well as the emotions surrounding this event, which reflected on the very nature of the relationship between the Old Rite and Russian state.

Figure 4.1 Damage to the Intercession Cathedral altar space after their reopening, Nikifor Zenin, April 16, 1905.

Figure 4.2 Damage to the Intercession Cathedral altar space after their reopening, Nikifor Zenin, April 16, 1905.

We went in [the Winter temple] and stopped. "Be careful, the floor will fail!" It is dark and musty – the darkness of the grave and the smell of a tomb. For half a century the altar did not see sunlight – the windows were barred by iron and the doors sealed. In the Summer Church, the windows were not blocked, and there almost everything remained. Light gives life. The darkness is of the dead.

The darkness of bigotry and ignorance shut the altar doors, but it disappears before the light of freedom of conscience. – Be careful, there is a hole! – A member of the clergy, E. I. Usov, very kindly helped me. I had stumbled upon the remains of the iron church chairs, the wood rotted, and I nearly fell into a deep hole in the collapsed floor.

[...] The floor is littered with icons and other debris – they collapsed a long time ago and now are covered in thick dust. To the right is the altar. What we see in the candlelight is not ordinary gray dust. This kind of dust has an unprecedented fervor, the color of darkness. A living, malevolent darkness.

Shaggy, plump dust, giving the impression of something living! Looking further into it, the more it appears to breath before the eyes, it rises, rising, and as if it is about to stir, continuing to rise – I think – and something terrible, very terrible, is about to crawl out from under it. As if from under the dust would come a monstrous wail, as if countless demons and monsters gathering their strength will climb and burst from the wreckage [. . .] it sickens the imagination to think that it was this countless multitude and its power that required so many to smash-in and break the doors open.

[. . .] We go into the altar. Our candles do not tremble, they do not flicker [. . .] And our footsteps become the voices of the dead as the dust muffles our steps. [. . .] The altar miraculously holds on to something [. . .] From a thick layer of dust, dressing it all, you can only guess at the contours of objects. [. . .] As we surround it the

Figure 4.3 Damage to the Nativity Cathedral's altar upon its reopening. Nikifor Zenin, April 16, 1905.

> heart muscles tighten, the soul hurts from this "Blasphemy of God's Holiness!" And now – Christ is risen![19]

Giliarovskii's essay perfectly conveys the first images and emotions that the Rogozhskoe Old Believers experienced once allowed to reopen their altars. As the community feared for decades, destruction greeted them as the decades of neglect due to the state's persecution left numerous treasures ruined.

As Giliarovskii's account reveals, undeterred by such devastation, the Rogozhskoe Old Believers wasted no time to begin cleaning and repairing the altars in order to have them as ready as possible for Easter services. Giliarovskii continues his account.

> As the day went on, more people, learning about the events, came to visit and arrived [at the temples]. They had questions, conversations, and shared their joy and jubilation.
>
> Up to forty people immediately began working to clean the altars of the churches, trying to ready them in any possible order for the

Figure 4.4 Damage to the Nativity Cathedral's altar upon its reopening. Nikifor Zenin, April 16, 1905.

> Easter services, which would take place at the altar for the first time after almost half a century of gloomy silence.
>
> Hastily they threw out the debris and decayed matter. The people took for their memory small fragments, scraps of matter, scraps of paper. And now before me a blackened piece of paper with a clearly written: "For the repose of Ivan. Remember for the Forty Day Mass." On the other side an inscription in pencil: "Vostryakov." And all of these pieces, were reminders of verses for these people.[20]

The Rogozhskoe Old Believers' attempts to repair the altars in order to hold any semblance of a proper Easter service emphasizes the significance of this moment in their history, as well as the community's spiritual ties to their Holy Moscow. Restoring the altars in time for Easter mirrored the very holiday itself. Specifically, as revealed by the Rogozhskoe Old Believers' shouts of "Christ is Risen . . . Now we have a Church!" just as Easter celebrates Christ's Resurrection, so too did Easter 1905 celebrate Rogozhskoe's resurrection of their Old Rite purity.[21]

The Rogozhskoe Old Believers' efforts proved successful as the community celebrated Easter Services in the Intercession Cathedral. Giliarovskii describes the scene:

> The people gathered in unprecedented numbers. The church filled, and crowds gathered all around the outside. There was a bright illumination from the outside. Even though the bells had not been restored, there was a solemn Easter ringing in the air, as it was in Macedonia and in Bulgaria before the wars of liberation.
>
> The procession moved inside the church, but could not move around it outside. "This was our most desired temptation" – said one of the Old Believers, when I asked him about the grand illumination and the procession.
>
> Prince Golitsyn, Count Sheremetev, and E. Volkov all attended the midnight liturgy. The service was extremely solemn and intimate. The mood was majestic. The persons joyful. The procession was over [. . .] they sang "Easter is Sacred," and sang out "Christ is Risen!" And all began to triple kiss.

> The Old-timers do not remember having such high spirits, such happy tears and warm embraces. The Easter greeting lasted about an hour.
>
> Soon all began repeating – Now we have a Church![22]

Giliarovskii's account reveals the outpouring of emotion throughout Rogozhskoe only hours after the announcement on religious toleration. Nicholas's *ukaz* heralded the beginning of a new era in Rogozhskoe's efforts at building the ideal Christian community. As the Rogozhskoe historian Makarov noted only a few years later, "[t]he day of April 16, 1905 will forever remain in the memory of the Moscow Old Believers as it completely shifted their history as it laid to rest their sad past of suffering, and brought on a new era to practice their religion freely."[23] Ultimately for the Rogozhskoe Old Believers, Nicholas's *ukaz* granted *de facto* recognition of everything Rogozhskoe Cemetery desired of itself and its community. With religious toleration, Rogozhskoe could now realize their efforts to build a community that embodied the spiritual and communal ideals of a pious Old Rite community.

Soon after the *ukaz*, the Rogozhskoe Old Believers elected a commission to give their thanks to Nicholas in person. On April 19, Rogozhskoe's elected commission met with Nicholas at Tsarskoe Selo, sharing their "joyful and heartfelt thanks on behalf of [their] Moscow Old Believer community for the kindness bestowed upon Rogozhskoe Cemetery with the reopening of their holy shrines" and the "mercy of religious toleration."[24] For the Rogozhskoe Old Believers, their *batiushka* finally undid the injustices of the past not only to return their altars but also to grant them the freedom to express their Faith in full.

In that one moment during Easter weekend 1905, the Easter greeting that "Christ is Risen" represented an even greater significance in Rogozhskoe. For the first time in Rogozhskoe's history, and the history of the Old Rite, these fervent believers could legitimately act as an Orthodox Church. Old Believers could legally attend a full Old-Rite Orthodox service, and they could legally refer to their sacred spaces as Churches and Cathedrals, thereby publically displaying their faith and spirituality. For the Rogozhskoe Old Believers, Easter 1905 not only allowed them to celebrate Christ's Resurrection, but the very

Resurrection of Old-Rite Russian Orthodoxy and the ability to achieve their ideal communal morality without restriction.

Rogozhskoe after Religious Toleration

The onset of religious toleration in Russia introduced numerous opportunities for the Rogozhskoe Old Believers to reshape their community in light of their newfound freedoms. In terms of immediate goals, Rogozhskoe's greatest concern focused on restoring and renovating their cathedrals to serve once again as symbols of the community's piety and grandeur. In addition, toleration also afforded the Rogozhskoe Old Believers with new opportunities to incorporate new construction projects and new symbols to reflect their communal ideals. Furthermore, with legal recognition of their community for the first time in their history, the Rogozhskoe Old Believers gained the opportunity to organize themselves without direct government oversight. Therefore, a major concern for Rogozhskoe in post-1905 Russia focused on the community's search for the best means of organizing and governing themselves to remain a model community for Moscow and Russian society. Under a new governing body that replaced their trustees, Rogozhskoe's leadership ushered Rogozhskoe into the era of religious toleration in Russia.

Shortly after the *ukaz* on religious freedom, the Rogozhskoe Old Believers came together on April 29, 1905 in order to discuss the critical issue on how to proceed with restoring and renovating the community's cathedrals' altars as well as the structures themselves.[25] The next day, the community elected a commission of some of their most esteemed and influential members under the expressed duty to determine the process and needs for renovation throughout the community. Over the next months, the commission (made up of Ivan and Grigori Rakhmanov, Matvei Kuznetsov, Ivan Pugovkin, Pavel Riabushinskii, Petr Rastorguev, Egor Malyzhev, Pavel Fedotov; and the priests Ioann Vlasov, Elisei Melekhin, and Prokopi Sorokin), first made the effort to determine the costs of not only restoring the altars and damaged icons, but also of repairing structural damage to the cathedrals.[26]

The committee's first meeting on May 25 revealed the many needs, both in terms of work as well as finances, to complete Rogozhskoe's restoration. The committee decided that the Intercession Cathedral required immediate repairs and restoration. After collecting as much information on the process as they could, the committee determined that the Intercession's altar required 5,600 rubles to restore its iconography. Furthermore, the Rogozhskoe's committee requested 8,000 rubles to hire Nikolai Safonov, a well-known iconographer throughout Central Russia for his icon and fresco restorations throughout Moscow, Vladimir, Novgorod, and even the Saint Sergius Trinity Lavra.[27] The committee considered completely restoring the dome on the Nativity Cathedral, however they postponed the decision until the next meeting when they determined not only to restore the dome, but also to wash the Nativity's walls and iconostasis.[28]

Restoring the cathedrals, the very symbols of Rogozhskoe's faith, therefore became the community's primary purpose in the immediate aftermath of religious toleration. The Rogozhskoe Old Believers spared no expense in their repair efforts. The final cost to restore both cathedrals reveals both how devastating tsarist oppression affected the physical embodiment of the Rogozhskoe Old Believers' faith as well as the community's resolve to undo the damage of decades past. For the Intercession Cathedral, the restoration's final total came to 38,100 rubles. In addition to the original restorations for the altars (5,600 rubles) and wall iconography (8,000 rubles), renovation of the Intercession Cathedral also included a new, gilded iconostasis (8,000 rubles) and new iron frames for the church (1,500 rubles).[29] The greatest expense, however, reveals the Rogozhskoe Old Believers' conviction that religious toleration would spark a spiritual renaissance in the community. In order to facilitate the use of the Intercession Cathedral for year-round services, the Rogozhskoe committee voted to install a new, steam heating system for the cathedral, totaling 15,000 rubles.[30] Installing a heating system for the Intercession Cathedral ensured that both cathedrals could be used simultaneously throughout the year in order to meet an expected increase in service attendance. No longer required to practice their faith in the privacy of their homes, the Rogozhskoe Old Believers could once again participate in a shared spiritual experience, and thereby reunite the community through the shared participation in the Old Rite.

Of the two buildings, however, the Nativity Cathedral found itself in even greater need for repairs than the Intercession Cathedral. Not only did tsarist oppression nearly leave the cathedral's altars in near complete ruin, but left the cathedral itself requiring structural repair and renovation. In all, the grand total for the Nativity Cathedral's restoration came to 43,100 rubles. The ravages of time left very little salvageable from the Nativity's altars, so the final cost for restoring the icons that could be saved totaled only 850 rubles.[31] However, too little remained of the altars themselves; in addition, much of the interior iconography all needed to be completely rebuilt. The costs for restoring the Nativity Cathedral included a new floor for the altar (10,000 rubles), a new iconostasis and wall paintings (13,750 rubles), and new sacred utensils such as candleholders, censers, and other materials (3,500 rubles).[32] As part of the Nativity Cathedral's renovation, the committee also paid for the installation of a new, steam heating system as well, for an additional 15,000 rubles.[33]

While renovating the cathedrals played an important role for Rogozhskoe after 1905, one of the newest rights granted to Old Rite communities allowed them to construct new religious buildings. For Rogozhskoe in particular, such an opportunity allowed the community to fill one of the few lacunae remaining after the age of toleration, their bells. Since the earliest days of Nicholas I's reign, legislation forbade Old Believers from using any belfries or bells in their services, granting sole privilege for such displays of piety only to the Orthodox Church. Rogozhskoe Cemetery too had their bells confiscated under Nicholas I's oppression of the Old Rite.[34] As bells and bell ringing play an important role in Russian Orthodox identity, as well as the history of the Orthodox Church,[35] the Rogozhskoe Old Believers wanted to restore bell ringing to their own spiritual experience. Therefore, in their meeting on June 16, 1905, the Rogozhskoe committee unanimously voted in favor of petitioning the Moscow authorities for permission to "erect a stone bell tower for our community, and while it is constructed, also build a temporary wooden belfry."[36] As the committee, and the Rogozhskoe community as a whole understood, the restoration of bell ringing in Rogozhskoe would further complete the spiritual experience and symbolism of Rogozhskoe's place within Orthodox Christianity.

However, even after religious toleration, the Rogozhskoe Old Believers faced continued resistance from critics and opponents still left in positions of power. For example, then Moscow Governor General Alexander Kozlov restricted any religious processions by the community to remain within the walls of the Rogozhskoe Cemetery.[37] Regarding

Old Rite communities, while the *ukaz* did allow new structures, it did not lay out the process for carrying out the new plans. Therefore, the ambiguity allowed opponents to continue interfering in Old Rite communities such as Rogozhskoe. For example, in response to Rogozhskoe's request for a bell tower, Kozlov dismissed the petition: "why would [you] build a temporary belfry and bell tower without the discretion of the Minister of Internal Affairs?"[38] With vague regulations on Old Rite construction projects, it appeared that the Rogozhskoe Old Believers' desire for a bell tower could remain unanswered.

However, even while thwarted by prejudiced officials, the Rogozhskoe Old Believers still moved ahead in their plans for a new bell tower by reviewing designs for a possible future project. The Rogozhskoe Old Believers desired a grand bell tower, designed both to express themselves as Orthodox Christians as well as to celebrate the era of religious toleration as the first new religious structure in Rogozhskoe in nearly a century. Furthermore, such a construction project also symbolized the Old Rite communities' sense of sacredness and legitimacy.[39] Therefore, in Rogozhskoe's case, the ability to build a bell tower both legitimized their freedom, as well as their sense that their Holy Moscow served as an affirmation of their morals and values. Designed by the architects Fyodor Gornostaev and Z. I. Ivanov, the estimated final cost of the bell tower totaled 155,847 rubles.[40] Therefore, the community needed to raise the necessary funds to build such a grand structure.

Beginning in 1906, and before ever receiving permission to build the bell tower, Rogozhskoe's leaders requested voluntary donations from the community, specifically for the construction of a bell tower.[41] Many of Rogozhskoe's members donated vast sums of rubles or purchased building materials for the project over the next three years. By the end of 1906, the community raised 2,081 rubles and 40 kopeks. By the end of 1907, Rogozhskoe's members donated a grand total of 82,438 rubles and 53 kopeks. In 1908 the community raised another 52,692 rubles and 11 kopeks. Finally, through 1909, Rogozhskoe raised an additional 60,903 rubles and 77 kopeks.[42] While a number of Rogozhskoe's most prominent families and individuals contributed vast sums of their own wealth for the bell tower project, such as Matvei Kuznetsov (10,000 rubles) and Stepan Riabushinskii (9,000 rubles),[43] none of Rogozhskoe's Old Believers rivaled the donations of the Morozov family.

Figure 4.5 Draft of the Rogozhskoe Bell Tower. F. F. Gornostaev and Z. I. Ivanov. *Tserkov'*, 1908.

Fedosiia Ervilovna and Maria Fedorovna, sisters-in-law and widows of the brothers Ivan and Timofei Morozov respectively, contributed the largest donations for Rogozhskoe's bell tower. For example, as a memorial to her recently deceased son, Sergei, Fedosiia donated 30,000 rubles in 1907 and "vast amounts of building materials including scaffolding, beams, and the entire fixture for the bells – all so the bells could ring in the memory of Sergei."[44] Similarly, Maria, who owned and managed her family's textile empire since 1889, devoted herself and her wealth, to both Rogozhskoe Cemetery and numerous charities throughout Moscow and the Russian Empire. Especially following the sudden, mysterious death of her youngest son, Savva, in 1905, Maria used her wealth to memorialize her son's memory.[45] Already one of

Moscow's most beloved and revered philanthropists, Maria increased her charitable efforts not only out of a sense of Christian duty, but also to memorialize Savva's memory and cement his own charitable legacy.[46] Maria quickly became one of Rogozhskoe Cemetery's most important patrons. Particularly for the bell tower project, Maria donated 20,000 rubles in 1908, and then an additional 45,000 rubles for the construction efforts.[47] Fedosiia and Maria's generosity reflected the high standards of the Rogozhskoe Old Believers' communal ideal of the ties between charity and Old Rite piety. Maria in particular received great praise directly from the Archbishop of Moscow and All Rus' Ioann in 1908, deeming her Rogozhskoe's "great benefactress" during one of the earliest ceremonies commemorating the groundbreaking event for Rogozhskoe's bell tower in 1908.[48]

Not until late 1907 did the Moscow authorities grant permission to the Rogozhskoe Old Believers' petition for a bell tower. On April 20, 1908, at a commemoration attended by thousands, the Rogozhskoe Old Believers consecrated the site for their future bell tower.[49] The community began the ceremony at 8:00 a.m. by celebrating the Divine Liturgy. All events took place under a large, white tent in view of representatives from both Moscow and tsarist authorities.[50] So many

Figure 4.6 Rogozhskoe Bell Tower Dedication Services on April 20, 1908. *Tserkov'*, 1908.

members of Rogozhskoe and other Old Believer communities attended that multiple processions took place around Rogozhskoe Cemetery, each procession with its own clergy and choir singers.[51]

Located between the Intercession and Nativity Cathedrals, the Rogozhskoe bell tower served as the very symbol of Rogozhskoe's efforts to tie themselves spiritually and ideologically to Moscow. As stated by the Old Believer Newspaper *Tserkov'*, founded by Rogozhskoe's Ivan Shibaev in 1908, "The Bell Tower's grand size and original, beautiful Russian-style architecture, will, no doubt, belong among the most prominent buildings in the area and one of the grandest examples of church architecture in the ancient capital."[52] The Rogozhskoe Old Believers intended to use the four-tiered bell tower to fill many needs. The first tier housed a small Church of the Resurrection, which could hold services for up to 200 people.[53] The second-tier served as the community's library and archives, housing both important community documents and correspondence, but doubled as a repository for Rogozhskoe's most valuable manuscripts and other antiquities.[54] The third and fourth tiers housed the bells, mounted in October 1908 after the construction of the bell tower's

Figure 4.7 Mounting of the Rogozhskoe Bells. *Tserkov'*, 1908.

basic structure.[55] The bell mounting too became a major celebration for the Rogozhskoe Old Believers as the community welcomed hundreds who gathered to witness the event on October 19.[56] By the end of the celebrations, the participating clergy issued a letter of thanks to the bell tower's great benefactress, Fedosiia Morozova, for her funding the bells' casting. "Your generous gift glorifies the name of God and the glory of our holy temples. Their powerful sound from these bells will now summon to prayer the faithful, who shall offer their prayers for the health of your pure heart and soul [. . .]."[57]

Architecturally, Rogozhskoe's new bell tower held great significance as it served as a very visible symbol of the new opportunities available to the community. Additionally, the tower and the Church of the Resurrection added to Rogozhskoe's physical representation of their Old Rite idealism. First, it symbolized both the first structure following the *ukaz* of 1905, as well as the first structure that the Rogozhskoe Old Believers constructed purely in old Russian architectural styles since the original Intercession Cathedral before its demolition by tsarist authorities in 1791. Unlike the Intercession and Nativity Cathedrals, which mixed and matched Russian and the neo-classical styles popular during their construction, the Rogozhskoe bell tower maintained a purely Russian architectural style, specifically that of the Early Moscow Period of the late fifteenth and early sixteenth centuries.[58] Rogozhskoe's bell tower represented the first spiritual structure that truly reflected the artistic and architectural styles of Pre-Nikonian Russian Orthodoxy, thereby allowing the Rogozhskoe Old Believers to produce a structure that itself reflected the cultural values of the Old Rite.

Second, and just as significantly, Rogozhskoe's new bell tower represented yet another effort to tie the community to Moscow historically, spiritually, and physically. Specifically, once completed, the Rogozhskoe's bell tower measured 80 meters tall, only one meter shorter than the Ivan the Great Bell Tower in the Moscow Kremlin.[59] For centuries, the Ivan the Great Bell Tower served as the tallest structure in all of Moscow. Only with the completion of the Cathedral of Christ the Savior in 1883 did another structure surpass the Ivan the Great Bell Tower. Just as in 1791 when Rogozhskoe originally designed the Intercession Cathedral as a larger replica of the Kremlin's Dormition Cathedral, Rogozhskoe's bell tower reconnected their community to an idealized symbol of Russian Orthodoxy, culture, and history. While Rogozhskoe did not directly copy the Ivan the Great Bell Tower, their tower still symbolized the community's efforts to reflect the Old Rite's ties to pre-Nikonian Russia.[60] Therefore, to the Rogozhskoe Old Believers, just as the Pre-Nikonian Church held the Moscow Kremlin's Cathedral Square as the seat of the Russian Orthodox Church, so now the Rogozhskoe Cemetery "cathedral square" served as the seat of their Old Rite community.

The bell tower took on a central role in the community's identity and activities in 1913.[61] On August 18 Rogozhskoe held a celebration for the bell tower's completion and the opening of the Church of the Resurrection. Emphasizing the moment's significance, a number of important figures from Moscow and high-ranking state officials either attended Rogozhskoe's celebrations or sent congratulatory telegrams. The list of dignitaries included the likes of the Chairman of the Council of Ministers Vladimir Kokovtsev, Minister of Internal Affairs Nikolai Maklakov, Director of the Department of Religious Affairs Evgeni Menkin, Chairman of the State Duma Mikhail Rodzianko, and Count Sergei Witte.[62] Although Witte did not attend the ceremonies, he sent a telegram to the Rogozhskoe Old Believers in which he expressed his "extreme joy" for his invitation and acknowledged the bell tower's construction as an important symbol of religious toleration in Russia.

> I feel joy, as your activities reveal the full vision of the extent of freedom by the decree, and even if it was applied to a smaller degree, this is a great benefit to all of Russia; I am saddened because for so long you had to remain relatively insignificant and could only rely on your hope. But without hope one could not live, but because of your continued hope we can give thanks to God and the Tsar for the passing of [religious toleration] so that you may receive full freedom.[63]

Ultimately, Rogozhskoe's bell tower served as another identifying symbol of the community's efforts to present their ideal community. One of most visible structures throughout all of Moscow in the early twentieth century because of its height,[64] Rogozhskoe's bell tower stood as a beacon of the community's opportunities in the future.

Governing the Community

Along with toleration, Nicholas's *ukaz* allowed communities like Rogozhskoe to determine the governance and organization for their community without outside interference by tsarist or Moscow authorities.

Figure 4.8 Rogozhskoe's Bell Tower, 1913. *Tserkov'*, 1913.

In post-1905 Russia, the Rogozhskoe Old Believers needed to determine how their community could exist in response to the political, social, cultural, and economic changes around them. Furthermore, as home to the Belokrinitskaya Archbishop of Moscow and all Rus', the Rogozhskoe Old Believers also needed to determine how religious toleration redefined the community's relationship to both the Hierarchy and the Old Rite as a whole. Toleration thereby provided the Rogozhskoe Old Believers with their first opportunity to determine how their community could fulfill their own expectations as an Old Rite community without fear of intervention by outside forces.

Rogozhskoe's first opportunity to determine how to organize their community in the era of toleration came in October 1906 following a decree sent from the Governing Senate on procedures for Old Believers to form and operate communities. In terms of historical significance, the decree became the first legislation to recognize the right for Old Rite communities officially to exist and organize their own governing bodies.[65] Taking the lead for the Rogozhskoe Old Believers in their organization efforts, Stepan Riabushinskii ultimately developed and registered Rogozhskoe Cemetery as the *Moskovskaya Staroobriadcheskaya Obshina Rogozhskogo Kladbisha* (MSORK) on January 25, 1907. Officially replacing the Rogozhskoe Trustees, MSORK served as the new organizational and political body for Rogozhskoe Cemetery and now determined all community matters.[66]

MSORK held its first communal meeting on February 24, discussing issues that included the election of clergy, determining the governing membership for the MSORK council, electing a board to oversee Rogozhskoe's charities, managing property and determining rules and regulations for both Rogozhskoe Cemetery and MSORK.[67] After deliberation the Rogozhskoe Old Believers decided to elect a Council of 40 members to serve as the leadership of MSORK. According to its governing documents, the primary duty for the MSORK Council was to "take care of the beauty and prosperity of the community and its churches, maintain order of the cemetery, and perform all duties to maintain the regular life of the charities and schools."[68] Members on the MSORK Council collectively managed all of the affairs for the entire community and served three-year terms. The head of the Council served as Chairman. Other officers included two Deputy Chairmen, a Treasurer, and Caretaker of the Churches.

MSORK also restored the Rogozhskoe Trustees as officers on the MSORK Council.[69]

Just as in the decades prior to toleration under the Rogozhskoe Trustees, the Rogozhskoe Old Believers now regularly elected the community's most successful and prominent businessmen to serve as MSORK officers. Individuals such as the Kuznetsovs (Matvei Sidorovich and his sons Sergei, Georgi, and Nikolai), Stepan and Pavel Riabushinskii, Arsenii Morozov, and Ivan Pugovkin all played leading roles in shaping Rogozhskoe while each serving multiple terms as some of MSORK's highest ranking officers.[70] Similar to the past role of Rogozhskkoe's Trustees, the MSORK officers controlled and invested the Rogozhskoe community's capital while overseeing Rogozhskoe's numerous charities. Given its members' business acumen, the MSORK Council proved effective in not only allocating community funds to restore buildings such as the hospitals, almshouses, hotel, schools, and the community's sacred structures and new bell tower, but also in ensuring that the community's finances remained strong. By January 1, 1915 Rogozhskoe's capital and investments totaled 2,487,881 rubles and 21 kopeks.[71]

While the MSORK Council regularly drew from Rogozhskoe's more affluent members, the Council still relied heavily on the group's membership to guide MSORK's efforts for the congregation. In particular, MSORK held at least one annual meeting each year for the community. At these meetings not only did they elect the MSORK Council, but also reviewed general finances, including both annual expenditures and budget forecasts for the Rogozhskoe.[72] Attendance at each annual meeting often numbered in the hundreds; participating members often added their voices to discussions concerning the community, most often means to cut expenses for projects going over budget, such as the bell tower.[73] Annual meetings also took into consideration other communal issues such as the approval of applications by Old Believers to join the Rogozhskoe Community. The MSORK Council drew up the application process in 1908 for new membership to include participation in the parish for at least one year prior to applying for membership.[74]

The annual meetings thereby became one of the main outlets for interaction between Rogozhskoe's leadership and its general membership. One of MSORK's primary duties also included providing annual reports prior to the general meeting to allow everyone to have all pertinent information up for consideration.[75] This often included council funding for many of the facilities used by Rogozhskoe's parishioners. One of the most important concerns for Rogozhskoe's general population in the years following toleration became the community's schools and medical facilities. MSORK often ensured that schooling for Rogozhskoe's nearly 200 school-aged children took place in acceptable facilities with adequate supplies.[76] Similarly, one of Rogozhskoe's regular budget expenditures went toward the salaries for the hundreds of employees who maintained Rogozhskoe's many facilities, a number of whom belonged to Rogozhskoe Cemetery itself.[77] With such oversight, while the MSORK Council often came from Rogozhskoe's political and economic elite, the council continued to serve on behalf of Rogozhskoe's general population.

One of MSORK's most important duties, however, concerned Rogozhskoe's spiritual organization. While the Belokrinitskaya Archbishop of Moscow still maintained its spiritual authority such as ordaining and maintaining a clergy, MSORK took authority over the spiritual life of the community. Specifically, one of MSORK's primary duties centered on ensuring an active clergy and spiritual experience for community members. These efforts included regulating priests' workloads, establishing requirements for serving as a deacon, and even outlining the expectations for the community's choir.[78] Furthermore, while the Archbishop could recommend clerical candidates or invite outside clergy to visit or perform services in Rogozhskoe, MSORK held sole rights of approval for all clergy within Rogozhskoe both permanent and visiting.[79]

MSORK's need to regulate Rogozhskoe's clergy resulted from some stipulations of the *ukaz* on religious toleration. Most salient was the idea that toleration did not legitimize the Belokrinitskaya Hierarchy, since its clergy still could not use titles such as "priest or bishop." Authorities required the Rogozhskoe Old Believers in particular to sign state documents guaranteeing that they would not permit the use of clerical titles or allow their clergy to conduct religious services outside of Rogozhskoe Cemetery.[80] However, the *ukaz* did recognize the right for Old Believer communities to regulate their own clergy as they wished.[81]

MSORK took it upon themselves to shape exactly how Rogozhskoe's Holy Moscow maintained its spiritual life by determining how the Belokrinitskaya clergy's duties would meet the community's spiritual needs. Furthermore, in 1910 tsarist authorities did ultimately recognize the Belokrinitskaya Hierarchy's legitimacy as an Old Rite Church, thereby granting its clergy the right to use clerical and episcopal titles.[82] Therefore, MSORK's duty to regulate spiritual functions within the community took on even greater significance. MSORK then needed to determine the best balance for selecting its priests, to ensure that on the one hand the congregants could determine some aspects of their spiritual lives, while on the other hand still respected and considered recommendations and suggestions from Archbishop Ioann.[83] The MSORK Council thereby took it upon itself to determine a set of regulations to guide Rogozhskoe's spiritual life from its clergy to its choristers. MSORK presented its "Internal Regulations for the Churches of Rogozhskoe Cemetery" listing the nine guidelines for spiritual duties within the community in 1913. A summary follows.

(1) Two priests must be present at all Sunday services.
(2) Two deacons must be present at all Sunday services.
(3) Priests must conduct services on Thursday, Friday, Saturday, and Sunday. Every priest will conduct services for four days and alternate who may take Sunday off.
(4) Deacons must attend services for Vespers, Matins, and Hours on weekday.
(5) Widowed priests must attend services on weekdays for Vespers, Matins, and Hours at least every other week.
(6) Choristers should be ready no later than ten minutes before services, without exception, when it is their turn to serve in the choir. If a member fails to attend the service, he will receive a warning the first time, the second time he will be punished for two weeks without performing, and the third time will be dismissed from his post.
(7) Choristers are selected by year. No chorister may be absent for more than 15 days, and if he misses more should be replaced.
(8) Any choristers dismissed or who lose their materials shall be fined.
(9) The older clergy and older community members may recommend priests and deacons, but they must be approved by the governing Council.[84]

By regulating church life at Rogozhskoe Cemetery, the MSORK Council not only established a uniform understanding of the spiritual experience for the community but also ensured that the laity remained an active part of the spiritual life of the whole.[85] Such control ensured that MSORK could both establish and maintain high expectations for the community's clergy in order to meet the spiritual standards for the Rogozhskoe Old Believers and their ideals.

The MSORK Council, as well as all Rogozhskoe Old Believers, required a specific standard for their clergy. As these clergy not only administered and maintained the community's spiritual life, they also embodied the Rogozhskoe Old Believers' expectations of Old Rite piety and morality. Therefore, the Rogozhskoe Old Believers and MSORK often commended outstanding clergy for their service to the community. One such example was Prokopi Sorokin.

First arriving at Rogozhskoe Cemetery in 1883, Father Sorokin became one of the most influential priests in Rogozhskoe's transition before and after religious toleration. Sorokin often served as council and personal confessor for many of Rogozhskoe's most notable parishioners and leaders such as Matvei and Sergei Kuznetsov, Stepan and Sergei Riabushinskii, Ivan Pugovkin, and Ivan Novikov.[86] To acknowledge his value as a priest, MSORK held a grand jubilee in Sorokin's honor for 25 years of service on May 6, 1908.[87] Because this celebration was the first to commemorate a priest's service following the *ukaz* on religious toleration, Father Prokopi's jubilee served as a means to celebrate his perseverance and devotion to both the Rogozhskoe community and the Old Rite during some of Rogozhskoe's most uncertain times. The jubilee included a prayer service in the Intercession Cathedral and messages of congratulations, of which a number compared Prokopi's career to the life of Job for experiencing the hardship of oppression, yet persevering until the onset of toleration. After receiving a number of valuable icons for his service, Sorokin reminded his parishioners that his experience was merely the shared experience of the community. "Although we have experienced much grief, we eventually received an ineffable joy with the reopening of the holy shrines and the freedom for our faith."[88] MSORK even further rewarded Sorokin's service by establishing a new educational scholarship in his name for the orphans and wards in Rogozhskoe's almshouses in October 1908.[89]

The formation of the MSORK ultimately established a governing body that ensured that the Rogozhskoe Old Believers' spiritual and communal needs fulfilled the community's sense of Old Rite purity in post 1905 Russia. MSORK and many of its prominent members continued to play a crucial role in shaping and maintaining Rogozhskoe Cemetery and its ideals. Under the leadership of MSORK, the Rogozhskoe Old Believers ultimately benefited from their history, recognition as one of the wealthiest and most charitable communities in Moscow, and their new spiritual freedom at last to create their idealized standard for both the Old Rite and early twentieth century Russia.

Rogozhskoe as a Spiritual Center after Toleration

As witnessed throughout their history, the Rogozhskoe Old Believers developed a specific identity and set of ideals that they presented to the world of a community devoted to true Christian piety, which they preserved in the face of the moral, religious, and economic corruptions of a westernized society. With the onset of religious toleration, the Rogozhskoe Old Believers sought, above all else, to affirm their community's status as a spiritual and cultural center for the priestly Old Rite, particularly now that they could do so mostly uninhibited. For the first time in the community's history, the Rogozhskoe Old Believers could fully use their many social, cultural, and economic influences not only to reaffirm their self-identity as defenders of Old Rite purity, but also to do so by participating openly with Moscow and Russian society.

In this new era of religious toleration, the Rogozhskoe Old Believers sought any means to affirm their place within both Moscow and Russia as the spiritual and cultural center for the priestly Old Rite. Consequently the Rogozhskoe Old Believers had to take advantage of any opportunities that arose from unprecedented changes after 1905 to redefine their community in relationship to the tsarist state, the Old Rite, and even the Belokrinitskaya Hierarchy. Through such efforts, the Rogozhskoe Old Believers at last hoped to realize the full potential of their ideals and in the process serve as a model society to impel Russia through times of social and political uncertainty.

While the *ukaz* on religious toleration granted the Belokrinitskaya clergy the right to conduct religious services and the hierarchy's bishops to ordain new priests, the *Belokrinitsy* did not receive legal recognition of their Church's place within the greater history of Russian Orthodoxy or Christendom. Rogozhskoe Old Believers therefore needed to gain legal recognition for their Church hierarchy as part of legitimizing their own self-identity. Hoping to build on the opportunities that arose in connection with religious toleration, the MSORK council, in particular, hoped to maintain and build the community's already close relationship with the Tsar and the Royal family by continuing traditions such as gifts for holidays and special occasions.[90] For example, the MSORK Council annually petitioned Nicholas to allow delegates from their community to celebrate Easter services with the Tsar and his family. An invitation to join the royal family at Tsarskoe Selo for Easter arrived in 1910. Rogozhskoe's delegation comprised of one Rogozhskoe's priest, Father Ioann Vlasov, and a number of MSORK's officials including Ivan Pugovkin, Sergei Solovyov, Petr Rastorguev, and Ivan Tregubov.[91] This audience was a major success for the Rogozhskoe Old Believers. Following a private exchange of Easter greetings with Nicholas, Alexandra, their children, and Maria Fedorovna, Father Ioann, acting on his own accord with no prior discussion with the other delegates, extended an invitation "on behalf of Archbishop Ioann" to visit Rogozhskoe Cemetery.[92] Surprising the delegation, Nicholas graciously accepted "with his supreme command, expressed his highest gratitude and returned his highest and warmest greetings to the Archbishop;" in this way he further acknowledged the Archbishop's position.[93]

While Nicholas did not visit Rogozhskoe Cemetery until Easter 1913, Nicholas's relationship with the Rogozhskoe Old Believers affirmed the community's influence as a religious, cultural, and social epicenter of the Old Rite in Late Imperial Russia.[94] Conversely, the relationship between Nicholas and the Rogozhskoe Old Believers also served the interest of the Tsar and Russian state, especially in the aftermath of 1905. At this time Nicholas willingly accepted support for his rule from any corner of the Russian Empire, particularly from the traditionalist community at Rogozhskoe.[95]

While continuing to build their relationship with the Tsar, the Rogozhskoe Old Believers next needed to reaffirm their position as the spiritual center for the Belokrinitskaya Hierarchy and the priestly Old Rite throughout Russia. The potential problem for the Rogozhskoe spiritual authority following the period of toleration derived from the *ukaz* allowing Old Rite communities to select their own clergy and religious leaders, thereby potentially weakening the spiritual authority of the Belokrinitskaya Hierarchy and Rogozhskoe to train or dispatch clergy to other Old Believers.[96] One such challenge stemmed from the fact that not all priestly Old Believers accepted the Belokrinitskaya Hierarchy such as the *beglopopovtsy* who continued using defrocked or runaway Orthodox priests. Furthermore, while the *okruzhniki* and most *neokruzhniki* concluded a major reconciliation in June 1906, some of the *neokruzhniki* still maintained their own groups within the Belokrinitskaya Hierarchy. However, while such movements potentially posed a moderate challenge to Rogozhskoe's influence as the ideological and physical spiritual center for priestly Old Rite, none could match the Rogozhskoe Old Believers' organization and resources.

Rogozhskoe's schools in particular positioned Rogozhskoe over other Old Rite communities. A critical part of any Old Rite community became the ability to educate future generations in their faith. Education of Old Believer children remained a historically contentious area between the State and the Old Rite; the secular authorities used education as yet another weapon in their efforts to stamp out the Old Rite. Many Old Rite communities proved resilient thanks to strong emphasis on parents' educating their own children. Yet a community like Rogozhskoe could also provide more formalized education for their school-aged children. Following 1905 Rogozhskoe found itself in an envious position for the community maintained two schools.[97]

Rogozhskoe's school stood as a source of pride in its role as a symbol of the Old Believers' continued existence in their faith. Particularly after the onset of toleration, Rogozhskoe's schools and students became models for other Old Rite communities, often being highlighted in articles in publications such as *Tserkov'*.[98] For example, news of the Rogozhskoe students' successful examinations in 1908 became worthy of publication.[99] Celebrating the successful exams, Archbishop Ioann praised the students: "Through the academic year you acquired much useful knowledge, and you can now further study the Law of God with more diligence, you will learn even more; and, by knowing the Law of God, and practice it, you will not only increase the delight of your parents, but you will be good Christians and true and useful citizens [. . .]."[100] By providing formal education for Rogozhskoe's children, their schools serve as yet another outlet for spreading the community's influence in both Moscow and the Old Rite.

In addition to subjects such as religion, history and mathematics, Rogozhskoe's students also sang in the choir. The children's choir also gained national prominence when they sang in events both in Rogozhskoe and throughout Moscow.[101] More importantly, Rogozhskoe's children's choir became a new means to contribute to the community's spiritual life. As one observer of the children's choir noted, "The children's participation in singing with the Rogozhskoe Cemetery choir completely transforms the already excellent choir [. . .] when they sing as one their innocence sends chills down the spine of the faithful [. . .] many could not contain themselves from crying with excitement [. . .] the Rogozhskoe Old Believer choir appears on the path to perfection, it is impossible not to rejoice."[102] Such an account reveals the significance of Rogozhskoe's ability to introduce new elements to the community's spiritual experience. Training their children to embody these new efforts at expressing Old Rite piety and purity thereby provided yet another means for Rogozhskoe to present itself as an idealized Old Rite community.

Rogozhskoe's new role as a symbol of Old Rite pedagogy did not only extend from the Rogozhskoe Old Believers themselves. In fact, many Old Rite communities looked to Rogozhskoe for guidance in teaching and training future generations. In the years immediately following the changes in 1905, Rogozhskoe quickly established itself as a collection and redistribution center of Old Rite texts and even schoolbooks.[103] However, while the Rogozhskoe Old Believers did produce new textbooks for Old Rite schools, they could not initially keep up with the increased demand for new, updated books after 1905.[104] Therefore, the years after toleration provided both new opportunities and new challenges for the Rogozhskoe Old Believers to shape and guide other Old Rite communities through their ties to Old Rite education.

Now that the Old Believers could express their faith freely, the Rogozhskoe Old Believers realized that many other communities also desired spiritual guidance. They saw that Old Rite communities might now seek training of their own spiritual leaders or even require experienced clergy from larger communities such as Rogozhskoe to meet their spiritual needs. In response the Rogozhskoe Old Believers not only offered training, but soon established theological instruction within Rogozhskoe Cemetery in order to prepare priests to minister to generations of future Old Believers.[105]

Fearing that a large influx of visiting priests or Old Believers seeking clerical training might overwhelm their own priests or prevent them from performing their duties to meet Rogozhskoe's needs,[106] the MSORK council soon took over the efforts to construct a theological seminary within Rogozhskoe Cemetery.[107] In 1911, seeking to meet the continually growing demand for spiritual training at Rogozhskoe, MSORK received permission from the Moscow Authorities to build a new theological institute. Opened on September 10, 1912 the Old Believer Theological Institute offered five-year courses for as many as

Figure 4.9 Rogozhskoe students after completing their exams. *Tserkov'*, 1912.

200 students and all "Old Believers who hold an ardent desire for both their faith and higher education."[108] Students enrolled in the Institute followed a curriculum that included catechism, liturgy, choir singing, Church Slavonic, Greek, icon painting, history of Orthodoxy and the Old Rite, pedagogy, and scripture. Students also regularly studied academic subjects such as geography, physics, and mathematics so that they could "be a benefit to both the parish and development of the Old Rite" and "provide enough practical training so that they may participate in Church social activities, become candidates for the priesthood, deacons, etc. and prepare them for responsible work in Russian society."[109]

The construction of the Old Believer Theological Institute at Rogozhskoe Cemetery serves as another example of the community's ability to adapt its identity and ideals to reflect trends in Russian society. Specifically, Late Imperial Russia witnessed a growing debate about how educational institutions could meet the varied needs of Russians throughout the empire in the face of the many social changes with the appearance of the working class and the rapid rise of urbanization. Various Russian state and church institutions as well as political and social groups all developed their own answer to questions regarding the place of education in Late Tsarist Russia. For example, some Orthodox Church institutions such as the Saint Petersburg Ecclesiastical Academy encouraged their students to use and practice their theological training by preaching in the city's working class neighborhoods. This practice not only encouraged the students to connect with their audience, but also helped provide a spiritual education for workers and other lower classes.[110] However, as a contrast to the educational efforts of Orthodox parish clergy, professional academics and universities also attempted to reshape Russia's educational system after 1905. During this period, academic institutions placed greater emphasis on curriculums focused on training in technical skills, politics, and civics to give students greater opportunities to participate in post-1905 politics and economics.[111]

Rogozhskoe's efforts to expand its educational outlets thereby fit into the larger social educational debates witnessed throughout Russia at the end of the tsarist period. Furthermore, MSORK and the Rogozhskoe Old Believers urged the faithful to maintain the Old Believer Theological Institute as a much needed institution. Even when the congregation generously suppported the Institute, it quickly became one of the greatest financial burdens for the community to build and maintain. Construction and materials for the Institute initially cost 300,000 rubles. Housing, feeding, stipends, and educational grants for the students totaled an additional 40,000 to 50,000 rubles annually.[112] Recognizing the Rogozhskoe Old Believers' devotion to their Institute, the MSORK leadership turned to them for funds to maintain the school. "Our community of Rogozhskoe Cemetery is already burdened by many other needs that require fixed costs, and they are gradually increasing. If we wish to ensure the existence and development of our Institute and its dedicated students, we need to raise more funds. To fully provide for and meet the Institute's requirements, we will need to raise a minimum of one million rubles in currency or other capital."[113] As witnessed in other financial drives during the construction of the new bell tower, among others, the Rogozhskoe Old Believers generously donated money and materials to the institute. Arsenii Morozov established himself as one of the most exemplary patrons of the Institute; in 1914 he purchased and donated the extensive library and icon collection from the family of Elisei Melekhin, one of Rogozhskoe's longest serving priests.[114] Also in 1916, Morozov purchased and donated a lavish collapsible iconostasis and altar from the descendants of one of Rogozhskoe's parishioners, Nikolai Yazinin, for the school's use.[115]

The Institute allowed Rogozhskoe to play a leading role in educating young, untrained Old Believers so that the students would return to their villages throughout the Russian Empire to offer spiritual leadership for their own Old Rite communities. Unfortunately, however, Rogozhskoe's Institute did not have the opportunity to develop its status or curriculum in order to attract greater attention. The outbreak of World War I placed a great strain on the Institute, as well as on the Rogozhskoe Old Believers to maintain the school. The Institute suffered financially with each year that the war dragged on. Supporting the war effort while contributing more of their capital and finances to the state now became a priority for the Rogozhskoe Old Believers.[116] Furthermore, over the years from 1914 to 1916 student enrollment diminished as a consequence of student enlistment or conscription into the military. Finally, in 1917, low enrollment and limited funding compelled Rogozhskoe to cancel all classes at the Institute indefinitely.[117]

World War I also necessitated that MSORK and the Rogozhskoe Old Believers delay their attempts to gain greater recognition for the legitimacy of the Belokrinitskaya Hierarchy in the Old Rite and Russia. Since the *ukaz* on religious toleration, the Rogozhskoe Old Believers hoped to gain the approval of both the Tsar and the Russian Orthodox Church to elevate the Belokrinitskaya Archbishop of Moscow and All-Russia to an Old Rite Metropolitanate. Archbishop Ioann in particular insisted adamantly that following religious toleration, the Old Rite not only needed official recognition of the legitimacy of the Belokrinitskaya Hierarchy within Russia, but also approval to establish a *Russian* Metropolitanate of their own.[118] However, not until shortly after Ioann's death on April 24, 1915, did MSORK finally petition the Holy Council of Bishops of the Russian Orthodox Church to consider Melety Kartushin, the new Belokrinitskaya Archbishop of Moscow and All-Russia, as an Old Rite Metropolitan of Moscow.[119] However, Melety himself eventually approached MSORK and the Holy Council of Bishops to request a delay; he felt that everyone should focus instead on Russia's war efforts. "We appeal to the love of the Holy Council of Bishops and request that, in view of the war and the Belokrinitskaya Archdiocese's devotion to the Russian state, that the council defer any decision on the elevation of Archbishop Melety as a Metropolitan until a more favorable time."[120]

War and the eventual rise of the Bolsheviks delayed the creation of the Old Rite Metropolitanate until 1988. Rogozhskoe's desire for a Metropolitan served several purposes. First, the creation of an Old Rite Metropolitanate would establish the Belokrinitskaya Hierarchy as a legitimate Church within the Russian Empire. Second, establishing an Old Rite Metropolitanate in Moscow would elevate Rogozhskoe to equal status with the Metropolitan in Belaia Krinitsa, thereby strengthening Rogozhskoe's position within the Old Rite Hierarchy. Finally, and most importantly, granting a Metropolitanate to Rogozhskoe would not only solidify Rogozhskoe Cemetery as the spiritual center for the *Belokrinitsy* in Russia, it would legitimize and bring the community closer to their idealized desire of a complete Christian Church. Not unlike the community's attempts to restore a relationship with the Tsar, recognition of a Metropolitanate would fully legitimize the Belokrinitskaya Hierarchy as an episcopal

Church in communion within the greater Russian Orthodox and Christian world.

Rogozhskoe's New Generation

Alongside the introduction of religious toleration, many of Rogozhskoe's more influential and established families such as the Morozovs, Riabushinskiis, and Kuznetsovs underwent generational changes. Specifically, many Rogozhskoe family dynasties from the late-nineteenth century made way for their sons to succeed them both in their own family businesses, as well as their leadership in Rogozhskoe. This new generation of Old Believer businessmen in a number of ways proved themselves more financially successful than their predecessors. Furthermore, this younger generation also took on new approaches of how best to promote their own, and the Rogozhskoe Old Believers', ideals as the community's new leadership.

Sharing similar transitions seen among other Moscow merchant and entrepreneurial families, the new generation of Rogozhskoe businessmen faced many very different social, economic, and political challenges than their elders. First, the new generation matured and witnessed first-hand the tumultuous political and economic atmosphere created by the social reforms and drive toward industrialization at the end of the nineteenth century. Second, the older generation of Old Believer entrepreneurial families ensured that their children received thorough educations in both Old Rite faith and history, but also in business and economics as well. As Alfred Rieber points out, the older generation of Old Believer merchants and entrepreneurs spared no expense to educate their heirs, to ensure that their sons and daughters could continue their families' legacies.[121]

Extensive studies in business and economics, then, became a shared characteristic among this younger generation of entrepreneurs. Specifically, this new generation received their training and education in some of the most prestigious business academies and universities throughout England, France, and Germany after completing their initial educations in Russia.[122] While never hiding their disdain for Western culture, and what they viewed as the social and human abuses created by Western industrialization, the late-nineteenth century patriarchs of the Old Rite entrepreneurial dynasties sent their sons off to Europe to make future business connections and educate themselves in Western economic development. However, even with direct exposure to Western European society, the younger generation returned to Russia not only still devoted to the Old Rite, but just as devoted to their forefathers' long-held values toward using capital and wealth as an outlet of Christian charity over individual pleasure and profit.[123] Furthermore, not only did these sons return with new ideas on how to maintain and advance their family businesses, but following the events of October 1905, also found themselves with new ideas on how to use their social and economic influence to play a role in Russian politics and social development.[124]

Because of this younger generation's affinity for trimmed beards and western suits, involvement in politics, and western-influenced business practices, modern historians have argued that the younger generation of entrepreneurs withdrew from their devotion to their communities as well as Old Rite ideals and morals.[125] William Blackwell best summarizes the arguments that this younger generation represented "[t]he communal solidarity of Preobrazhenskoe and Rogozhskoe giving way to the spirit of capitalist individualism and materialism."[126] By lumping Rogozhskoe's new generation of entrepreneurs into the larger economic and societal trends in early-twentieth century Russia, modern historians present a disturbingly bleak conclusion that this younger generation abandoned their families' long-held values of Christian charity and morality in favor of the very traits the Old Rite merchants and entrepreneurs despised for generations.

Contrary to such arguments, particularly regarding Rogozhskoe's and Russia's most prominent entrepreneurial dynasties such as the Riabushinskiis and Morozovs, evidence reveals that this younger generation, in fact, remained fully devoted to Rogozhskoe, the Old Rite, and their families' ideals of Christian morality. The younger generation of Rogozhskoe's entrepreneurial elite remained fully devoted to their predecessors' ideals, not only establishing themselves as Rogozhskoe's next leaders, but also accepting their wealth as a gift from God to share with the rest of society, rather than spend on individual frivolity. As stated best by Vladimir Riabushinskii, "The Lord hath sent three gifts. Yea, the first gift is the cross and prayer. The second gift is love and charity. The third gift is the night orison."[127] Ultimately, then, contrary to what some historians see as the degradation of communal solidarity,

Rogozhskoe's merchant elites continued their devotion and embodied their community's Christian morals and ideals on a much grander scale than their predecessors.

Following 1905, politics also provided a new outlet for influential Old Rite families. As explored in the works of Roy Robson and James West, families such as Rogozhskoe's Riabushinskiis openly attempted to unify the Old Rite and its various factions into a political entity as a means of bringing Old Believers into the larger political discussions in Russia.[128] The effort to involve the Old Rite into national politics may suggest broader efforts by some of Rogozhskoe's more affluent families to drift outside of their immediate community; but I argue that the forays into the political sphere rather reveal an active effort to shape the Old Rite through the filter of Rogozhskoe's own sense of morality and mission in preserving the Old Rite. Therefore, while discussed briefly, this work focuses more on how Rogozhskoe and the community's idealism rather served as a model for Rogozhskoe's more influential families in their efforts to unify the Old Rite and emulate their understanding of Rogozhskoe's "Holy Moscow."

As evidence for this argument that the younger generation upheld their communal ties and the previous generations' sense of morality and values, the Rogozhskoe Old Believers regularly elected many representatives from the most prominent business families such as the Kuznetsovs, Riabushinskiis, Morozovs, and Pugovkins to serve as officials on the MSORK Council.[129] Election to the MSORK council reflected the respect and esteem for that individual throughout Rogozhskoe. The Rogozhskoe Old Believers elected individuals to the council based on those representatives serving as model community members who upheld the values and ideals of the entire group. Therefore, while an individual's business acumen often did play a role in their election as MSORK dealt with community finances, the Rogozhskoe Old Believers placed greater value on that person's ability to maintain and protect the Rogozhskoe Cemetery itself, and by extension the community's very social and religious ideals. Therefore, the fact is that the Rogozhskoe Old Believers regularly elected members from this younger generation of businessmen to serve on the MSORK council for more than one term. Their success in governing Rogozhskoe affirms that these entrepreneurs represented a continuation, not a deviation, of Rogozhskoe's communal bonds and a shared duty to their Old Rite morals and piety.

In the early twentieth century, a number of the most influential of these younger entrepreneurs not only established themselves as some of the wealthiest individuals in Russia, but also served as model members of Rogozhskoe's traditions, values, and ideals. Among Rogozhskoe's successful entrepreneurial dynasties in the early twentieth century, the new generations in the Morozov and Riabushinskii families in particular embodied the ideals of Rogozhskoe's community while becoming some of the most economically influential families throughout Russia at the end of the Tsarist Era.

During this period, both the Morozov and Riabushinskii dynasties changed hands, and came under the control of some of the most celebrated, and historically remembered members of each family: the brothers Savva and Sergei Timofeyevich Morozov and their cousin Arsenii Ivanovich, and the famous Riabushinskii brothers, Pavel, Sergei, Vladimir, Stepan, Nikolai, Mikhail, Dmitri, and Feodor Pavlovich. While the newest generation of some of Rogozhskoe's and Moscow's oldest manufacturing and industrialist families, the young Morozovs and Riabushinskiis found themselves in an unprecedented situation with many new economic, social, and political opportunities in the aftermath of 1905. Furthermore, the young Morozovs and Riabushinskiis now took control of two of Russia's wealthiest families when they inherited two well-established industrialist dynasties, predominately in textiles and paper mills, that placed vast amounts of capital at their disposal.[130] Seizing on the new economic, social, and political opportunities presented to them, the Morozovs and Riabushinskiis both expanded their family businesses and influences into areas such as banking, railroads, and cultural patronage of the arts. However, even while growing and diversifying their entrepreneurial dynasties, the younger generation of Morozovs and Riabushinskiis adhered to their families' traditional principles, ultimately serving as models of their predecessors' and Rogozhskoe's values of using capital for charity and the betterment of both their community and society. Just as their dynasties' progenitors emphasized nearly a century before, the younger Morozovs and Riabushinskiis not only represented their financial success, but also served as a reminder to use their success to help those less fortunate than themselves.

The Morozov family often equated their sense of Old Rite Christian morality and charity through establishing strong bonds with the workers in their factories. As the founder of the Morozov Dynasty, Savva Vasilievich divided his holdings among his sons in the mid-nineteenth century, the youngest, Timofei, receiving control over the family's largest firm, the Nikol'sk factory of the Savva Morozov Company. Throughout the eighteenth century, the Morozovs continued to epitomize "moral capitalism" that reflected the family's duality between industrialist modernity and Old Rite senses of morality.[131] However, while one of the most influential and charitable of both Rogozhskoe's and Moscow's entrepreneurs, Timofei's managerial practices resulted in an overbearing, patriarchal approach toward his workers. Still highly successful, the rapid growth of the Nikol'sk workforce throughout the 1880s, combined with the "natural resistance" among the Old Rite and peasant workers, led to the outbreak of a major strike in 1885.[132] While Timofei reestablished order at the Savva Morozov Company, the next generation endeavored to restore favorable relations between management and their workers.

Emulating their grandfather, Savva, and hoping to reverse the worker-management trends in their factory, the young Morozovs sought to restore their family's ties to using their wealth not only to benefit themselves, but also to better the lives of their workers. For example, beginning in the 1890s, under the direction of Sergei and Savva Timofeyevich (and with their cousin Arsenii as their accountant), the Morozovs introduced a number of charity and welfare funds for their workers, including paid maternity leave for expectant and new mothers.[133] The Morozovs also made great efforts to educate their workers and managers and often paid for training some workers to enroll in technical universities in Russia or abroad.[134] As a result, the Morozov factory workers were often noted as far more literate than any other workers throughout Russia.[135] Savva, in particular, took great interest in the wellbeing of the Morozov factory workers by insisting that all locations have on-site hospitals to provide aid to any sick or injured workers since "[t]here are hardly any hospitals in Russia that uphold either the character or definition of such an institution."[136] While significantly more liberal and politically radical than his brother, or than his mother Maria, with whom he clashed regularly over his political views, Savva saw his efforts to provide greater charity and philanthropy to his workers meet some significant success.[137] Savva ultimately believed that under his guidance the Morozov workers would experience a new era of welfare and prosperity, going so far as to proclaim to his brother, "If I live another fifty years, our Nikol'skii factory and its streets will be covered in gold!"[138]

In addition to improving the lives of their workers, Savva and Sergei soon expanded their patronage to include Russian art and culture. Sergei and Savva in particular became major cultural influences in Moscow. For example, Savva used his wealth to support his love of the theater, particularly by donating vast sums to revitalize the failing Moscow Art Theater, now the Chekhov Moscow Art Theater and the Gorky Moscow Art Theater. Furthermore, in 1902, Savva personally financed the construction of a new theater designed by his close friend, and personal architect, Fyodor Shekhtel, even helping paint and decorate the interior.[139] Sergei, too, quickly became one of Russia's biggest patrons in Russian folk art, eventually purchasing the Moscow Museum of Handicrafts in 1903.[140] Under Sergei Morozov's management, the Museum of Handicrafts grew to display the largest collection of Russian folk relics, including numerous works by rural Old Believer communities, from all of Russian history.[141] Similarly, Savva and Sergei's cousin, Arsenii Ivanovich, also used his wealth to find and collect many Russian antiquities. For example, Arsenii, not only enjoyed recognition for his family's multi-generational monetary donations to Rogozhskoe Cemetery, but also for his regular donations of icons, altarpieces, and manuscripts to Rogozhskoe's already extensive collection.[142]

Charity, however, remained at the very heart of the Morozovs' worldview. The Morozovs regularly donated significant sums of wealth to Rogozhskoe Cemetery both for the community's general funds, as well as to meet various needs such as the construction of Rogozhskoe's new bell tower. In addition, the Morozovs also donated extensively to charitable projects throughout Moscow. Sergei and his mother, Maria, became two of Moscow's greatest patrons of many charities throughout the city. In 1909, for example, Maria and Sergei provided the monies to build two new wards at Moscow's St. Catherine's Hospital, one donated as a memorial to Savva after his death in 1905.[143] Ultimately then, while Russia's drive toward industrialization at the end of the Tsarist Period saw the Morozovs obtain greater wealth, the new generation remained devoted to upholding long traditions of using wealth for compassion and Christian charity. Therefore, the Morozovs, in the early twentieth century still championed Rogozhskoe's values as the basis for a strong, moral society as a model of Russian piety.

During this same period, the Riabushinskii merchant family also underwent its own generational transition. Pavel Mikhailovich's eight sons – Pavel, Sergei, Vladimir, Stepan, Nikolai, Mikhail, Dmitri, and Feodor – quickly established themselves as economic and business geniuses as they oversaw the family's fortune and influence soar economically, socially, and politically in Late Imperial Russia. Pavel Mikhailovich, himself a successful, outspoken, and influential merchant in Moscow, spared no expense to provide his sons with extensive educations in business, sending his five eldest sons (Pavel, Sergei, Vladimir, Stepan, and Nikolai) to the Academy of Commercial Sciences. In the hope of preventing discord among his sons, Pavel Mikhailovich founded the P. M. Riabushinskii and Sons Manufactory Association to manage the family's cotton dynasty, granting each of his sons equal stake in the family business before his own death in 1899.[144]

Unlike the Morozovs, who predominately built their wealth from their textile mills, the Riabushinskii brothers became so financially successful because of their willingness to invest in new businesses and ventures to diversify their family's holdings. While the Riabushinskiis' textile factories remained the heart of the family fortune, the brothers utilized their entrepreneurial skills as well as a willingness to take financial risks in order to meet many new opportunities provided by Russia's newest manufacturing and economic needs such as for banks or even new industries for consumer goods. For example, in 1902 Sergei, Vladimir, Stepan, and Mikhail combined some of their wealth in order to found the Riabushinskii Brothers' Bank, later renamed in 1912 as the Moscow Bank.[145] Similarly, in 1916 Vladimir, Stepan, Pavel, and Sergei established the first automobile manufacturing plant in Russia, the Moscow Automobile Plant, (which now exists as the present day Likhachev Plant), to provide cars for the tsarist government and army.[146] Furthermore, in order to aid Russia's war efforts, the Riabushinskii brothers, with the help of their brother Dmitri, a member of the Moscow Mathematical Society, drafted plans and gained approval to develop an aircraft factory. However, the plans never came to fruition owing to the outbreak of the Revolutions of 1917.[147]

The Riabushinskii brothers also established themselves as great patrons of the arts throughout Moscow and Russia. Art served as a shared hobby among the brothers. Mikhail, for example, acquired one of the largest private collections of Russian and European art in all of Russia.[148] Sergei himself took up sculpting, and even became a close friend of the artist Ilya Repin.[149] However, reflecting their ties to their Old Rite roots, most of the Riabushinskiis, particularly Stepan and Vladimir, acquired some of the most valuable collections of ancient Russian icons. Following the onset of religious toleration in 1905, when many Old Believers registered their faith publically, the brothers often traveled to or contacted Old Believers and Orthodox alike throughout Russia in order to purchase their icons. The Riabushinskiis then paid all fees to have the icons restored; ultimately they donated many of the icons to Rogozhskoe Cemetery, as well as Moscow's Tretiakov Gallery, of which the Riabushinskii collection remains as the largest icon collection in the museum to this day.[150] More importantly, however, the Riabushinskiis' efforts to collect and restore old Russian icons reflects the family's connection to their Old Rite traditions to preserve the icons for their spiritual, cultural, and historical value. For example, Vladimir in particular equated collecting icons as preserving the very essence of Russian spirituality. "Icons blossomed in Russia [. . .] nowhere have there been more zealous icon lovers [. . .] they remind us that God's presence is all around [. . .] that is why we, the Russian people, easily and joyfully pray with holy icons."[151] Therefore, the Riabushinskiis' affinity for icons reveals their ties to their Old Rite heritage, as well as to the values instilled in Rogozhskoe's Old Believer community.

Rogozhskoe's merchants, such as the Riabushinskiis and Morozovs, upheld their families' and community's principles, traditions, and values even while building some of Russia's wealthiest merchant dynasties. However, what did set the new generation of Old Rite merchants apart from their predecessors became their ability to become more public and vocal figures in Russian politics. The turmoil of the early twentieth century provided a new outlet for the younger generation of entrepreneurs to establish themselves as a political influence in both Moscow and the Russian Empire and become some of the most vocal participants in late-tsarist politics. The younger merchants' political endeavors, particularly those of Savva Morozov and the Riabushinskii brothers, often is used as evidence of their "breaking away" from their ties to their family and Old Rite morals and traditions because of their liberal political leanings.[152] On the contrary, the political endeavors of the younger generation of merchants represented yet another adaptation to their desires to create a Russia based on their understanding of their Old Rite morals and piety.

While in ways more radical than their predecessors, many of the ideas held by the younger Riabushinskiis and notably Savva Morozov actually reflect a changing attitude shared among the Rogozhskoe Old Believers: their moral and civic duties should transfer into national politics. The young merchants' politics incorporated many of the same ideals and morals found in Rogozhskoe's long held values for a proper Christian society that emphasized providing aid and comfort to the needy. For example, Savva Morozov's liberal political leanings led him to adopt new ideas on how to use his own wealth and influence to better the lives of his workers. He even distributed pamphlets encouraging workers at the Morozov's Nikolskoi factory to organize. Savva also promised to discuss any labor issues personally. Furthermore, following the outbreak of revolutions in 1905, Savva publically announced that he would discuss profit sharing for the workers with his family.[153] Unfortunately, the Nikolskoi workers joined the nation-wide general strike in February; consequently, Savva's mother, Maria, removed him from his post as Directing Manager of the factory because of his role in inciting the workers.[154] However, while he distanced himself from his family politically, Savva's intentions still reflected many of the shared ideal of his grandfather and other Rogozhskoe merchants that profit and capital remained for bettering the lives of others rather than personal gain.

Whereas Savva Morozov used his influence to restore the philanthropic relationship between management and his workers, the Riabushinskii brothers saw the political reforms following 1905 as an opportunity to enter politics on behalf of the Old Rite. The Riabushinskiis' upbringing and experience as social and religious outsiders as Old Believers directly influenced their outlook on politics following the Revolution of 1905.[155] Those who became Old Rite politicians, such as Pavel and Vladimir Riabushinskii, realized that the Old Rite required strong self-representation in order to have their movement's interests considered since many Orthodox officials and politicians remained hostile toward the Old Rite. Alfred Rieber notes that, the Riabushinskiis realized that in Russia's new political atmosphere, the Old Rite would attract lobbying from both extreme leftist and rightest political groups in an attempt to rally Old Believers to their own causes. Namely, leftist political groups hoped the Old Rite's history as victims of oppression might encourage Old Believers to move against the tsarist regime; while parties on the political right hoped that the Old Rite's ties to Russian traditionalism might likewise bolster conservatism in the face of political radicalization.[156] Therefore, fearing that political chaos might lead to the Old Rite's losing any independent political voice, Pavel and Vladimir realized that Old Believers needed to unify and organize themselves politically to avoid exploitation at the hands of extremist political parties only looking to gain support for their own political agendas.[157]

The basis for the Riabushinskiis' drive into politics was "the incentive of being an outsider" and a desire to unite all sects of the Old Rite to "join in the struggle for political and religious freedom."[158] The greatest political problem that the Old Rite faced as an interest group after 1905 was that even when Old Rite political leaders did seek to ally with other political organizations, the Old Rite found itself isolated in the political center. For example, for groups to the left, such as the Constitutional Democrats, the Old Rite held "far too narrow class interests" to support their agenda.[159] Conversely, individuals on the right, such as Timofei Butkevich, still viewed the Old Rite as a subversive entity both to the stability of the state and especially to the Russian Orthodox Church. Since 1906 Butkevich even appealed directly to Nicholas and eventually the State Duma for the need to rescind all of the rights granted to Old Believers since the 1905 *ukaz* on religious toleration. For example, in a letter dated from 1909, Butkevich stated that "[t]he essence of the *raskol* is not in its religious foundations, but in its sociopolitical motivations, in its permanent opposition to government power."[160]

Therefore, the Riabushinskiis' efforts to bring the Old Rite into national politics extended from their need to legitimize their co-religionists as a political entity.[161] To ensure an Old Rite political presence, Pavel and Vladimir realized that they needed to galvanize the Old Rite into a coherent constituency in order to represent their faith in the new Russia. The Riabushinskii brothers then organized mass meetings of fellow Old Believer merchants throughout central Russia, often meeting in Moscow or Nizhni Novgorod. In 1906, in one grand attempt to unify the Old Rite into a political body, the Riabushinskiis even called for an All-Russian Congress of Old Believer Peasants in Moscow.[162]

Unfortunately little came of such gatherings as a result of the diversity of the Old Believers themselves. Spiritual divisions between priestly and priestless Old Believers, as well as the social and cultural divide between urban and rural faithful, prevented participants from coming to any consensus on how to unify the Old Rite as a whole politically, or even culturally.[163] Undeterred, Vladimir saw the new freedoms in post-1905 Russia as an opportunity to take upon himself the personal duty to help organize Old Believers and bring the Old Rite out of social and political obscurity. In such a critical time for Russia, Vladimir viewed Old Rite organization and unity as vital to the very survival of Russia. Reflecting the ideal he shared with the Rogozhskoe Old Believers, Vladimir believed that the Old Rite remained as the only "pure" form of Russianness remaining in Russia, particularly following the political and social upheavals of the Late Tsarist period.

In one such important example, Vladimir openly professed that the Old Rite embodied Russia's natural, cultural destiny of the Third Rome Doctrine. Vladimir clearly viewed the Old Rite as the sole inheritor of the only uniquely Russian idea.

> The idea [of Moscow the Third Rome] filled the Russian soul with pride and awe, for it warned that only through the wickedness of the Third Rome – Moscow – and the collapse of piety give the world over to the power of the Antichrist. Thus our ancestors grew a sense of responsibility not only for ourselves but for others, and therefore feared falling into heresy [...] Therefore, for the enlightenment of the Russian spirit one must understand the meaning of the Old Believers and need to consider what role they played in the history of Russian culture [...] for it is the Old Believers, and their religious phenomenon, that are most acquainted with the history of this spiritual feeling in Russia, especially in the period from the late seventeenth century to the present day, and therefore becoming all the more important to gain a proper understanding of Russian Orthodoxy, and indeed the Russian reality.[164]

As Russia faced numerous political and social challenges in the early twentieth century, Riabushinskii clearly understood that at the very heart of the Old Rite remained a true understanding of Russian identity and cultural destiny. Like the Rogozhskoe Old Believers, Riabushinskii saw that thanks to its ties to traditional Russian values and morals, the Old Rite served as a unifying force for Russia in this era of uncertainty.

While Vladimir openly portrayed the Old Rite and its traditions as the defenders of a pure form of Russian identity and culture, he similarly compared himself and his fellow Old Rite merchants as the primary example of Russian *muzhiks*, the very embodiment of the every-day Russian. In Vladimir's eyes, the concept of the *muzhik* represented only the most ardent of Russian patriots, which the Old Believers naturally emulated out of their shared devotion to their faith and traditional Russian culture.

> The well-read, rich merchant-Old Believer, with a beard and long Russian dress, is a talented industrialist, the manager of hundreds, sometimes thousands, of working people, and at the same time, he is an expert on ancient Russian art, an archeologist, a collector of icons, books, manuscripts, he is greatly versed in historical and economic issues, he loves his job, but he also strives to meet his spiritual needs – this person is a *muzhik*.[165]

As the foil to the Old Believer *muzhik*, and thereby a danger to Russia itself, Vladimir placed the *barin*: "The petty clerk, clean-shaven, in his western dress, seized some elite education but is essentially uncultured, he often takes bribes, and secretly criticizes and condemns those above him, he despises the *muzhik*, his ancestors created the intelligentsia, he is a *barin*".[166]

One can argue then, that to Vladimir Riabushinskii, the Old Believer *muzhik* as a whole needed to politicize himself in post-1905 Russia. Not only could the Old Rite best represent its own interests, but the situation in Late Tsarist Russia necessitated that Old Believers embrace Russian politics in order to defend Russia from the Westernized *barin*, who neither knew anything nor cared about Russia's history, traditions, and culture. Ultimately the political and social changes in post-1905 Russia created the opportunity for outspoken leaders such as the Riabushinskii brothers to participate in the public sphere as well as in mass politics; thereby they could bring the Old Rite into the larger discussion of national politics. However, as witnessed in the failed efforts to unify the Old Rite into a political entity, the Riabushinskiis and other

Rogozhskoe Old Believers realized that the Old Rite itself faced an identity crisis of its own in the new Russia. To that end, under the leadership of the likes of the Riabushinskiis, the Rogozhskoe Old Believers used the opportunities of post-1905 Russia to attempt to establish their community as a leading center of the Old Rite, and thereby invigorate the movement under the direction of their values.

Rogozhskoe and the Efforts to Define the Old Rite after 1905

Like some of their prominent families such as the Riabushinskiis and Morozovs, following the onset of religious toleration, Rogozhskoe's members envisioned a grand role for their community in shaping the Old Rite in Post-1905 Russia. Their history, as well as their established relationship with both tsarist and Moscow officials, predicated that the Rogozhskoe Old Believers, took upon themselves the duty to intercede and guide the Old Rite socially and politically in this new era. While individuals from Rogozhskoe, such as Pavel and Vladimir Riabushinskii, used their morals and ideals in an effort to guide the Old Rite into mass politics, Rogozhskoe took on an effort to present its community as a champion and guiding force in defining the Old Rite movement in the Russian Empire.

As they did in the period of the Great Reforms, the Rogozhskoe Old Believers envisioned themselves as intercessors for both their immediate community as well as the Old Rite as a whole. For example, Rogozhskoe Old Believers took roles in the Moscow city government when Ivan Pugovkin, Grigori Rakhmanov, and Petr Rastorguev all won election to the Moscow City Duma.[167] The Rogozhskoe Old Believers serving on the City Duma, working closely with the MSORK council, most often took up the issue of establishing proper schools for Old Believer children and orphans. Under this same premise, the Rogozhskoe Old Believer petitioned and received permission to build the Rogozhskoe Theological Institute.[168]

While politics served as a newer outlet for Rogozhskoe's efforts to bring the Old Rite into post-1905 Russia, the community's influence as an Old Rite cultural center remained Rogozhskoe's greatest asset. Building on Rogozhskoe's own historical role as a leader of Old Rite self-identity, and similarly build on the historical approach by tsarist authorities to view the community as a definitive representation of the

Old Rite, the Rogozhskoe Old Believers now sought to become a leading presence in the quest to define the Old Rite after toleration. Rogozhskoe first started small by opening its community to the public by hosting lectures, choir concerts, and open public debates about the state of the Old Rite, the Old Believers' place in Russia and Russian history, as well as forums on contemporary politics, economics, and other events.[169] The expressed intent of these gatherings served as the Rogozhskoe Old Believers' attempt to "put the community on display to the public," in order to share their history, knowledge, and faith with other Old Believers, as well as openly engage with religious scholars, historians, and journalists from Moscow and the empire.[170]

In one of their earliest victories, in August 1906, the Rogozhskoe Old Believers obtained permission to conduct religious processions and services outside of Rogozhskoe Cemetery, thereby allowing public displays of their faith.[171] However, the decisions on when to hold such public processions remained under the authority of the MSORK Council, rather than at the discretion of Rogozhskoe's priests, or even their Archbishop. Eventually, the religious processions became a vital representation of the Rogozhskoe Old Believers' Old Rite identity, providing a public view into the community's life when as many as thousands of parishioners participated in grand processions around Rogozhskoe Cemetery's walls, while they carried their religious banners and icons.[172] Furthermore, Rogozhskoe's influence spread beyond its own community, for Rogozhskoe often sent their own delegations and processions to participate in religious celebrations and holidays in other Old Believer communities. These acts revealed the reverence other Old Rite communities held for Rogozhskoe. For example, the Rogozhskoe Old Believers often participated in religious processions with the Old Rite community in the near-by village of Borisovo (now part of Southeastern Moscow), bringing their priests and other religious relics, such as icons, as part of these shared celebrations.[173]

Following the freedoms of 1905, the Rogozhskoe Old Believers also played a significant role in aiding in the formation of new communities and Old Rite churches. As Old Believers could now openly practice their faith, Moscow and the surrounding area witnessed the development of a number of Old Rite communities. Many of these new communities in turn invited Rogozhskoe's priests and parishioners to participate in services consecrating new communities and temples.[174] Particularly in

Moscow, Rogozhskoe's spiritual and community leaders regularly took part in celebrations, even offering models for these new communities to emulate as they looked toward Rogozhskoe for spiritual and political guidance.[175]

Rogozhskoe Old Believers regularly celebrated with the smaller community that developed around the Cathedral of the Assumption of the Virgin Mary on Apukhtinke, a short distance west of Rogozhskoe Cemetery. The Rogozhskoe and Apukhtinke Old Believers regularly celebrated holidays and other events together. Rogozhskoe clergy and parishioners participated in the original consecration of the new cathedral on Apukhtinke.[176] The Rogozhskoe Old Believers often led processions with the Apukhtinke Old Believers and even carried many of Rogozhskoe's own sacred icons and holy texts, while Rogozhskoe's choir often led the processional singing.[177] In like manner, Rogozhskoe Old Believers regularly participated in major holiday services with the Apukhtinke Old Believers; Rogozhskoe's clergy often led both congregations at each community's Easter celebrations.[178] Rogozhskoe's growing profile after 1905 then allowed them to establish a greater public presence among other Old Rite communities throughout the region, thereby aiding the community's efforts to become a spiritual center for the priestly Old Rite.

After 1905, the Rogozhskoe Old Believers also used their ability to perform public processions as an effort to tie their community and the Old Rite to Russian society as a whole. Rogozhskoe Old Believers regularly held public processions celebrating important dates and events in Russian History. Some of Rogozhskoe's largest processions coincided with empire-wide celebrations in 1912 commemorating the 100-year anniversary of Napoleon's expulsion from Russia.[179] Two years later, on August 17, 1914 the Rogozhskoe Old Believers and others from neighboring villages held one of the community's largest religious processions as thousands joined together to pray for Russia's armed forces and for victory for Russia following the outbreak of World War I.[180] On a more personal note to the Rogozhskoe Old Believers, the community also held a major celebration and religious procession, offering thanks and prayers to Nicholas for the Russian Army's capture of Bukovina in early 1915, the home region of the Belaia Krinitsa monastery "from the hands of infidels, villains, and Russia's and God's enemies."[181] Ultimately, Rogozhskoe processions clearly served both as a display of the community's spirituality and as their attempts to continue to tie their Holy Moscow to Imperial Russia socially, religiously, and historically.

The onset of religious toleration, furthermore, allowed the Rogozhskoe Old Believers to utilize new methods in their efforts to shape and define the Old Rite after 1905. Publishing in particular became one of Rogozhskoe's most important tools in this new era. Shortly after the introduction of toleration, fully comprehending the opportunity for both Rogozhskoe and the Belokrinitskaya Hierarchy to shape the Old Rite, Archbishop Ioann openly beseeched the Rogozhskoe leadership to establish a printing house within the community in 1906. Seeing the significance of such a potential for publication, Ioann wrote to Rogozhskoe's MSORK Council.

> Our Sacred Council believes it to be both useful and necessary to open an Old Believer printing house in Moscow to print ecclesiastical and liturgical educational books and reproductions of rare ancient Christian manuscripts of our fathers, kept in the library of the Rogozhskoe Almshouse. We beseech you gentlemen and proud Trustees: If you do not find it possible to open the mentioned printing house for use of the Holy Church and community at Rogozhskoe Cemetery, then consider it for God and to call upon and spread His Holy Word.[182]

After receiving approval from the MSORK Council in 1908, Rogozhskoe's printing house opened in 1910 with its first publications a Psalter and a beginner's alphabet book in both Russian and Church Slavonic.[183]

Publishing by far became one of Rogozhskoe's and the Old Rite's most important tools after 1905 in both shaping and defining the Old Rite for Old Believers themselves, but also the very understanding of the movement's place within Russian history and Russian identity. With restrictions on Old Believer publications lifted with the *ukaz* of 1905, the Old Rite could now freely discuss and present their understanding of their Orthodox faith in the Russian public sphere. Most importantly, however, the period from 1905 to 1917 became a significant period for Old Rite publishing as the Old Believers now obtained the very first opportunity since the schism *to define themselves*, their faith, and their own history and place in Orthodoxy among themselves and with the Russian public.[184]

Prior to 1905, the Russian State and the Russian Orthodox Church monopolized the only legal and official narratives concerning the *raskol* and Old Rite. Such control over the public perception of Old Rite history allowed state and church authorities to paint the Old Believers as ignorant, stubborn, and even dangerous schismatics.[185] More damaging to the persona of the Old Rite, the earliest efforts to establish a historiography on the Old Rite began during the reign of Nicholas I, an era of the greatest repression of the Old Rite since its founding. Such an effort on the part of tsarist and church authorities in the mid-nineteenth century, then, allowed some of the Old Rite's greatest critics and opponents, such as Metropolitan Filaret and the historian Nikolai Subbotin, to create a historical narrative that painted Old Believers as heretical traitors to the Russian State and Russian Orthodoxy. In his historical analyses of the Rogozhskoe Old Believers, Subbotin openly applauded Nicholas's attempts to destroy what he proclaimed as the "deplorable" and "shameful" existence of Rogozhskoe Cemetery following the community's adoption of the Belokrinitskaya Hierarchy.[186] As a mouthpiece for the "official" narrative on the Old Rite, Subbotin took upon himself to provide a historical explanation of Rogozhskoe's "stubborn" and "insulting" existence in order to justify the State's and Church's open hostility and efforts to force Rogozhskoe into submission to Russian Orthodoxy.

However, the Old Rite and Old Believer communities like Rogozhskoe refused to remain passive in these versions and narratives of their image and identity. Not only did Old Believers defy oppression and create a number of successful communities like Rogozhskoe, they directly challenged the "official" narrative through publications of their own well before 1905. In order to circumvent many restrictions preventing Old Believers from publishing any materials, Old Rite publications relied on either illegal printing by private individuals, or on arduously copying works by hand.[187] Ironically, while the "official" narrative on the Old Rite throughout the nineteenth century portrayed Old Believers as "ignorant" for their rejection of the Nikonian reforms, the Old Rite remained revered for their book culture and high rates of literacy. Even though church and tsarist authorities often vilified the Old Rite, opponents like Subbotin himself often noted and praised Old

Believers for their literacy and love for religious texts.[188] The Rogozhskoe Old Believers in particular became famous throughout Late Tsarist Russia for their library and collection of ancient Russian manuscripts and religious service books.[189]

Book culture and literacy became one of the defining characteristics of the Old Rite as communities often actively collected pre-Nikonian texts and manuscripts in order to "protect" them from corruption or destruction. Additionally, Old Rite communities relied heavily on illegal publishing as a means of preserving their reverence for book culture, but also as a means of ensuring their faith's survival with each successive generation. Not only did Old Rite publishing aid their own faith, but the Old Rite's reverence for their books and literacy sparked fear among the Orthodox clergy and state officials that Old Believers would prey upon the often less educated and illiterate Orthodox populations. Communities such as Rogozhskoe Cemetery therefore became prime targets as a direct threat to their "teach[ing] the schismatic ways."[190] Such concern on the part of the authorities about the Old Rite, the many prohibitions placed on Old rite publishing, and internal dialogue and debate on the Old Rite itself often proved difficult among communities.

In the years following 1905, publishing provided a vital opportunity for Old Rite communities such as Rogozhskoe to define and debate their faith and movement openly in order to present their sense of an ideal Christian community. Publishing not only provided the opportunity for the Old Rite to offer their own narrative of their history and faith, but also to aid their efforts to play a role in Russia's religious, social, cultural, and political progress after 1905. First, however, various Old Believer individuals, communities, and printing houses needed to ask themselves how religious freedom would, and should, shape Old Believers' ability to express their own faith and ideals. Publishing therefore served a critical tool for Old Rite communities, and particularly for the Rogozhskoe Old Believers in their efforts to guide the Old Rite into a new era.

As seen above, some of Rogozhskoe's prominent members saw the need to take a lead role in developing the Old Rite in response to the many changes after the events of 1905, predominately Pavel and Vladimir Riabushinskii. The Riabushinskiis realized the critical need for the Old Rite to participate openly in post-1905 politics in order to best represent the movement's own interests. Following the various failures to unify the Old Rite, particularly the defeated endeavor of the

All-Russian Congress of Old Believer Peasants, the Riabushinskiis realized that the Old Rite remained highly divisive about not only spiritual concerns, such as between the priestly and priestless branches, but also social and political issues dividing the rural and urban Old Believers. More worrisome to the Riabushinskiis and other prominent Rogozhskoe Old Believers became the realization that the Old Believers throughout Russia lacked a common consensus of the movement's own beliefs and understanding of the movement's history. To that end, the Riabushinskiis and other Old Believers now realized the full potential that toleration provided particularly in allowing Old Believer publications. Increased publishing could alleviate misconceptions held by Old Believers and Orthodox alike about the Old Rite by defining and discussing the very tenets of the Old Rite in the public sphere.

In order to bring debate on the Old Rite into the public forum, as well as provide an outlet to help guide the Old Rite toward a consensus of the very tenets and history of the movement as well as its future, Old Believers turned to publishing regular periodicals. Two journals published by Rogozhskoe Old Believers led the charge in establishing periodicals directed to Old Believer audiences. Pavel Riabushinskii's *Narodnaia gazeta* founded in 1906, and Ivan Shibaev's *Tserkov'* founded in 1908 (changed later to *Slovo Tserkvi* in 1914) with a shared investment from the Riabushinskiis and edited by a number of Rogozhskoe Old Believers, provided a fresh medium for the priestly Old Believers to publish articles and news regarding the Old Rite in past and contemporary Russia. These periodicals provided opportunities for Old Believers throughout Moscow and Russia to engage in a larger debate over the Old Rite's place within Russian society and the very tenets of their faith. For example, while *Narodnaia gazeta* focused more on Old Rite political matters than its culturally-focused counterpart *Tserkov'*, both regularly printed question and answer columns responding to general inquiries about Old Rite practices and beliefs as well as growing concerns for Old Believers in the early twentieth century. However, both *Narodnaia gazeta* and *Tserkov'* regularly professed their goal as the hope to be able to mold the Old Rite into a unified cultural-political movement. *Narodnaia gazeta* specifically urged that the Old Rite refuse to rest on the "victories" of 1905. These Rogozhskoe publications reflected the Old Rite ideology that the Old Believers remained the only pure defenders of Russia's Third Rome destiny. For example, *Narodnaia gazeta* insisted that the Old Rite must unify its identity and goals for they remained as the only "moderate force" that could save Russia from the anarchy of the "Reds" and reestablish the Old Regime by the "Blacks."[191] Similarly, *Tserkov'* further championed the Old Rite historical narrative that the Russian Orthodox Church and the State that betrayed their people by causing the *raskol*, left the Old Rite as the sole representation of the true "Russian religious soul," and only could a united Old Rite defend it in the current political chaos.[192]

However, the fact that the Old Rite remained far from unified along spiritual, social, and cultural lines, and lacked a shared historical narrative, made such lofty goals for the Old Rite seem impossible. As seen in reader letters to *Tserkov'*, Old Believers possessed little consensus on any understanding of various Old Rite beliefs, disagreements with the mainstream church, or the relationship between branches.[193] As a result, *Tserkov'* openly urged that the Old Rite needed to "end artificial divisions" and create "one spirit, one soul, bound by family ties, one history, one centuries-long suffering."[194] With such a sentiment then, for communities like Rogozhskoe with its members such as Shibaev and the Riabushinskiis, the Old Rite desperately needed to define this "one soul" for themselves and for Russia.

Publishing therefore became even more critical for the Old Rite because it served as a medium that provided the opportunity for Old Believers to create their own public identity and define their movement free from outside narratives. More specifically, legally able to publish for the first time, many Old Believers and their communities saw the opportunity to present their "version" of the schism and explain their own ideology to the Russian public. One of the primary, and most important narratives that Old Believers could now present of their own self-identity returned to the narratives of the mid-seventeenth century that the Old Rite championed Russia's true destiny, the Third Rome Doctrine.

Unfortunately, as noted by the editors of *Narodnaia Gazeta* and *Tserkov'*, Old Believers remained divided or confused about their own history and justification for their discrepancies with the Russian Orthodox Church. Publishing therefore provided new opportunities for Old Believers to remedy these gaps within the Old Rite movement. One publication in particular attempted to explain the very historical and spiritual foundations of Old Rite identity as the sole defenders of the

Third Rome Doctrine and true Russian Orthodoxy. Fedor Permiakov's "*Vypiski*" of 1910, or its full title, *Vypiski iz Sviashennogo i sviattootecheckago Pisaniia i tvorenii sviatikh ottsov i uchitelei tserkvi. O vnesenii patriarkhom Nikonom i ego preemnikami novizne i lozhnago ucheniia* (*Extracts from the Holy Scriptures and Holy Teachings of the Church Fathers and Teachers. About the Introduction of False Teachings by Patriarch Nikon and His Successors*), attempted to serve as the definitive collection, explanation, and justification of each of the Old Rite's disagreements with the Russian Orthodox Church and defend the Old Rite's claim as the last true Orthodox Christian faith. Permiakov's *Vypiski* provided the first, and most complete published collection of Old Rite rituals, theology, and ideology and represents one of the most important documents published by Old Believers to define the Old Rite movement.

Published by Pavel Riabushinskii's printing house in 1910, Permiakov's *Vypiski* embodies the efforts by the Old Rite to define itself historically, culturally, and ideologically in the era after religious toleration. Combining scripture, spiritual texts by ancient Church Fathers, and Old Rite and Russian Orthodox Church writings the *Vypiski* provided an overview of the Old Rite from the Old Believers' perspective. However, only the first volume was published out of the intended two-volume set. While incomplete, Permiakov's *Vypiski* still represented the most complete collection of Old Rite rituals, practices, beliefs, and religious and historical disagreements with the Russian Orthodox Church ever collected to that point. Therefore, the *Vypiski* represents the growing trend among Old Rite publications to provide a unified understanding of the Old Rite as a religious and cultural movement in Russian and Christian history.

Permiakov's *Vypiski* perfectly reflects the Old Believer mindset that the Old Rite remained as the only pure embodiment of Russian Orthodoxy, and lays blame for the schism on the Russian Orthodox Church's betrayal of Russia's spiritual and cultural destiny. The *Vypiski* opens immediately with a scathing rebuttal of the "official" narrative that the Orthodox and tsarist officials painted of the Old Rite, stating:

> The missionaries, theologians and pastors of the dominant church, have over the past two and a half centuries, accuse us Christians for separating from their church. They claim that Patriarch Nikon and the council of 1666–1667 we had no reason for succession,

> that the mainstream Orthodox Church and Patriarch Nikon did not bring in any errors to our articles of faith, rites, and customs to the established church. This accusation is false [. . .] In 1654, Patriarch Nikon announced his so-called book-correction [. . .] and "corrected" the ancient Greek and Slavic manuscripts. It was established even then that the "correct" books were printed in Venice and brought to Southern Russia through the aid of Roman Jesuits. Nikon still made no correction to his error and his books distorted and brought in many heresies [. . .] Finally, the Council of 1666 – 1667, cursed and betrayed the ancient traditions of the Holy Church and legalized these Venetian heresies [. . .] as a result the mainstream Church embarked on a false path and departed from the holy church and ancient piety, violated the teachings of the gospel, the apostles and the Holy Fathers [. . .][195]

One of the major goals Permiakov intended with his work explains the very history of the Old Rite and the split with the church from the Old Believers' perspective. Predominately, his efforts focus on how the Russian Orthodox Church fell into heresy, thereby leaving the Old Believers as the sole inheritors of Russia's ancient piety. Elaborating on many of the points Permiakov made in his introduction, the *Vypiski's* fifth and sixth chapters, "About the Ancient Russian Church" and "The Criteria of the Withdrawal of Piety," respectively, explain how the Russian Orthodox Church abandoned its spiritual and cultural destiny. Chapter 5 in particular relies on numerous historical texts pertaining to the foundations of Russia's spiritual identity such as the letters of Patriarch Theophanes of Jerusalem and Patriarch Jeremiah of Constantinople recognizing the elevation of Patriarch Job as the First Patriarch of Moscow. Additionally, Permiakov includes and explains the legend of the White Cowl of Novgorod and the famous letter by the monk Filofei to Vasili III establishing the idea of the "Third Rome Doctrine" as a basis for the Ancient Russian Church: the Church of the Old Rite.[196]

After Permiakov presents his case for the foundations of Russia's spiritual and cultural destiny, he uses his sixth chapter to explain how the Russian Orthodox Church under Nikon and his successors betrayed the Third Rome Doctrine and Russian Orthodoxy. Providing evidence from the Gospels and other religious and prophetical texts, predominately from the Book of Daniel and Gospels of Mark and

Luke, Permiakov highlights entries proclaiming the eventual reign of Antichrist by a power-hungry "beast."[197] Permiakov even notes in his introduction to the chapter, "Temptations will come. False prophets will create heresy, changing the Divine Law, and rise in the ranks of the Church. The Antichrist will sit on the throne of the Church, will attack people, and will drive away the faithful. These were the prophecies for 1666. Nikon's treason of Orthodoxy."[198]

Furthermore, Permiakov emphasizes the heretical origins for Nikon's efforts to edit Russian liturgical texts. Particularly, Permiakov notes that Nikon's primary advisors for his "corrections" to Russian texts, the monk Arsenii the Greek and former Uniate Bishop and Metropolitan of Giza Paissi Ligarid, were both excommunicated from the Orthodox Church due to their ties to the pro-Papal, Uniate Church in the Ukraine.[199] Referring to Arsenii as "A Jesuit and traitor to Orthodoxy" and providing evidence from letters from Constantinople to Nikon and Tsar Alexis revealing Arsenii and Paissi's excommunication, Permiakov argues that these two heretics' influence, combined with Nikon's hunger for power, introduced "the Catholic heresies into Russia."[200] Permiakov argues further that, "[The Ancient Russian Church] had made no corrections or distortions. The new books were translated from modern Jesuit publications. The new Greek books contained the heresies of Catholicism. The Ancient Slavic books agreed with our ancient and holy manuscripts."[201] The introduction of "Catholic heresies" remains a recurring theme throughout the *Vypiski*'s early chapters; buttressing the long-held Old Believer notion that only the Old Rite truly defended the sole remaining pure form of Orthodoxy and the Third Rome Doctrine.

Permiakov explains and justifies the Old Rite's long-held views of their historical origins and devotion to their faith. Additionally, one of the most important aspects of the *Vypiski* is Permiakov's effort to explain many of the origins of Old Rite rituals and practices that served as the very basis for disagreements with the mainstream church. For example, the *Vypiski* presented the origins of one of the most significant, visible, and well-known disagreements with the mainstream church – the Old Rite's insistence on using two fingers to make the sign of the cross. Relying heavily on ancient Christian texts by a number of Church Fathers, Permiakov justifies the Old Rite's insistence on this particular ritual. In one such example Permiakov uses the works of St. Ephrem the Syrian in which the Saint stated, "the sign of the cross is a weapon for the

Christian, it is the conqueror of death, it sows hope in the faithful, gives light to the meek, deposes heresy, and the symbol of an Orthodox faith and salvation of the Church."[202] Permiakov also includes the works of St. Peter of Damascus and St. John Chrysostom, emphasizing the sanctity of the two-fingered cross as one of the earliest declarations of the Church Councils. Permiakov quotes Peter, "it was passed by the saints and Holy Fathers to refute the heretics and unbelievers; for two fingers and a single hand represents the crucified Lord Jesus Christ in two natures, and in a single hypostasis."[203] Knowing that the two-fingered sign of the cross plays a crucial role in defining the Old Rite, the *Vypiski* attempts to provide a historical and spiritual justification for one of the Old Believers' most important expressions of their faith and representation of their divide from the mainstream church.

The *Vypiski* also explains the history and origins of various Old Rite spiritual rituals, but also explains the historical contexts of Old Rite culture. One such example comes from an entire chapter devoted to the question of men shaving their beards. Following Peter the Great's effort to introduce Westernization, a common identifying trait of Old Believer men came from their refusal to shave or trim their beards thereby making them targets of Peter's infamous "beard tax."[204] Furthermore, Old Believers' insistence on maintaining their beards served as one of the sources of the state's criticism of the Old Rite's "superstitious" nature. Once again, Permiakov uses ancient spiritual texts justifying the Old Believers' insistence on not shaving. The *Vypiski's* first example starts with Mosaic Law in Leviticus 19:27, "You shall not shave around the sides of your head, nor shall you disfigure the edges of your beard." Permiakov also provides views of the Church Fathers and their insistence on the need for men to maintain beards, such as St. Jerome: "If a man shaves with a razor, that deprives him of [God's] beauty."[205] Beards served as one example, out of many chapters of the *Vypiski* that reveal an effort to provide a uniform understanding of Old Rite cultural preferences. By relying on historical texts, Permiakov's work made the first efforts to openly define and explain the very symbols of the Old Rite for both Old Believers and Orthodox Christians alike.

Conclusively Permiakov's *Vypiski* fits into the greater trends in Old Believer publishing aimed to provide a greater understanding of the Old Rite and greater uniformity for Old Believers in Late Imperial Russia. The purpose of works like the *Vypiski* served the dual goal to both define the Old Rite historically, spiritually, and culturally as well as guide Old Believers toward unity into a single movement. For prominent Old Believers such as the Riabushinskiis, open dialogue and publishing Old Believer ideology became the best means to define the Old Rite in the Russian public sphere, as well as the rest of Russia.

While Rogozhskoe Old Believers played a critical role in Old Rite publishing, the community also served as a repository of Old Rite cultural artifacts that contributed to their efforts to shape the Old Rite after 1905. As seen in Archbishop Ioann's original request for a printing house at Rogozhskoe Cemetery, the Rogozhskoe Old Believers took great pride in the community's collection of ancient Russian and Orthodox manuscripts, icons, and other relics. However, the contents of the community's collection, for much of Rogozhskoe's history, remained known only to the Rogozhskoe Old Believers themselves and the few outsiders who came to view the collections.[206]

In order to make Rogozhskoe's collection more accessible, in June 1907, the MSORK Council established the Commission for Protection of Antiquities, headed by Stepan Riabushinskii, to oversee proper cataloguing and maintenance of all collected materials. One of the most significant moments in this effort was the invitation for the photographer Karl Fischer to take photographs to catalog the community's icons from their cathedrals, almshouses, and private collections. Fischer later published the photographs in 1913.[207] Prominent Rogozhskoe families, such as the Riabushinskiis and Rakhmanovs, also provided greater access for historians, theologians, and even numerous students and classes to view their private collections, some which also served as the basis of articles in the journal *Tserkov'*.[208]

As home to one of the largest collection of ancient Russian manuscripts and icons, as well as an extensive collection of Old Believer texts and literature, Rogozhskoe's collection received extensive interest from art connoisseurs, historians, theologians, and others. Due to the increased interest in the community's collections the MSORK Council ultimately voted to incorporate a new library into their bell tower after hearing testimony from one of the community's librarians, Iosef Khromov who stated:

> We have a large collection of valuable books and manuscripts which are still not published in any directory. At such a time as

> now when interest in all things old has awoken in broad sectors of society we need to open a library for use for those who wish to use it, and must strive to ensure that everyone knows about what is held within. It is hoped that such an initiative will serve as an impetus for the transformation of our book storage into one intact gathering that is valuable for all in Russia, in the Old Rite, and in the memory of posterity and to our special treasures from antiquity, and therefore would not end up in foreign depositories.[209]

By providing greater access to their collection, Rogozhskoe Cemetery became a research center on the history of the Old Rite. The community maintained their extensive collection until the 1920s when Soviet officials began confiscating materials and depleted Rogozhskoe's holdings. With greater organization, a new library, and more open access to the community's collections of antiquities, Rogozhskoe Cemetery played a vital role in shaping numerous academic works on the Old Rite for the next 20 years. For example, Rogozhskoe's materials provided the basis for numerous works by noted early twentieth century religious historians such as Vasili Druzhinin and Nikolai Nikol'skii, as well as contemporary theologians such as Feodor Mel'nikov.[210] Rogozhskoe's efforts to build their ideal Old Rite community appeared to be near fully realized in the years after 1905. The Rogozhskoe Old Believers could now openly express their own ideals and identity and similarly attempt to shape the Old Rite entirely.

Conclusion

Nicholas II's *ukaz* on religious toleration provided the opportunity for the Rogozhskoe Old Believers to define themselves and their community free of outside interference. Under the guidance of their new governing board, MSORK, the Rogozhskoe Old Believers experienced even greater efforts to display their moral and cultural devotion to upholding their sense of Old Rite purity physically, ideologically, and culturally. The period immediately following the *ukaz* of April 17, 1905 provided the first opportunity for the Rogozhskoe Old Believers to fully realize and practice their idealized society and attempt to shape the Old Rite throughout the Russian Empire. Larger efforts by Rogozhskoe's members to guide the Old Rite toward spiritual, cultural, and political unification failed as the era of toleration was not everything the Old Believers hoped. Toleration was too short lived as not only did the Old Rite continue to meet political and spiritual resistance at the hands of tsarist and Orthodox officials, but with the onset of World War I and Bolshevik Revolution, the Old Rite once again found its goals disrupted by the political and societal forces affecting Russia.

EPILOGUE AND CONCLUSION

TRAGEDY AND NEW CHALLENGES

I am confident that the Russian Orthodox
Old-Rite Church and the Rogozhskoe Old Believers
will continue to be a beacon for Russia as
a testament of civility, peace, and of
high spiritual and moral values.
Vladimir Putin (2005)[1]

. . . History does not disappear. We cherish every brick.
Metropolitan Kornily of Moscow and All-Rus' (2009)[2]

On November 5, 1917 Agniia Rakhmanova, a member of Rogozhskoe's prominent Rakhmanov merchant family, made one of the last recorded gifts to Rogozhskoe Cemetery with the donation of an early-sixteenth century icon of Our Lady of Tenderness for Rogozhskoe's Intercession Cathedral.[3] Seemingly foretelling Rogozhskoe's and Russia's troubles ahead, attached to the back of the icon was a note stating:

> This icon of the Holy Mother of God of Tenderness is a gift to the temple of the Intercession of the Holy Virgin and this community so that She may keep it in her memory and deliver it from the danger of the events from October 28 to November 3, 1917.[4]

Unfortunately for the Rogozhskoe Old Believers, such prayers for the community's salvation remained unanswered as the Bolsheviks soon took control of Russia.

Like the rest of Russian society the February and October Revolutions in 1917 forever changed Rogozhskoe Cemetery and its community of Old Believers. In a Russia without a Tsar, and soon with the rise of the Bolsheviks, Rogozhskoe faced an even greater uncertainty than it experienced at any point in the community's history. Following the Bolshevik takeover the Rogozhskoe Old Believers found that their history and influence in the Old Rite served as a double-edged sword. On one hand, Rogozhskoe Cemetery became the target of severe persecution under Soviet anti-religion policies. On the other hand, the community's history and universal recognition as a spiritual and cultural center for the Old Rite offered Rogozhskoe Cemetery some protection for its buildings as the community received special designations as a museum in 1919, and later recognized as the Museum of the Old Rite in 1926.[5]

However, Rogozhskoe's museum status did not keep Soviet oppression at bay as the state confiscated all of the library's materials, books, manuscripts, and all of the community's records in 1923. The authorities placed these collections in the Rumiantsev Museum and later the Lenin State Library, eventually becoming the extensive Rogozhskoe Archive.[6] Eventually, under increased pressure from state authorities, Rogozhskoe lost its museum status on October 1, 1928. Just as Metropolitan Filaret believed a century earlier, Soviet officials viewed Rogozhskoe's survival as contrary to the Soviet state itself and soon dismantled all of Rogozhskoe's bells as well as some other structures in the community such as the Nativity Cathedral's dome.[7]

Yet Rogozhskoe persevered. While the Soviet world penetrated Rogozhskoe Cemetery's physical boundaries and surrounded the community on all sides with factories, highways, and apartments, enough of the Old Believer community remained to allow the community to survive into the present day. Rogozhskoe survived after a long and difficult period, remaining true to the community's self-identity as a beacon of Old Rite piety.

Eventually Rogozhskoe finally fulfilled one of the key missing components of their spiritual experience. On July 24, 1988, coinciding with the celebrations for 1,000 years of Christianity in Russia, the Rogozhskoe Old Believers called for a council of Belokrinitskaya

Bishops with the sole purpose of elevating the Archbishopric of Moscow to an Old Rite Metropolitanate. In response, the council elected Alimpii Gusev as the first Metropolitan of All Rus' of the Russian Orthodox Old Rite Church.[8] Under Alimpii's guidance the Rogozhskoe community experienced a significant spiritual and influential resurgence as he sought to reestablish Rogozhskoe Cemetery as a spiritual center for the Old Rite. For example, Alimpii successfully negotiated with Soviet officials for the return of what remained of the Nativity Cathedral and the icons held in the community's old library.[9] Following the Soviet Union's collapse, Alimpii also negotiated with the new Russian State to return more structures to the community, expanding Rogozhskoe Cemetery to the largest it had been since before the October Revolution.[10] Due to his poor health the Metropolitan rarely traveled away from Rogozhskoe Cemetery. However, Alimpii regularly performed services for the community often disregarding those concerned about his health, one time noting "I hear what you are saying! But with every service I attend, I feel ten years younger."[11] Ultimately, Alimpii's tenure as Metropolitan, until his death in December 2003, and his strong influence in rebuilding Rogozhskoe Cemetery allowed the Rogozhskoe Old Believers to transition through the Soviet collapse and helped usher the community into the twenty-first century.

In the twenty-first century Rogozhskoe continues on a path of revival. Coinciding with celebrations for the 100th Anniversary of the *ukaz* of 1905 on religious toleration, the community received special recognition as a National Heritage Site.[12] Furthermore, the state began an extended process of community restoration for Rogozhskoe. The main intention for the project called for the demolition of a number of structures built on Rogozhskoe's property since 1917 in order to restore the area to its "historical essence" including the rebuilding of Rogozhskoe's hotels and charity offices.[13] The efforts did complete extensive restoration to many of the Rogozhskoe structures that remained, including completely rebuilding the dome on the Nativity Cathedral in 2008.[14] After nearly two and a half centuries, and the many trials faced at the hands of an oppressive tsarist and then Soviet regimes, Rogozhskoe Cemetery still thrives both as a community of Old Believers and as the spiritual center and symbol for Old Believers spread throughout the world.

Conclusions

Over the course of the community's history, Rogozhskoe Cemetery developed and adapted both as a physical sanctuary from the outside world and as an opportunity to create new ideals of Christian identity and community for its Old Believers. Unlike Old Believer communities spread throughout the Russian Empire that escaped to the periphery and wilderness, the Moscow Old Believers created their own community within the heart of the empire and defined their self-identity in direct contrast to the "corrupt" world around them. For the Rogozhskoe Old Believers, their community served as an opportunity to build an entirely new understanding of the Old Rite's spiritual purity in the post-*raskol* Russian Empire.

The Rogozhskoe Old Believers brought into being a physical and ideological embodiment of their attempt to create the ideal Christian community in its fundamental organization and its interaction with the outside world. Rogozhskoe particularly emphasized the role of Christian charity and piety, not only by offering aid to the sick and destitute, but also by instilling these virtues in Rogozhskoe's merchant families to use their morality not only to set themselves apart from Russia's more westernized populace but also to bring to the fore Rogozhskoe's ideals.

Furthermore, Rogozhskoe's merchant families such as the Morozovs, Soldatenkovs, Rakhmanovs, and Riabushinskiis all proved to be vital to Rogozhskoe's portrayal and understanding of their communal ideals. The Rogozhskoe Old Believers looked to these families not only in hope that their business acumen would aid the community's finances, but also because these families developed their own unique approach to a "Christian capitalism." These families served as the greatest symbols of Rogozhskoe's ideals thanks to their extensive patronage and charity both in and outside of Rogozhskoe Cemetery. Additionally, these and other families' financial success, along with their charitable donations directly helped the Rogozhskoe community to build and maintain the physical structures used by the community. Rogozhskoe's financial success and recognition as the most charitable institution in Moscow led to significant concessions from tsarist authorities, who feared alienation of such wealthy families would compel them to curtail, or even cut off economic contributions to Moscow and the Russian Empire.

Ultimately, the Rogozhskoe Old Believers constructed their very ideal of a sacred Old Rite community. However, rather than portray themselves exclusively as a testament to their ties to the Old Rite, they actively emphasized their place as a part of Imperial Russia as well through their choices of various architectural styles and especially through their extensive charitable enterprises. Such efforts then emphasized the dual nature of Rogozhskoe: a community that championed "pure" pre-Nikonian Russian Orthodoxy but remained an active part of contemporary Russia.

Even under extreme oppression from the likes of Nicholas I, Metropolitan Filaret, and Konstantin Pobedonostsev, the Rogozhskoe Old Believers persevered. Despite the obstacles placed on them by both secular and spiritual authorities, Rogozhskoe's Old Believers strove to maintain their communal morality and piety and present it as an integral part of Late Imperial Russia. Under the leadership of some of Rogozhskoe's prominent individuals, the community reshaped the ideal of their community to work actively and directly with the tsarist authorities to incorporate both Rogozhskoe Cemetery and the entire Old Rite into the Great Reforms. The ultimate change to Rogozhskoe's identity arrived with their conscious decision to restore the place of the Tsar within their own historical narrative.

Yet it was ultimately the autocracy's own attempts to stave off the disturbances of 1905 that truly allowed the Rogozhskoe Old Believers to flourish anew, even if only briefly. With Nicholas II's *ukaz* on religious toleration, the Rogozhskoe Old Believers received not only legal toleration for their faith but also the return of full control of their sacred spaces. Once again, Rogozhskoe's community could serve as both a spiritual and physical representation of the ideal Christian community and the purity of the Old Rite. For Rogozhskoe, restoration of their sacred spaces became one of the earliest goals for the community after 1905. Furthermore, not only did the Rogozhskoe Old Believers seek to restore the grandeur of their cathedrals, but also to complete their own version of the Cathedral Square of the Moscow Kremlin with the construction of a bell tower.

At the same time, Rogozhskoe's own influence continued to grow under the guidance of a new generation of merchants and industrialists within many of Rogozhskoe's wealthiest families. Contrary to many historical interpretations of these younger Old Believers, such as the Morozov and Riabushinskii brothers, this new generation not only continued to play a significantly active role in shaping the Rogozhskoe community during this time of toleration, but also to uphold the community's ideals through their extensive use of charity and patronage in their businesses and throughout contemporary Russia. In this process, they even developed and refined a different idea of and approach to Christian capitalism. Individuals such as Vladimir and Stepan Riabushinky, for example, expanded and diversified their families business to become some of the wealthiest people in the Russian Empire; yet all the while they remained devoted to their Old Rite roots. They reflected the very ideals of Rogozhskoe's community by using their capital for the greater good of both Rogozhskoe and the Russian people as a whole.

For the Rogozhskoe Old Believers, then, their history is the story of a community devoted to the Old Rite as a faith but also as a means to build a community that embodied their ideals of Old Rite piety and morality. They understood themselves as an Orthodox Christian community free of Western corruptions spiritually, socially, and economically and devoted to what they designated traditional Russian culture and values. This ideology remained as part of the shared self-identity of all members of the Rogozhskoe community, the general parishioners, the clergy who served the community, and Rogozhskoe's wealthiest families and merchants. Yet while the Rogozhskoe Old Believers continually and stubbornly defended their community under the ebbs and flows of oppression by tsarist and Russian Orthodox authorities, their very understanding and presentation of their ideals reflected the community's ties to contemporary Russia. Rogozhskoe Cemetery, then, embodied the very essence of its community. From the outside, the Rogozhskoe Old Believers upheld themselves as loyal, patriotic members of contemporary Russia, while their community exemplified true Christian piety and morality. Inside the community's walls and structures, their ideals remained devoted solely to championing the Old Rite. Ultimately, the Rogozhskoe Old Believers' ability to adapt and participate in the world around them, provided them with the opportunity to serve as a spiritual and moral ideal to guide their own community, other Old Believers, Russian citizens, and Christian society as a whole to this day.

NOTES

Introduction

1. Feodor Permiakov, *Vypiski iz Sviashchennago i sviatootecheskago pisaniia, i tvorenii sviatykh ottsov i uchitelei tserkov: o vnesenii patriarkh Nikonom i ego priemnikami novizn i lozhnago ucheniia; chast I*, (Moscow: P. P. Riabushinskii, 1910), viii.
2. Vladimir P. Riabushinskii, *Staroobriadchestvo i russkoe religioznoe chuvstvo* (Moscow-Ierusalim: "Mosti," 1994), 12–13.
3. While commonly referred to as "Old Believers" in English, the Russian term, *staroobriadtsy*, is more properly translated as "Old Ritualists." This is an important distinction in order to understand the origins and history of the Old Rite movement as the *staroobriadtsy* maintained dogmatic orthodoxy with the Russian Orthodox Church, but objected to ritualistic and liturgical changes introduced in the mid-seventeenth century. Therefore, throughout this work the more popular term "Old Believers" and the proper term "Old Ritualists" appear interchangeably, as do references to the movement that appear as either "Old Belief" or "Old Rite."
4. See, E. M. Iukhimenko, *Staroobriadcheskii tsentr za Rogozhskoi zastavoiu* (Moscow, 2005), V. E. Makarov, *Ocherk istorii Rogozhskogo kladbisha v Moskve (K 140-letiu ego sushestvovaniia: 1771–1911 gg.)* (Moscow: BARC, 1994) and F. E. Mel'nikov, *Kratkia istoriia drevlepravoslavnoi (staroobriadcheskoi) tserkvi* (Barnaul: Barnaul State Pedagogical University, 1999).
5. For examples of studies on Old Rite communities see, Robert O. Crummey, *The Old Believers and the World of Antichrist* (Madison, WI: University of Wisconsin Press, 1970); Irina Paert, *Old Believers, Religious Dissent and Gender in Russia, 1760–1850* (Manchester: Manchester University Press, 2003); and "Regulating Old Believer Marriage: Ritual, Legality, and Conversion in Nicholas I's Russia," *Slavic Review*, Vol. 63 No. 3 (Fall 2004), 555–76; Roy R. Robson, *Old Believers in Modern Russia* (DeKalb, IL: Northern Illinois University Press, 1995); and Serge A. Zenkovsky, *Russkoe*

staroobriadchestvo: Dukhovnye dvizheniia semnadtsatogo veka (Munich: Wilhelm Fink Verlag, 1970).

6. Emile Durkheim, "The Elementary Forms of Religious Life," in W. S. F. Pickering, ed., *Durkheim on Religion* (Atlanta: Scholars Press, 1994), 123–35.
7. Guilford Dudley III, *Religion on Trial: Mircea Eliade and His Critics* (Philadelphia: Temple University Press, 1977), 50–8.
8. A. S. Provorikhina, "Moscovskoe staroobriadchestvo," in *Moskva v ee proshlom i nastoiashchem*, 10th edn (Moscow, 1912), 51.
9. See Isabel de Madariaga, *Ivan the Terrible: First Tsar of Russia* (New Haven: Yale University Press, 2005), 16–19.
10. Ibid.
11. Fr. John Meyendorff, *Rome, Constantinople, Moscow: Historical and Theological Studies* (Crestwood, NY: St. Vladimir's Seminary Press, 1996), 105–6; Michael Cherniavsky, "The Reception of the Council of Florence in Moscow," *Church History*, Vol. 24, No. 4 (December 1955), 347–59; Gustave Alef, "Muscovy and the Council of Florence," *Slavic Review*, Vol. 20, No. 3 (October 1961), 389–401. Also see Joseph Gill, *The Council of Florence* (Cambridge: Cambridge University Press, 1959).
12. Meyendorff, *Rome, Constantinople, Moscow*, 105.
13. Quoted in Meyendorff, *Rome, Constantinople, Moscow*, 108.
14. Ibid., 107.
15. Ibid.
16. Ibid., 108–9.
17. Cherniavsky, "Reception of the Council of Florence," 352.
18. Previously, the head of the Russian Orthodox Church held the title of Metropolitan of Kiev and All Rus', even though the Metropolitan did not reside in Kiev since the late thirteenth century. Ioan's election further reflected the growing political divide between Muscovy and Kiev, the latter resenting Moscow's growing influence. In response, Kiev elected its own Metropolitan in 1458, Gregory II, recognized by both the King of Poland, Casmir, and Pope Calixtus III. The mutual resentment for Muscovy shared by some in Kiev and Muscovy's Western advisaries eventually set the foundations of the Uniate Church in Polish-controlled Russian lands. However, since Gregory was a disciple of the deposed Metropolitan Isidore, the Moscow Metropolitanate proved far more successful in establishing its authority over Orthodoxy throughout the Russian lands. See Meyendorff, *Rome, Constantinople, Moscow*, 108–10, 134–6; Stremooukhoff, "Moscow the Third Rome," 87–9; and Alef, "Muscovy and the Council of Florence," 399–401.
19. Meyendorff, *Rome, Constantinople, Moscow*, 117–19.
20. For the entire *Legend of the White Cowl*, see *Medieval Russia: A Source Book, 850–1700*. Basil Dmytryshyn trans. ed., (Gulf Breeze, FL: Academic International Press, 2000).
21. Ibid.
22. Nicolas Zernov, *Eastern Christendom: A Study of the Origin and Development of the Eastern Orthodox Church*, (New York: Putnam, 1961), 140–2.

23. Dimitry Pospielovsky, *The Orthodox Church in the History of Russia* (Crestwood, NY: St. Vladimir's Seminary Press), 62–4.
24. George Maloney, *A History of Orthodox Theology Since 1453* (Belmont, MA: Nordland Publishers, 1976), 30.
25. These concerns remained at the core of the Old Rite even centuries later. For an excellent example of the Old Rite teachings on these reforms and changes see Fedor Permiakov's *Vypiski* of 1910 which will be described in detail later in this work. F. Permiakov, *Vypiski*.
26. Paul Meyendorff. *Russia, Ritual, and Reform: The Liturgical Reforms of Nikon In the 17th Century* (Crestwood, NY: St Vladimir's Seminary Press, 1991), 39–45.
27. Ibid., 62–4.
28. Crummey, *The Old Believers and the World of Antichrist*, 11–15.
29. *Polnoe sobranie zakonov Rossiiskoi Imperii* Ser. I Vol. 2, (Saint Petersburg, 1830), 647–50. Hereafter *PSZ*.
30. Crummey, *The Old Believers and the World of Antichrist*, 14.
31. James Cracraft. *The Revolution of Peter the Great* (Cambridge, MA: Harvard University Press, 2003), 123.
32. For detail on individuals who protested either the Russian Orthodox Church, the Nikonian Reforms, or both yet did not identify themselves as Old Believers, see, Georg Michels, *At War with the Church: Religious Dissent in Seventeenth-Century Russia* (Stanford: Stanford University Press, 1999). On the *khlysti* see, John Eugene Clay, "Russian Peasant Religion and its Representation: The Christ-faith (Khristovshchina) and the Origins of the 'Flagellant' Myth, 1666–1837," (Ph.D. diss., University of Chicago, 1989).
33. The two major branches of the Old Rite are broadly known as the "priestly" (*popovtsy*) and "priestless" (*bespopovtsy*), the term *staroobriadtsy* refers to the followers of the Old Rite movement as a whole. All Old Believers shared these common disagreements with the Russian Orthodox Church while dividing themselves along questions of gender relations, marriage, social interaction, social organization, and the role of a clergy in Post-Nikonian Orthodoxy. While there was no monolithic Old Rite movement, in the most general sense the division between the priestly and priestless arose from the question over the legitimacy of the priesthood and certain sacraments in the Post-Nikonian world. Whereas the priestless groups rejected both priests and some sacraments as illegitimate as no Old Rite bishops existed to ordain priests, the priestly maintained both priests and all sacraments through taking in defrocked or runaway priests from the Russian Orthodox Church who agreed to perform services using Old Rite methods. Michels, *At War with the Church*, 13–14; Zenkovsky *Russkoe staroobriadchestvo*, 7–12; and Robert O. Crummey, "Old Belief as Popular Religion: New Approaches," *Slavic Review*, Vol. 52 No. 4 (Winter 1993), 701.
34. I. F. Nil'skii, *Semeinaia zhizn' v russkom raskole* (Saint Petersburg: Pechatano v tip. departmenta Udielov, 1868), and V. V. Andreev, *Raskol' i ego znachenie v' narodnoi russkoi istorii* (Osnabruck: Otto Zeller, 1965).

35. See, A. Shchapov, *Russkii Raskol' staroobriadstva, razsmatrivaemyi v sviazi s vnutrennim sostoianiem russkoi tserkvi i grazhdanstvennosti v XVII veke i pervoi polovine XVIII* (Kazan': Isdanie knigoprodavtsa Ivana Dubrovina, 1859) and Michels, *At War with the Church*, 217–19.
36. Michael Cherniavsky, "The Old Believers and the New Religion" in *The Structure of Russian History: Interpretive Essays*, Michael Cherniavsky, ed., (New York: Random House, 1970), 141–7; Robert O. Crummey, *Old Believers in a Changing World*, Robert O. Crummey, ed., (DeKalb, IL: Northern Illinois University Press, 2011), 6–7; "Old Belief as Popular Religion," 701–2; and Serge A. Zenkovsky, "The Russian Church Schism: Its Background and Repercussions" *Russian Review*, Vol. 16 No. 4 (Oct. 1957), 40–3.
37. Avvakum, *Archpriest Avvakum the Life Written by Himself*, Kenneth N. Brostrom, trans., (Ann Arbor, MI: Michigan Slavic Publications, 1979), 51–2.
38. Ibid., 52–8.
39. See for example the language (ignorance, fairy tales, etc) used to describe *raskol'niki* and Old Believers and their beliefs in some documents of the Holy Synod in the *Sobranie postanovlenii po chasti raskola sostoiavshikhsia po vedomstvu Sv. Sinoda*, (Saint Petersburg 1860), Vol. 1, 5–20. Hereafter *SppcrSVS*. See also, I. S. Belliustin, *Description of the Clergy in Rural Russia: The Memoir of a Nineteenth-Century Parish Priest*, Gregory L. Freeze trans., (Ithaca, NY: Cornell University Press, 1985), 173–4.
40. See *SppcrSVS*, Vol. 1, 44, 185–6, 231–8, 259–63, 304–9, 680–1, 689–90, and Vol. 2, 69–71.
41. Robert O. Crummey, *Old Believers in a Changing World*, (DeKalb, IL: Northern Illinois University Press, 2011), 76–9, and *Old Believers in the World of Antichrist*, 94–8.
42. Crummey, *Changing World*, 77–8.
43. Donald Ostrowski, "'Moscow the Third Rome' as Historical Ghost," in *Byzantium: Faith and Power (1261–1557): Perspectives on Late Byzantine Art and Culture*, Sarah T. Brooks, ed., (New York: Metropolitan Museum of Art, 2006), 170–9.
44. Marshall Poe, "Moscow, the Third Rome: The Origins and Transformations of a 'Pivotal Moment,'" *Jahrbucher fur Geschichte Osteuropas*, Vol. 49, No. 3 (2001), 413.
45. Daniel B. Rowland, "Moscow – The Third Rome or the New Israel?" *Russian Review*, Vol. 55, No. 4 (Oct. 1996), 594.
46. See for example, Crummey, *Old Believers and the World of Antichrist*; Paert, *Old Believers, Religious Dissent and Gender*; Robson, *Old Believers in Modern Russia*; and Douglas Rogers, *The Old Faith and the Russian Land: A Historical Ethnography of Ethics in the Urals*, (Ithaca, NY: Cornell University Press, 2009).
47. Crummey, *Old Believers and the World of Antichrist*, 70–85.
48. See Paert, *Old Believers, Religious Dissent and Gender*.
49. Crummey, *Old Believers in a Changing World*, 68–70.
50. Ibid., 77–8.

51. Rogers, *The Old Faith*, 2–19.
52. Riabushinskii, *Staroobriadchestvo*, 12–13.
53. Ibid., 15–20.
54. See for example, I. A. Kirillov, *Tretii Rim: Ocherk istoricheskogo razvitiia idei russkogo messianizma* (Moscow Izdatel'stvo "Tretii Rim," 1996), 47–62 and V. G. Senatov, *Filosofiia istorii staroobriadchestva* (Moscow: Biblioteka zhurnal "Tserkov'," 1995).
55. Vladimir P. Riabushinskii, *Kupchestvo moskovskoe* (Moscow: Rodina, 1992), nos. 8–9, 176.
56. *Materialy k istorii Prokhorovskoi trekhgornoi manufaktury i torgovo-promyshlennoi dieiatel'nosti sem'i Prokhorovykh: gody 1799–1915* (Moscow 1996), 108–9, 124–5.
57. Makarov, *Ocherk istorii*, 7.
58. See, Riabushinskii, *Staroobriadchestvo*, 41–51.
59. By the "public sphere," I build off of the arguments put forward by Jurgen Habermas in which the public sphere became a forum for interaction between a populace and authority. This work emphasizes that the conflict between the Old Rite, Rogozhskoe Cemetery in particular, and Imperial Russia occurred within the public sphere. While Habermas's arguments predominately focus on the rise of the bourgeoisie, and many historians debate the extent to which pre-Revolutionary Russia ever had an identifiable "bourgeoisie" this work reveals that the Rogozhskoe Old Believers utilized the public sphere as a critical means to present their ideological claim to Russia's historical destiny, and challenge the "narrative" put forward by tsarist and Russian Orthodox Church authorities. See Jurgen Habermas, *The Structural Transformation of the Public Sphere: An Inquiry into a Category of Bourgeois Society*, Sixth Edition, (Cambridge, MA: The MIT Press, 1991).
60. See, Crummey, *Old Believers and the World of Antichrist* and *Old Believers in a Changing World*; Hugh D. Hudson, "Lords of the Urals: The Demidov Entrepreneurial Family and the Rise of the Iron Industry in Eighteenth-Century Russia," (Ph.D. diss., University of North Carolina at Chapel Hill, 1981; Paert, *Old Believers, Religious Dissent and Gender*; Alfred J. Rieber *Merchants and Entrepreneurs in Imperial Russia* (Chapel Hill, NC: University of North Carolina Press, 1982); Robson, *Old Believers in Modern Russia*; and Lyudmila Vorontsova and Sergei Filatov, "Paradoxes of the Old Believer Movement," *Religion, State and Society*, Vol. 28, No. 1, 2000, 53–67.
61. Roy R. Robson, "An Architecture of Change: Old Believer Liturgical Spaces in Late Imperial Russia," in *Seeking God: The Recovery of Religious Identity in Orthodox Russia, Ukraine, and Georgia*, Stephen K. Batalden, ed. (DeKalb: Northern Illinois University Press, 1993), 161.
62. Ibid., 165.
63. See for example, William Blackwell, "The Old Believers and the Rise of Private Industrial Enterprise in Early Nineteenth Century Moscow." *Slavic Review*, Vol. 24 No. 3 (Sep. 1965), 407–24; and Jo Ann Ruckman, *The Moscow*

Business Elite: A Social and Cultural Portrait of Two Generations, 1840–1905 (DeKalb: Northern Illinois University Press, 1984).
64. Robson, *Old Believers in Modern Russia*, 10–13.
65. Crummey, *Old Believers in a Changing World*, 101.
66. Ibid., 100–15.
67. See Nicholas Breyfogle, *Heretics and Colonizers: Forging Russia's Empire in the South Caucasus* (Ithaca, NY: Cornell University Press, 2005).
68. Ibid.
69. Heather Coleman, *Russian Baptists and Spiritual Revolution, 1905–1929* (Bloomington: Indiana University Press, 2005), 5.
70. See Coleman, *Russian Baptists* and Sergei I. Zhuk, *Russia's Lost Reformation: Peasants, Millennialism, and Radical Sects in Southern Russia and Ukraine, 1830–1917* (Baltimore: Johns Hopkins University Press, 2004).
71. Vera Shevzov, *Russian Orthodoxy on the Eve of Revolution* (Oxford: Oxford University Press, 2004), 3.
72. Ibid., 8.

Chapter 1 Old Believers and the Opportunities of Imperial Russia

1. Unfortunately, many documents from Rogozhskoe during this period were lost. However, the community's origins were well known to later scholars such as two of Rogozhskoe's critics, Pavel Mel'nikov and Nikolai Subbotin, as well as Rogozhskoe's own historian Vladimir Makarov, who collected documents from various sources on Rogozhskoe's early history. E. M. Iukhimenko notes that tsarist authorities claimed that a fire in Rogozhskoe in 1840 likely destroyed many of the community's early records. Iukhimenko, *Staroobriadcheskii tsentr*, 10–13.
2. For an explanation of difficulties of determining population figures for the Old Rite, see Irina Paert, "'Two or Twenty Million?' The Languages of Official Statistics and Religious Dissent in Imperial Russia," *Ab Imperio*, 3 (2006), 75–98.
3. See Andreas Kappeler, *The Russian Empire: A Multi-Ethnic History* (Harlow, UK: Pearson Education Ltd, 2001); Nicholas Breyfogle, *Heretics and Colonizers*; and Rieber, *Merchants and Entrepreneurs*.
4. Brian E. Strayer, *Huguenots and Camisards as Aliens in France, 1598–1789: The Struggle for Religious Toleration* (Lewiston, NY: The Edwin Mellen Press, 2001), 5.
5. Ibid., 12.
6. Ibid., 95–102.
7. Ibid., 144–5. See also, John M. Hintermaier, "The First Modern Refugees? Charity, Entitlement, and Persuasion in the Huguenot Immigration of the 1680s," *Albion*, Vol. 32 No. 3 (Fall 2000), 429–49.
8. Paul Werth, *The Tsar's Foreign Faiths: Toleration and the Fate of Religious Freedom in Imperial Russia*, (Oxford: Oxford University Press, 2014), 3–6, 45.

9. See, Ernest Zitser, *The Transfigured Kingdom: Sacred Parody and Charismatic Authority at the Court of Peter the Great* (Ithaca, NY: Cornell University Press, 2004).
10. Evgenii V. Anisimov, *The Reforms of Peter the Great: Progress through Coercion in Russia*, John T. Alexander trans. (Armonk, NY: M. E. Sharpe, Inc., 1993), 26–8.
11. Ibid., 203–7.
12. *PSZ*, Ser. I, Vol. 6, 641–2, 720, and Vol. 10, 624–6.
13. See for example, Paert, "'Two or Twenty Million?'"
14. Other large Old Rite communities developed a working relationship with the Russian state. The Vyg Old Believer community in Karelia received numerous privileges, including full payment of all taxes by the Admiralty and even state protection from harassment by the Orthodox Church in exchange for supplying iron ore to the State. Similarly the Demidov family, all ardent Old Believers, received noble status from Peter the Great, granted the right to own and purchase serfs (made illegal out of fear of Old Believers serfs to the Old Rite), and eventually built the largest metallurgical empire in the Urals. See, Crummey, *Old Believers in the World of Antichrist* and Hudson, "Lords of the Urals".
15. Lindsey Hughes, *Russia in the Age of Peter the Great* (New Haven: Yale University Press, 1998), 454–5; and West, "A Note on Old Belief," in James L. West and Iuri A. Petrov, eds, *Merchant Moscow: Images of Russia's Vanished Bourgeoisie* (Princeton: Princeton University Press, 1998), 15–16.
16. James L. West, "A Note on Old Belief," 15–16.
17. Andreas Kappeler, "Czarist Policy toward the Muslims of the Russian Empire," *Muslim Communities Reemerge: Historical Perspectives on Nationality, Politics, and Opposition in the Former Soviet Union and Yugoslavia*, Edward Allworth, ed., (Durham, NC: Duke University Press, 1994), 142–3.
18. Matthew Romaniello, "The Profit Motive: Regional Economic Development in Muscovy after the Conquest of Kazan," *The Journal of European Economic History*, Vol. 33 No. 3 (Winter 2004), 663–4. Also see, Matthew Romaniello, *The Elusive Empire: Kazan and the Creation of Russia, 1552–1671* (Madison: University of Wisconsin Press, 2012).
19. Romaniello, "The Profit Motive," 672–78.
20. Rieber, *Merchants and Entrepreneurs*, 54.
21. Ibid., 56–7.
22. Ibid., 60–1.
23. On the Vyg community see, Crummey, *The Old Believers and the World of Antichrist*. For greater detail of the Preobrazhenskoe Cemetery, see, Irina Paert, *Old Believers, Religious Dissent and Gender*.
24. See for example the overview of the Old Rite's early history in the early Twentieth Century work by Old Believer Historian F. E. Mel'nikov in *Kratkia istoriia.*
25. John T. Alexander, *Bubonic Plague in Early Modern Russia: Public Health and Urban Disaster* (Baltimore: Johns Hopkins University Press, 1980), 181–3.

26. N. I. Subbotin, "Iz istorii Rogozhskago Kladbisha." *Bratskoe Slovo: zhurnal, posviashennii izucheniy raskola.* 1891, Vol. 2, 479.
27. *PSZ*, Ser. I, Vol. 2, 1102.
28. Ibid.
29. Paert, "'Two or Twenty Million?'" 77.
30. Ibid.
31. *PSZ* Ser I. Vol. 5, 166, 200, Vol. 6, 248–49, 513–14, Vol. 10, 624–6 and *SppchSVS*, Vol. 1, 1–2.
32. *PSZ*, Ser. 1, Vol. 9, 551. Empress Anne took a much stricter approach toward the Old Rite than her predecessors; she attempted to require Old Believers to baptize only in the Orthodox Church, as well as forbid the teaching of the Old Rite or allow Old Believers to marry one another. See *PSZ*, Ser. 1, Vol. 9, 789–91. Also see, *PSZ*, Ser. 1, Vol. 10, 624–26 concerning punishments for civil and Church officials who did not properly register Old Believers.
33. Irina Paert, "'Two or Twenty Million?'", 79.
34. *PSZ* Ser. I, Vol. 21, 745.
35. Paert, "'Two or Twenty Million?'", 81–2.
36. John T. Alexander, *Emperor of the Cossacks: Pugachev and the Frontier Jacquerie of 1773–1775* (Lawrence, KS: Coronado Press, 1973), 11.
37. Catherine II of Russia, "Catherine to Volkonskii, 31 July 1774," *Osmnadtsatyi vek: istoricheskii sbornik*, P. I. Bartenev, ed., Vol. I (Moscow, 1868), 116–17.
38. E. E. Lebedev, *Edinoverie v protivodei'stvii russkomu obriadovomu raskolu: Ocherk po istorii i statistike edinoveriia s obzorov sushestvuoshich o nem mnenii i prilozheniiami* (Novgorod: M. O. Selivanova, 1904), 1.
39. M. V. Pervushin, "Edinoverie do i posle mitropolita Platona (Levshina)," http://www.bogoslov.ru/text/315404.html, 15 February 2009; and Vladimir Karpets, "Chto takoe Edinoverie?" http://www.pravaya.ru/faith/118/2777, 31 March 2004.
40. Ibid.
41. Quoted in Archimandrite Platon (Levshin), "Yveshanie k staroobriadtsam." In *Polnoe sobranie sochinenii mitropolita Platona*, (Saint Petersburg: P. P. Soikina, 1913) v. 2, 419–64.
42. James Matthew White, "A Bridge to Schism: Edinoverie, Russian Orthodoxy, and the Ritual Formation of Confessions, 1800–1918," (Ph.D. diss., European University Institute, 2014), 36–46 and Yu. A. Katunin and A. V. Belskii, "Etapi bor'bi za sozdanie tserkvi u staroobriadtsev," in *Kul'tura narodov prichernomor'ia*, No. 81, 2006, 107–8.
43. Ibid.
44. Ibid.
45. *Sobranie postanovlenii po chasti raskola*, (Saint Petersburg, Ministry of the Interior, 1875) Hereafter, *SobranieMVD*, 7–16 and *PSZ* Ser. I, Vol. 23, 880–1.
46. White, "Bridge," 46–54.
47. *PSZ* Ser 1. Vol. 25, 133.
48. White, "Bridge," 2.

49. Paert, "'Two or Twenty Million?'" 81–2.
50. *PSZ* Ser. I, Vol. 16, 140–1.
51. *SppcrSVS* Vol. 1, 586–90, 593–5; *SobranieMVD*, 1; and *PSZ* Ser. I, Vol. 16, 129–32, 140–1.
52. *PSZ* Ser. I, Vol. 16, 129–32.
53. Ibid.
54. Makarov, *Ocherk istorii*, 7–9, and Galina Ulianova, "Old Believers and New Entrepreneurs: Religious Belief and Ritual in Merchant Moscow," in *Merchant Moscow: Images of Russia's Vanished Bourgeoisie*, James L. West and Y. A. Petrov, eds, (Princeton: Princeton University Press, 1998), 67–70.
55. Ibid.
56. Alexander, *Bubonic Plague*, 70–1.
57. Ibid.
58. Galina N. Ulianova, "Old Believers and New Entrepreneurs." 68–9.
59. Makarov, *Ocherk istorii*, 5–7.
60. For a detailed account on how Catherine's Court and elite Russian society, particularly the elite of Saint Petersburg, viewed Moscow in the late eighteenth century, see, Alexander M. Martin, *Enlightened Metropolis: Constructing Imperial Moscow, 1762–1855.* (Oxford: Oxford University Press, 2013).
61. Alexander, *Bubonic Plague*, 70.
62. Ibid., 70–2.
63. Martin, *Enlightened Metropolis*, 14–18.
64. Alexander, *Bubonic Plague*, 70–2.
65. Ibid., 212–7.
66. Makarov, *Ocherk istorii*, 19–24. Moscow priestless Old Believers also petitioned tsarist and city officials for the right to establish their own community. Under similar terms as guaranteed by the priestly Old Believers, authorities approved for the creation of what became Preobrazhenskoe Cemetery.
67. RGB, f. 246, k. 2, ed. 5, ll. 222–229ob and k. 3, ed. 3, ll. 60–60ob.
68. Makarov, *Ocherk istorii*, 10 - 13.
69. Ibid.
70. RGB, f. 246. k. 3, ed. 3, ll. 60-60 ob. Also see Makarov, *Ocherk istorii*, 6–10. This "monastic" communal organization became common among Old Believer communities. As in the Russian tradition, monasteries often developed throughout the Russian wilderness in order to allow for these monastic communities to remove themselves from the corruptions of the world outside of the monasteries. See Fr. Seraphim Rose, *The Northern Thebaid: Monastic Saints of the Russian North*, (Plantina, CA: Saint Herman Press, 1995). A number of historians argue that Old Believers often emulated monastic communities as a means for both order and communal structure as well as to protect the purity of their Orthodoxy through strict adherence to spiritual customs and observations similar to monasteries. See for example, Crummey,

The Old Believers and the World of Antichrist and *Old Believers in a Changing World*. Also see Irina Paert, *Old Believers, Religious Dissent and Gender*.

71. Makarov, *Ocherk istorii*, 12–13.
72. Ibid., 14–15.
73. Mikhail V. Posochin, *Pamiatniki architektury Moskvy. Okrestnosti staroi Moskvy (iugo-vostochnaia i iuzhnaia chasti goroda)* (Moscow, Iskusstvo, 2007), 93.
74. Ibid., 8–9.
75. "Petition to Prince A. A. Prozorovskii," Reproduced in Makarov, *Ocherk istorii*, 14.
76. *PSZ*, Ser. 1, Vol. 4, 87–8.
77. "Prozorovskii to Catherine II, 25 October 1792," Reproduced in Makarov, *Ocherk istorii*, 14–24.
78. Ibid.
79. Ibid.
80. Concerning the symbolism, the Moscow Kremlin as well as its interiors and structures represented for Russian culture, including for the Old Rite in the immediate aftermath of the *Raskol*, see Catherine Merridale, *Red Fortress: History and Illusion in the Kremlin*, (New York: Metropolitan Books, 2013).
81. Gabriel, Metropolitan of Novgorod and Saint Petersburg, "Petition to Catherine II," Reproduced in Makarov, *Ocherk istorii*, 12–14.
82. Makarov, *Ocherk istorii*, 25.
83. Posochin, *Pamiatniki arkhitekturi Moskvy*. 94.
84. Document reproduced in Makarov, *Ocherk istorii*, 25.
85. P. I. Mel'nikov, *Istoricheskie ocherki popovshchini* (Moscow: Katkov, 1864), 214–15.
86. RGB, f. 246, k. 10, ed. 5, l. 4.
87. Makarov, *Ocherk istorii*, 26.
88. Ibid., 6–8. And Iukhimenko, et al., eds, *Drevnosti i dukhovni sviatini staroobriadchestva: Ikoni, knigi, oblacheniia, predmeti tserkovnogo ubranstva Arkhiereiskoi riznitsi i Pokrovskogo sobora pri Rogozhskom kladbishe v Moskve* (Moscow: Interbuk-biznes, 2005), 24–30.
89. "Iz rasskazov i zapisok V. A. Sapelkina." *Russkii vestnik*. M. N. Katkov ed., (Moscow, 1864). No. 11. 190–1.
90. Oleg Tarasov, *Icon and Devotion: Sacred Spaces in Imperial Russia*, Robin Milner-Gulland, trans., (London: Reaktion Books Ltd., 2002), 119–20.
91. Ibid., 24–6.
92. Avvakum, quoted in ibid.
93. Engelina Smirnova, "The Icons of Moscow and Local Artistic Schools, 15th – early 16th centuries," in *A History of Icon Painting*, L. M. Evseeva and Kate Cook eds, (Moscow, 2005), 143–4.
94. Makarov, *Ocherk istorii*, 9–10.
95. Iukhimenko, et al., eds, *Drevnosti i dukhovni sviatini staroobriadchestva*, 23–4.
96. Makarov, *Ocherk istorii*, 9–10.
97. Ibid.

98. Photographs of many of these icons can be found in *Snimki drevnikh ikon i staroobriadcheskikh khramov Rogozhskago kladbisha v Moskve*, (Moscow: Rogozhskoe kladbishche i Tipo-litographa T-vo I. N. Kushnerev i Ko., 1913); and Iukhimenko, et al., eds, *Drevnosti i dukhovni sviatini staroobriadchestva*.
99. Iukhimenko, *Staroobriadcheskii tsentr*, 17.
100. Ibid.
101. For photographs of such icons, see Iukhimenko, et al., eds, *Drevnosti i dukhovni sviatini staroobriadchestva*.
102. In March 2012, the Russian Orthodox Old-Rite Church unveiled plans to erect a monument to Avvakum on the grounds of Rogozhskoe Cemetery in commemoration of his martyrdom for the Old Rite. See "Na Rogozhskom sostoialos' zasedanie Moskovskoi eparkhii," March 19, 2012. http://rpsc.ru/news/novosti-mitropolii/2012/na-rogozhskom-sostoyalos-zasedanie-moskovskoj-eparhii.
103. S. Bulgakov, *Handbook for Church Servers*, (Kharkov, 1900), 22.
104. Ibid.
105. As Alexander Martin notes, one of the difficulties tsarist authority faced was that while Saint Petersburg represented political authority, Moscow remained the city of "Russia's heartland," and in the eyes of the citizens of the Russian Empire, its principle city. For tsarist officials, however, Saint Petersburg represented "progress" and "enlightenment" while Moscow remained emblematic of Russia's larger social and cultural backwardness. Martin, *Enlightened Metropolis*, 1–5.
106. Ibid., 216–19.
107. Ibid., 5.
108. Ibid., 215–19.
109. See, Martin, *Enlightened Metropolis*, and "Moscow Society in the Napoleonic Era: Cultural Tradition and Political Stability," (Washington, DC: National Council for Eurasian and East European Research, 2004).
110. *Tserkov'*, 1912. No. 35. 834–7.
111. Quoted in Makarov, *Ocherk istorii*, 44.
112. *Tserkov'*, 1912. No. 35. 834–6.
113. Ibid., 835–6.
114. T. P. Morozov and I. V. Potkina, *Savva Morozov* (Moscow: "Russkaia kniga," 1998) 3–7.
115. Vladimir P. Riabushinskii, *Kupchestvo moskovskoe*, 176.
116. Anonymous, quoted in Makarov, *Ocherk istorii*, 8.
117. For more on the history of the Prokhorov family see *Materialy k istorii Prokhorovskoi trekhgornoi manufaktury i torgovo-promyshlennoi dieiatel'nosti sem'i Prokhorovykh: gody 1799–1915*.
118. Ibid., 10–15.
119. Ibid., 108–9, 124–5.
120. Ulianova, "Old Believers and New Entrepreneurs," 63.

121. Makarov, *Ocherk istorii*, 7.
122. Ibid., 7–10.
123. RGB, f. 246, k. 2, ed. 5, ll. 93-96 ob.
124. Ibid., 94–94 ob.
125. See Iukhimenko, *Staroobriadcheskii tsentr*, 13.
126. RGB, f. 246, k. 3, ed. 3, ll. 60–60ob.
127. RGB, f. 246, k. 2, ed. 5, ll. 93-96 ob.
128. Makarov, *Ocherk istorii*, 40–1.
129. Ibid.
130. Ibid.
131. Ibid., 7–9.
132. Ulianova, "Old Believers and New Entrepreneurs," 62–4; and Makarov, *Ocherk istorii*, 7–9.
133. Makarov, *Ocherk istorii*, 7–9.
134. Ibid.
135. Ibid., 40. The ties between the Cossacks and the Old Rite is well studied as it often became a source of conflict between some Cossacks and Imperial Russia. See for example John T. Alexander, *Emperor of the Cossacks: Pugachev and the Frontier Jacquerie of 1773–1775*; A. N. Bartenev, *Staraia vera kazakov* (Moscow, 2001); Nicholas V. Fedoroff, *History of the Cossacks* (Commack, NY: Nova Science Publishers, Inc., 1999); N. N. Firsov, *Pugachevshchina: Opyt sotsial'no-psikhologicheskoi kharakteristiki* (Moscow, 1921); I. Z. Kadson, "Vosstanie Pugacheva i Raskola" in *Ezhegodnik muzeia istorii religii i ateizma.* Vol. 4, (Akademia nauk SSSR: Muzei istorii religii i ateizma, Moscow i Leningrada, 1960), 222–38 and Shane O'Rourke, *The Cossacks* (Manchester: Manchester University Press, 2007).
136. Makarov, *Ocherk istorii*, 40–1.
137. "Iz rasskazov i zapisok V. A. Sapelkina." 190–1.
138. RGB, f. 246. k. 6, ed. 1, l. 197 ob., and Makarov, *Ocherk istorii*, 30–2.
139. Ibid.
140. Mel'nikov-Piercheskii, *Ocherki popovshchini*, 215–16.
141. RGB, f. 246, k. 153, ed. 3, l. 6.
142. RGB, f. 246, k. 2, ed. 5, l. 94ob.
143. Makarov, *Ocherk istorii*, 67.
144. RGB, f. 246, k. 2, ed. 5, l. 94ob.
145. Ibid.
146. Mel'nikov-Piercheskii, *Ocherki popovishchii*, 232–6.
147. Ibid.
148. On other minority groups' relations with Tsarist Russia see, Breyfogle, *Heretics and Colonizers*; Crummey, *Old Believers and the World of Antichrist*; Hudson, "Lords of the Urals;" and Benjamin Nathans, *Beyond the Pale: The Jewish Encounter with Late Imperial Russia* (Berkeley: University of California Press, 2002).

Chapter 2 Faith and Identity Under Siege, 1822–56

1. For a look at how tsarist officials desired how to shape Moscow after the Fire of 1812, see Martin, *Enlightened Metropolis*.
2. Thomas Marsden, *The Crisis of Religious Toleration in Imperial Russia: Bibikov's System for the Old Believers, 1841–1855*, (Oxford: Oxford University Press, 2015), 3–6.
3. Writing in the last quarter of the nineteenth century, the historian and hostile critic of both the Old Rite and Rogozhskoe Cemetery, Nikolai Subbotin applauded Nicholas's attempts to destroy the "shameful" and "deplorable" existence of Rogozhskoe Cemetery. Subbotin made it his own goal to provide a historical explanation of Rogozhskoe's errors, thereby justifying Nicholas's and Filaret's attempts to oppress Rogozhskoe Cemetery into submission to the tsarist state and the Russian Orthodox Church. N. I. Subbotin, "Iz istorii Rogozhskago Kladbisha" in N. I. Subbotin, ed., *Bratskoe Slovo*, 1891, Vol. 2, 446–7.
4. For more on Nicholas I see, Nicholas V. Riasanovsky, *Nicholas I and Official Nationality in Russia, 1825–1855* (Berkeley: University of California Press, 1959) and Marsden, *The Crisis of Religious Toleration*.
5. Filaret, quoted in N. Subbotin, ed., *Bratskoye Slovo*, 445–6.
6. Ibid., 41.
7. RGADA. f. 1183. op. 11, d. 1, l. 2.
8. Ibid., ll. 8ob–9.
9. "Delo Sinoda 1823 g. o Rogozhskom kladbishe." Quoted i, Makarov, *Ocherk istorii*, 42.
10. *PSZ* Ser. II, (Moscow, 1911) Vol. 2, 1130–31 and *SobranieMVD*, 81–2, 84, 148.
11. Paert, "Regulating ...," 555.
12. RGADA. f. 1183, op. 11, d. 151, l. 28–34.
13. Paert, *Old Believers, Religious Dissent and Gender*, 193–204.
14. *PSZ* Ser. II, Vol. 1, 946, Vol. 11, 446–7, and *SobranieMVD*, 92.
15. *SobranieMVD*, 187.
16. N. I. Subbotin, "Na Rogozhskoe kladbishe" in N. I. Subbotin, ed., *Bratskoe Slovo*, 1885, Vol. 2, 226–7.
17. Filaret, quoted in Subbotin, *Bratskoye Slovo*, 445–6.
18. For an overview of the many agencies created to investigate the Old Rite under Nicholas, see Marsden, *The Crisis of Religious Toleration*.
19. *SobranieMVD*, 109.
20. RGADA, f. 1183.,op. 11, d. 46, ll. 15-25.
21. RGB, f. 246, k. 3, ed. 3, l. 79.
22. E. M. Iukhimenko, *Staroobriadcheskii tsentr*, 71.
23. RGB, f. 246, k. 2, ed. 2. ll. 84–84ob and k. 3, ed. 6, ll. 34–34ob.
24. Paert, *Old Believers, Religious Dissent and Gender*, 86.
25. *SobranieMVD*, 101–2, 108.
26. Ibid.

27. Ibid., 138–9.
28. Ibid., 142–3.
29. Ibid.
30. Regulations permitted Rogozhskoe to keep any priests currently living with the community. However, any future priests discovered after 1827 faced immediate exile. This left Rogozhskoe with only five priests in 1827 and only four priests, all elderly, by 1841. *SobranieMVD*, 95 and Mel'nikov-Piercheskii, *Ocherki popovshchini*, 215–17.
31. "Delo Sinoda 1823 g. o Rogozhskom kladbishe" quoted in Makarov, *Ocherk istorii*, 42.
32. Ibid.
33. Ibid., 43.
34. Mel'nikov-Piercheskii, *Ocherki popovshchini*, 205.
35. Ibid., 211–13.
36. Quoted in Makarov, *Ocherk istorii*, 44.
37. RGADA, f. 1183, op. 11, d. 61, ll. 27–27ob.
38. *Tserkov'*, 1908, No. 18, 655.
39. Mel'nikov-Piercheskii, *Ocherki popovishini*, 215.
40. Ibid.
41. Makarov, *Ocherk istorii*, 42–43.
42. Iukhimenko, *Staroobriadcheskii tsentr*, 21–2.
43. RGADA, f. 1183, op. 11, d. 1, ll. 8ob–9.
44. Ibid.
45. Ibid.
46. *SppcrSVS*, v. 2, 124–26 and RGADA, f. 1183, op. 11, d. 1, l. 11.
47. RGADA, f. 1183, op. 11, d. 1, ll. 8–11.
48. *SobranieMVD*, 68–70.
49. Ibid.
50. RGADA, f. 1183, op. 11, d. 61, l. 27–27v.
51. Mel'nikov-Piercheskii, *Ocherki popovshchini*, 215.
52. Ibid., 265–8.
53. N. I. Subbotin, *Istoriia Belokrinitskoi ierarkhii*, (Moscow, 1874), 378 and Mel'nikov, *Kratkaia istoriia*, 205–17.
54. Ibid.
55. Quoted in Subbotin, *Istoriia Belokrinitskoi*, 393–4.
56. Ibid.
57. Makarov, *Ocherk istorii*, 31–3.
58. Mel'nikov, *Kratkaia istoriia*, 271–2.
59. Mel'nikov-Piercheskii, *Ocherki popovishchini*, 230.
60. *SobranieMVD*, May 13, 1847.
61. N. I. Subbotin, ed., *Materiali dlia istorii tak nazyvaemoi avstriiskoi, ili belokrinitskoi ierarkhii* (Moscow 1897), 250–97.
62. Marsden, *The Crisis of Religious Toleration*, 44–55.
63. Ibid., 54.

64. *PSZ* Ser. II, Vol. 11, Book 2, 1, Vol. 19, 881–83 and Rieber, *Merchants and Entrepreneurs*, 140–2.
65. M. N. Vasil'evskii, *Gosudarstvennaia sistema otnoshenii k staroobriadtsam v tsarstvovanie imperatora Nikolaia I* (Kazan, 1914), 39.
66. *Tserkov'*, 34 (1908), 1006.
67. Mel'nikov-Piercheskii, *Ocherki popovshchini*, 230.
68. Makarov, *Ocherk istorii*, 37.
69. RGB, f. 246, k. 221, ed. 1, ll. 1ob–2.
70. Subbotin, "Iz istorii Rogozhskago Kladbisha," 448.
71. Metropolitan Filaret, quoted in Ibid., 448–9.
72. Ibid., 449.
73. Writing in 1891, Nikolai Subbotin disputed the original number of *edinovertsy* converts in Rogozhskoe at only 100 as a fabrication of "the adherents of that Austrian priesthood." However, he does not provide any figures or estimates of his own but only suggests that the number provided was a low misrepresentation. Subbotin, "Iz istori . . .," 448.
74. Metropolitan Filaret, "Donesenie m. Filareta Sv. Sinodu 25 sent. 1854 g." in Subbotin, "Iz istorii . . . 451". See also "Iz rasskazov i zapisok V. A. Sapelkina."
75. Iukhimenko, *Staroobriadcheskii tsentr*, 35.
76. Subbotin, "Iz istorii Rogozhskaogo Kladbisha," 452.
77. Ibid., 452–4.
78. Ibid.
79. Ibid.
80. RGB, f. 246, k. 3, ed. 3, l. 60ob.
81. Subbotin, "Iz istorii Rogozhskago Kladbisha", 455–6.
82. RGADA, f. 1183, op. 11, d. 151, l. 12ob.
83. Ibid., and *Op.cit.*, d. 156, ll. 7–19.
84. Subbotin, "Iz istorii Rogozhskago Kladbisha", 456.
85. Marsden, *The Crisis of Religious Toleration*, 204–8.
86. Metropolitan Filaret, "Pis'ma k ober-prokuroru 4 marta 1855," *Sobranie mnenie i otsivov Filareta, mitropolita Moscovskago i Kolomenskago, po dielam pravoslavnoi tserkvi na Vostokie*, Vol. 4, (Saint Petersburg, 1888), 8. Similarly, Alfred Rieber notes that between 1828 and 1855, roughly 350,000 Old Believers converted either to Orthodoxy or to *Edinoverie*, but stresses the difficulty of maintaining accurate records on the Old Believers. Rieber, *Merchants*, 141–2.
87. Filaret, *Sobranie mnienie*, Vol. 4, 8.
88. RGADA. f. 1183, op. 11, d. 148, ll. 11ob.–12.
89. Filaret, *Sobranie mnienie*, Vol. 4, 45–7.
90. A. A. Zakrevskii to Minister of the Interior Sergei Lanskoi, Sep. 4, 1855, RGADA. f. 1183, op. 11, d. 148, ll. 9ob.–10.
91. Ibid., ll. 13ob–14.
92. Ibid., Also see, Mikhail Longinov, "Report of 18 February 1856." And "Letter of Count Zakrevskii to Minister of Internal Affairs Lanskoi;" both reproduced in Subbotin, "Iz istorii Rogozhskago Kladbisha," 617–33.

93. "Pis'ma k gospodinu NN" quoted in Iukhimenko, *Staroobriacheskii tsentr*, 36.
94. RGADA, f. 1183, op. 11, d. 151, l. 26, and d. 153, l. 12.
95. See "Report to the Ober-Procurator and Secret Committee," quoted in Subbotin, "Iz istorii Rogozhskago kladbisha," 515–17.
96. Filaret, Metropolitan of Moscow, "Report of Metropolitan Filaret to the Holy Synod of February 16, 1856." Reproduced in Subbotin, "Iz istorii Rogozhskago Kladbisha." 636–39.
97. See Mikhail Longinov, "Report of 18 February 1856" and "Letter of Count Zakrevskii to Minister of Internal Affairs Lanskoi." Both reproduced in Subbotin, "Iz istorii Rogozhskago Kladbisha," 617–33.
98. RGADA. f. 1183, op. 11, d. 148.
99. Ibid., l. 66–8.
100. Ibid., l. 41.
101. RGB, f. 246, k. 5, ed. 1, l. 9.
102. Reproduced in Makarov, *Ocherk istorii*, 52.

Chapter 3 Rogozhskoe in the Reform Era, 1856–1905

1. Makarov, *Ocherk istorii*, 31–3.
2. Ibid.
3. See, N. I. Subbotin, ed., *Belokrinitskoi ierarkhii*, 250–97.
4. See Arsenii, Bishop of the Urals, *Zhizn' i podvigi Antoniia, staroobriadcheskogo arkhiepiskopa Moskovskogo i Vladimirskogo* (Moscow: MP "Pechatnik," 1995).
5. Ibid., and *Tserkov'*. 1908, No. 1. 23–4.
6. Ibid.
7. Ibid.
8. Antonii's predecessor and first Old Rite bishop in Russia, Sophroni of Simbirsk (appointed in 1849), attempted to create his own Old Rite hierarchy by ordaining his own bishops and naming himself Metropolitan of Moscow. However, Sophroni attracted few followers and Kirill excommunicated him and his bishops for simony in 1853. This eventually led to Kirill's decision to create three Old Rite archdiocese for Russia and place Antonii as the Archbishop of Vladimir with spiritual authority of all *Belokrinitsi* Old Believers in Russia while the archdiocese of Moscow remained under Kirill's authority. N. I. Subbotin. "Istoriia tak nazyvaemogo avstriiskogo, ili belokrinitskogo, sviachenstva," in *Bratskoe Slov'*, 1895, Vol. II, 299.
9. N. I. Popov, "Okruzhnoe Poslanie Popovchini," in *Sbornik iz istorii staroobriadchestva* (Moscow, 1866), Vol. I, 99–100.
10. Ibid., 96–7.
11. "Xenos" (I. G. Kabanov), *Okruzhnoe poslanie Rossiiskikh arkhipastirei Belokrinitskoi ierarkhii*, Feb. 24, 1862.
12. RGB, f. 247. no. 397, ll. 24–24ob.
13. "Xenos," *Okruzhnoe poslanie.*
14. Ibid.

15. Ibid.
16. Ibid.
17. Ibid.
18. Ibid.
19. Ibid.
20. Iukhimenko, *Staroobriadcheskii tsentr'*, 92.
21. N. I. Subbotin, "Sovremennie dvizheniia v raskole," *Tserkov'u*, 1863 Vol. I, 18, and Popov, "Okruzhnoe Poslanie Popovchini," 94–7.
22. Popov, "Okruzhnoe Poslanie Popovchini," 94–6.
23. Ibid., 97.
24. Ibid.
25. Ibid.
26. Ibid., 98–100, and "Pervie godi suchestvovaniia Belokrinitskoi ierarkhii. Bor'ba vokrug 'okruzhnogo poslaniia'" in *Iz istorii Belokrinitskoi ierarkhii: sbornik*, T. A. Ivanova, ed., (Moscow, 2007), 104–5.
27. Bishop Arsenii, *Zhizn' i podvigi Antoniia*.
28. Popov, "Okruzhnoe Poslanie Popovchini," 100.
29. With Antonii's election, his old position as Archbishop of Vladimir became part of his jurisdiction in Moscow until 1876 when Vladimir transferred to the authority of the Bishop of Nizhni Novgorod and Kostroma. "Pervie godi suchestvovaniia Belokrinitskoi ierarkhii," 106.
30. Ibid.
31. Ibid., 106–7.
32. Ibid.
33. Popov, "Okruzhnoe Poslanie Popovchini," 100–2.
34. Metropolitan Ambrose, "Gramota Mitropolita Ambroseia iz Tsilli v Moskvu k Antoniu i prochim episkopam. 28 oktiabria 1863 g," in *Iz istorii Belokrinitskoi Ierarkhii*, 123–6.
35. Ibid.
36. "Pervie godi suchestvovaniia Belokrinitskoi ierarkhii," 106–7.
37. Ibid., 107–9.
38. Vera Shevzov also explores similar issues faced by Russian Orthodox parishes as Orthodox laity sought to take a larger role in parish organization in the late nineteenth and early twentieth century. See Shevzov, *Russian Orthodoxy on the Eve of Revolution.* In like fashion, many other religious groups faced similar needs for organization. For other examples see Breyfogle, *Heretics and Colonizers* and "Prayer and Politics of Place," Coleman *Russian Baptists and Spiritual Revolution*, and Laura Engelstein *Castration and the Heavenly Kingdom* (Ithaca, NY: Cornell University Press, 1999).
39. RGB, f. 246, k. 2, ed. 2, ll. 26–26ob, and k. 2, ed. 5, ll. 97–8.
40. RGB, f. 246, k. 2, ed. 5, ll. 141–3.
41. D. E. Raskov, *Ekonomicheskie instituty staroobriadchestva*, (Saint Petersburg: Saint Petersburg State University, 2012), 242–5.
42. Iukhimenko, *Staroobriadcheskii tsentr*, 68.

43. Iukhimenko et al., *Drevnosti i dukhovnie sviatini staroobriadchestva*, 11.
44. RGB, f. 246, k. 3, ed. 3, ll. 114–114ob.
45. Ibid., ll. 111–112.
46. RGB, f. 246, k. 3, ed. 5, l. 1.
47. Iukhimenko, *Staroobriadcheskii tsentr*, 71.
48. RGB, f. 246, k. 2, ed. 5, ll. 186–186ob.
49. Ibid.
50. RGB, f. 246, k. 3, ed. 3, ll. 68ob and 79.
51. Ibid., l. 68.
52. RGADA. f. 1183, op. 11, d. 146, ll. 38ob–39.
53. RGB, f. 246, k. 5, ed. 1, l. 127.
54. RGB, f. 246, k. 3, ed. 6, l. 6; k. 5, ed. 4, l. 16; k. 6, ed. 4, ll. 35–36; k. 7, ed. 3, ll. 15–17; k. 2, ed. 2, l. 44; k. 9, ed. 1, l. 3.
55. RGB, f. 246, k. 7, ed. 4, ll. 75–76ob.
56. RGB, f. 246, k. 8, ed. 1, l. 123.
57. Raskov, *Eknomicheskie*, 242–3.
58. Manfred Hildermeier, "Old Belief and Worldly Performance: Socio-economic and Sociocultural Aspects of the Raskol in Early Industrial Russia" in *Russia's Dissident Old Believers, 1650–1950*, Georg B. Michels and Robert L. Nichols, eds, (Minneapolis: University of Minnesota Press, 2009), 132.
59. Ibid.
60. *Materialy k istorii Prokhorovskoi Trekhgornoi manufaktury*, 108–9.
61. *PSZ*, Ser. III, Vol. 3, 219–21.
62. Jo Ann Ruckman, *The Moscow Business Elite: A Social and Cultural Portrait of Two Generations, 1840–1905* (DeKalb, IL: Northern Illinois University Press, 1984), 24–5.
63. G. N. Ulianova, "Not for Wealth but for God," *Russian Studies in History*, Vol. 39, No. 2 (Fall 2000), 28–9.
64. Ibid., 31.
65. Ibid.
66. Jo Ann Ruckman explores this phenomenon and its effects in Moscow merchant culture, politics, and society in her work *The Moscow Business Elite* in greater detail. Also see, Alfred Rieber, *Merchants and Entrepreneurs*.
67. Rieber, *Merchants and Entrepreneurs*, 145–7. Also see Linda Bowman, "Moral Economies and Management at the Morozov Mills, 1885–1905" in *Social History*, Vol. 28, No. 3 (October 2003), 322–45.
68. Prince V. P. Meshcherskii, *Ocherki nyneshnei obshchestvennoi zhizni Rossii: Pis'ma iz srednykh Veliko-Russkikh gubernii* (Saint Petersburg, 1868), 119.
69. Rieber, *Merchants and Entrepreneurs*, 147.
70. Ibid., 143.
71. Many other religious communities faced similar situations over questions and concerns regarding public and private forms of spiritual expression. See for example, Breyfogle "Prayer and Politics of Place;" Paert, *Old Believers, Religious*

Dissent and Gender; and Peter Waldron, *The End of Imperial Russia, 1855–1917* (New York: St. Martin's Press, 1997).

72. RGB, f. 246, k. 5, ed., 1, ll. 39–39ob.
73. Makarov, *Ocherk istorii*, 49.
74. RGADA. f. 1183, op. 11, d. 153, l. 42.
75. RGB, f. 246, k. 5, ed. 1, l. 50.
76. See for example the works of N. I. Subbotin and his *Istoriia Belokrinitskoi ierarkhii*.
77. Iukhimenko, *Staroobriadcheskii tsentr*, 46–8.
78. RGB, f. 246, k. 5, ed. 1, l. 50.
79. Daniel Field, *Rebels in the Name of the Tsar* (Boston: Houghton Mifflin, 1976), 1–5, 22, and 24.
80. Iukhimenko, *Staroobriadcheskii tsentr*, 46–7.
81. RGB, f. 246. k. 5, ed. 1, ll. 28–30.
82. RGB, f. 246, k. 2, ed. 5, ll. 215–216ob and k. 91, ed. 9, ll. 1–16.
83. *Tserkov'*, 1908, No. 20, 714–716.
84. *Tserkov'*, 1908, No. 19, 689.
85. RGB, f. 246, k. 3, ed. 1, ll. 21–2.
86. *Bratskoie Slovo*, 1889 T. 2, 320– 1.
87. RGB, f. 246, k. 3. ed. 3.l. 9.
88. Ibid., l. 21.
89. Ibid.
90. Ibid., ll. 23–23ob.
91. Ibid., l. 24.
92. Ibid., l. 25ob.
93. Ibid.
94. Ibid., l. 26.
95. Ibid., l. 69ob.
96. Ibid., ll. 70–70ob, 72.
97. Ibid., l. 86.
98. Ibid., l. 69ob.
99. Ibid., l. 86.
100. Ibid., l. 33.
101. Ibid., ll. 20, 77.
102. Werth, *Tsar's Foreign Faiths*, 173–4.
103. Ibid., 177–8.
104. Ibid.
105. RGB, f. 246, k. 4, ed. 3, l. 568.
106. RGB, f. 246, k. 4, ed. 1, l. 46.
107. RGB, f. 246, k. 2, ed. 2, ll. 35–35ob.
108. The Rogozhskoe Old Believers held a long established relationship with Alexander Abramovich Suvorov. In one paragraph of the minutes of the community election of Trustees held in late 1875, it appeared: "As we all know that we have repeatedly asked His Serene Highness Prince Alexander Suvorov

to intervene in our affairs, and he always had full sympathy for our cause and to the most useful extent possible. On January 1, 1876 Duke Suvorov, will celebrate 50 years of service in the officer ranks. On this occasion, some supposed to celebrate its 50th anniversary [. . .] and therefore, we should acknowledge and commemorate this event." At the meeting, the community decided to provide Suvorov with a gift of an icon of St. Alexander Nevsky. (RGB, f. 246, k. 3, ed. 3, l. 15ob.). Rogozhskoe's representatives at the anniversary reported to the elected assembly on January 15, 1876: January 1, the day of the Grand Duke Suvorov's anniversary we handed him the holy image . . . He kissed us repeatedly, and was very pleased and said: "I would like to say a few words, but cannot: I am terribly excited! However, I heartily thank you for your well-wishes and memories. I am very grateful!" (Ibid., l. 33).

109. Ibid., l. 93–104. The Apostle of America, St. Innocent (Benjamin), serves as a great contrast to his predecessor, Filaret, and approached the Old Rite with significantly more compassion. The Rogozhskoe Old Believers acknowledged Innocent's kindness in a memorandum to members of the State Council on February 9, 1883: "When our most loyal petition to the late Emperor Alexander Nikolayevich, submitted in 1878, concerning the reopening of our altars by the chief prosecutor, [the petition] was assigned for preliminary consideration by the Moscow Spiritual Consistory, most memorably the Metropolitan of Moscow Innocent afterward told our deputies with words of truth: "I find myself in this issue in a painful situation: if I say that I agree on the freedom of your service, then I will be the focus of great criticism, and if I said that this should not be allowed, it would be against my conscience. And therefore I tell you only that it would be better for this government [to grant your freedoms] but I cannot ask for it." (RGB, f. 246, k. 6. ed. 1, ll. 6–6ob).

110. The Rogozhskoe Trustees also kept records of the cost for these eggs, for example: 537 rubles and 60 kopeks in 1885 (RGB, f. 246, k. 6, ed. 4, l. 45); 610 rubles and 80 kopeks in 1886 (Ibid., l. 46); 654 rubles in 1887 (Ibid., l. 133); 651 rubles in 1888 (RGB, f. 246, k. 7, ed. 4, l. 51); 710 rubles and 40 kopeks in 1889 (Ibid., l. 76); and 1155 rubles and 60 kopeks in 1890 (Ibid., l. 99).

111. Iukhimenko, *Staroobriadcheskii tsentr*, 61.

112. RGB, f. 246, k. 7, ed. 4, l. 35.

113. RGB, f. 246, k. 5, ed. 1, l. 38.

114. Leonid Heretz and Nicholas Breyfogle both point out the relationship between religious communities in Russia and their conceptualization of their place within the Russian Empire based on their understanding of the authority and rule of the Tsar. See Breyfogle, *Heretics and Colonizers* and Leonid Heretz, *Russia on the Eve of Modernity: Popular Religion and Traditional Culture Under the Last Tsars* (Cambridge: Cambridge University press, 2008).

115. *PSZ* Ser. I Vol. 2, 647–50.

116. Crummey, *The Old Believers and the World of Antichrist*, 14.

117. See for example, James Cracraft. *The Revolution of Peter the Great*, (Cambridge, MA: Harvard University Press, 2003), 123.
118. *PSZ* Ser I, Vol. 6, 169, and *SppcrSVS*, Vol. 1, 185–6, 231–8.
119. V. N. Tatishchev "O soderzhaniitserkveiishkol," quoted in Hudson, "Religious Persecution and Industrial Policy," 27–9.
120. See for example, Crummey, *Old Believers and the World of Antichrist*, Irina Paert, *Old Believers, Religious Dissent and Gender in Russia, 1760–1850*, and Hugh D. Hudson, Jr. "Lords of the Urals." Non-Old Believer, and even non-Christian groups also benefited from this relationship, see for example: Breyfogle, *Heretics and Colonizers*, Kappeler *The Russian Empire*, and Nathans, *Beyond the Pale.*
121. Ibid.
122. RGB, f. 246, k. 5, ed. 1, l. 51.
123. *Slovo tserkvi'*, 1915 No. 12, 292.
124. RGB, f. 246, k. 5, ed. 1, l. 51.
125. RGB, f. 246, k. 6. ed. 6. l. 78.
126. RGB, f. 246, k. 2, ed. 2, l. 124.
127. Ibid., l. 244.
128. RGB, f. 246, k. 5, ed. 5, l. 6.
129. RGB, f. 246, k. 4, ed. 5, l. 43.
130. RGB, f. 246, k. 6, ed. 1, l. 60
131. RGB, f. 246, k. 5, ed. 1, l. 57.
132. Ibid., ed. 8.
133. *PSZ*, Series III, Vol. 3, 219–221.
134. Ibid.
135. RGB, f. 246, k. 5, ed. 5, l. 6.
136. *PSZ*, Series III, Vol. 3, 219–221.
137. *PSZ*, Ser. III, Vol. 3, 219–221.
138. RGB, f. 246, k. 6, ed. 4, l. 7ob.
139. RGB, f. 246, k. 92, ed. 10, ll. 1–10.
140. RGB, f. 246, k. 92, ed. 1, l. 2.
141. For more on Pobedonostsev see, A. Iu. Polunov's *Pod vlastiu ober-prokurora: gosudarstvo i tserkov' v epokhu Aleksandra III*, (Moscow, AIRO-XX, 1996), for greater detail on Pobedonostsev.
142. Makarov, *Ocherk istorii . . .*, 54.
143. Ibid.

Chapter 4 A New Beginning, 1905–17

1. For greater detail on the Revolution of 1905, see Abraham Ascher, *The Revolution of 1905* Vol. 1 and 2, (Stanford: Stanford University Press, 1992).
2. *PSZ*, Ser. III, Vol. 25, 257–58.
3. Konstantine Pobedonostsev, Quoted in Makarov, *Ocherk istorii*, 56.
4. *PSZ*, Ser. III, Vol. 25, 257.

5. Konstantin Pobedonostsev, Quoted in Makarov, 55–6.
6. Ibid.
7. See Ascher, *The Revolution of 1905*.
8. *PSZ*, Ser. III, Vol. 25, 257–58. A number of historians have also looked at the effects the *ukaz* had for various groups throughout the Russian Empire. See for example, Nicholas Breyfogle, *Heretics and Colonizers*, Heather Coleman, *Russian Baptists and Spiritual Revolution*, Laura Engelstein, *Castration and the Heavenly Kingdom*, V. I. Iasevich-Borodaevskaia, *Bor'ba za veru* (Saint Petersburg, 1912), Vera Shevzov, *Russian Orthodoxy on the Eve of Revolution*, Peter Waldron, *The End of Imperial Russia*, and "Religious Toleration in Late Imperial Russia," in *Civil Rights in Imperial Russia*, Crisp, Olga and Linda Edmondson eds, (Oxford: Clarendon Press, 1989), 103–20, Paul W. Werth, *The Tsar's Foreign Faiths*, and *At the Margins of Orthodoxy: Mission, Governance, and Confessional Politics in Russia's Volga-Kama Region, 1827–1905*, (Ithaca, NY: Cornell University Press, 2002) and "Orthodoxy as Ascription (and Beyond): Religious Identity on the Edges of the Orthodox Community," in, *Orthodox Russia: Belief and Practice under the Tsars*, Kivelson, Valerie A. and Robert H. Greene, eds, (University Park, PA: Pennsylvania State University Press, 2003).
9. *PSZ*, Ser. III Vol. 25, 257–8.
10. Ibid.
11. Ibid.
12. Ibid.
13. Nicholas II, quoted in: A. V. de Shamborant, *Raspechatanie altarei v khramakh staroobriadcheskogo Rogozhskogo kladbisha 16 apr. 1905 g.* (Moscow 1905), 11.
14. Ibid., 11–12.
15. See, B. I. Esin, *Reportazhi Gilyarovskogo*, (Moscow: Moskovskogo universiteta, 1985). Giliarovskii is also well known for posing as the "Laughing Cossack in White Hat" in Ilya Repin's famous painting "Cossacks Writing a Letter to the Sultan of Turkey."
16. V. A. Giliarovskii, "Raspechatanie altarei Rogozhskogo kladbisha," in *Staraia vera Khrestomatiia*, A. C. Ribakov, ed., (Moscow, 1911), 392.
17. Ibid.
18. Ibid.
19. Ibid., 395–8.
20. Ibid., 393.
21. Ibid., 394.
22. Ibid.
23. Makarov, *Ocherik istorii*, 59.
24. RGB, f. 246, k. 9, ed. 8, l. 84.
25. Ibid.
26. Ibid., ll. 111, 113–14.
27. Ibid., l. 126.
28. Ibid., ll. 126–129ob.

29. RGB, f. 246, k. 92, ed. 25, l. 5.
30. Ibid.
31. Ibid., l. 6.
32. Ibid.
33. Ibid.
34. *PSZ* Ser. II, Vol. 1, 946, Vol. 11, 446–7, and *SobranieMVD*, 92.
35. For greater elaboration see, for example: Archpriest Seraphim Slobodskoi, "Bells and Russian Orthodox Peals," in *The Law of God* (Jordanville, NY: Holy Trinity Monastery, 1996), 623–5.
36. RGB, f. 246, k. 9, ed. 8, l. 140.
37. RGB, f. 246, k. 6, ed. 6, l. 90.
38. Ibid.
39. Robson, "An Architecture of Change," 164–5.
40. The final estimate for the tower itself was 143,847 rubles plus an additional 12,000 rubles to build a heating and ventilation system for the tower. RGB, f. 246, k. 10, ed. 3, ll. 1–15ob.
41. RGB, f. 246, k. 10, ed. 3, l. 31.
42. Ibid., ll. 21–22ob.
43. Ibid., l. 29.
44. Ibid., l. 31.
45. See for example, Ulianova, "Not for Wealth, but for God." For a further analysis of the general approach toward private charity and philanthropy in Late Imperial Russia see, Adele Lindenmeyr, *Poverty is Not a Vice: Charity, Society, and the State in Imperial Russia* (Princeton, NJ: Princeton University Press, 1996).
46. The questionable nature of Savva's death in Cannes, France led to some of Savva's friends, such as Maxim Gorky, Savva's wife and family, and even the Moscow Governor-General Kozlov to reject the Cannes police's ruling of suicide, eventually allowing Savva to receive a Christian burial at the Morozov family crypt in Rogozhskoe Cemetery. Hoping to maintain Savva's "good name," and also distance Savva's legacy tied to the increasingly revolutionary Social Democrats (Maria originally suspended Savva from managing any of the family's factories following strikes at the Morozov's Nikol'skoi plant in February 1905, and openly accused the Social Democrats of murdering Savva for no longer funding the party or their newspaper *Iskra*), Maria and her surviving son, Sergei, took great efforts to maintain many of Savva's charities and other organizations. See, T. P. Morozova and I. V. Potkina, *Savva Morozov.*
47. RGB, f. 246, k. 6, ed. 1, ll. 121–122 and RGB, f. 246, k. 10, ed. 3, ll. 21–22ob.
48. RGB, f. 246, k. 6, ed. 1, l. 122.
49. *Tserkov'*, 1908 No. 17, 622.
50. Ibid., 622–3.
51. Ibid.
52. Ibid.

53. Ibid.
54. Ibid., 622.
55. *Tserkov'*, 1908 No. 36, 1231, and No. 43, 1318.
56. *Tserkov'*, 1908 No. 43, 1318.
57. Ibid., 1319.
58. Posochin, *Pamiatniki arkhitekturi Moskvi*, 97.
59. *Tserkov'*, 1908 No. 17, 622 and Posochin, *Pamiatniki arkhitekturi Moskvi*, 97.
60. *Tserkov'*, 1908 No. 17, 622–3.
61. Work on the bell tower slowed or ceased briefly from the end of 1911 until July of 1912 as the community diverted all available funds and donations to provide aid to victims of a series of crop failures in European Russia. RGB, f. 246, k. 17, ed. 14, l. 61ob and RGB, f. 246, k. 17, ed 15, l. 12ob.
62. RGB, f. 246, k. 17, ed. 16, ll. 41–41ob.
63. RGB, f. 246, k. 156, ed. 2, l. 9.
64. Posochin, *Pamiatniki architektury Moskvy*, 97–98.
65. *PSZ*, Ser. III, Vol. 26, 904–914.
66. RGB, f. 246, k. 14, ed. 7, l. 10.
67. Ibid., l. 11.
68. RGB, f. 246, k. 10, ed. 4, ll. 12–14ob.
69. Ibid. Furthermore, Rogozhskoe's efforts to organize under a larger governing body shares similar trends throughout Russia during this period among communities and religious groups in order to participate in Russia's public sphere. See for example, Joseph Bradley, *Voluntary Associations in Tsarist Russia: Science, Patriotism, and Civil Society* (Cambridge, MA: Harvard University Press, 2009). Nicholas Breyfogle also looks at similar organization amongst the sectarian group of Molokans through efforts such as church building in Late Imperial Russia in "Prayer and the Politics of Place."
70. A detailed, chronological catalogue of all Rogozhskoe Trustees and later MSORK officers appears in Iukhimenko, *Staroobriadcheskii tsentr*, 163–5.
71. *Slovo Tserkvi'*, 1915 No. 14, 342.
72. *Tserkov'*, 1908 No. 11, 381–2.
73. Ibid., 382.
74. Ibid., 381.
75. *Tserkov'*, 1909 No. 10, 354.
76. Ibid.
77. Ibid., 354–5.
78. RGB, f. 246, k. 10, ed. 4, ll. 12–14ob.
79. Ibid.
80. RGB, f. 246, k. 6, ed. 6, l. 86.
81. *PSZ*, Ser. III, Vol. 25, 258.
82. RGB, f. 246, k. 6, ed. 6, ll. 99–99ob.
83. Ibid.
84. Ibid., ll. 39–39ob.

85. This is very similar to the arguments presented in the works by Robert Crummey, Irina Paert, and Roy Robson. Crummey, *Old Believers in the World of Antichrist* and *Old Believers in a Changing World*, Paert, *Old Believers, Religious Dissent and Gender*, and Robson, *Old Believers in Modern Russia.*
86. *Tserkov'*, 1908 No. 20, 716–18.
87. Ibid.
88. Ibid., 716.
89. RGB, f. 246, k. 92, ed. 33, l. 2ob.
90. RGB, f. 246, k. 6, ed. 6, ll. 99–99ob.
91. RGB, f. 246, k. 17, ed. 12, l. 13.
92. Ibid.
93. Ibid.
94. As relayed in the MSORK Council minutes of April 22, 1913: Upon Nicholas's arrival, Ivan Pugovkin, as representative of MSORK, and Archpriest Procopius, acting for the ailing Archbishop Ioann, welcomed Nicholas on behalf "of the entire Rogozhskoe community" and exchanged the traditional Easter greetings with the Emperor and his delegation. While both Pugovkin and Procopius both invited and implored Nicholas to tour the Rogozhskoe Cathedrals, Nicholas declined, stating that the next time he was in Moscow, and "had the time, [he] would willingly and gladly visit Rogozhskoe's grand temples." RGB, f. 246, k. 17, ed. 16, ll. 19ob–20.
95. See, Richard Wortman, *Scenarios of Power: Myth and Ceremony in Russian Monarchy*, Vol. II (Princeton: Princeton University Press, 1995).
96. *PSZ*, Ser. III, Vol. 25, 258.
97. *Tserkov'*, 1909 No. 10, 354.
98. *Tserkov'*, 1908 No. 21, 710.
99. Ibid.
100. Ibid., 711.
101. *Tserkov'*, 1908 No. 18, 621.
102. Ibid.
103. *Tserkov'*, 1910 No. 43, 1060.
104. Ibid.
105. RGB, f. 246, k. 6, ed. 6, l. 2.
106. Ibid., ll. 39–39ob.
107. Dmitri Urushev, "Nuzhno nam staroobriadcheskogo uchitelya," *Nezavisimaya*, July 12, 2011.
108. RGB, f. 246, k. 6, ed. 6, l. 2, *Russkoe Slov*, 1914 No. 17 (May 4), 131, and Urushev, "Nuzhno nam staroobriadcheskogo uchitelya."
109. Ibid.
110. For more on the role Russian Orthodox parish clergy played in social activities in Late Imperial Russia see, Jennifer Hedda, *His Kingdom Come: Orthodox Pastorship and Social Activism in Revolutionary Russia* (DeKalb: Northern Illinois University Press, 2008).

111. See, David Wartenweiler, *Civil Society and Academic Debate in Russia, 1905–1914* (Oxford: Clarendon Press, 1999).
112. RGB, f. 246, k. 6, ed. 6, ll. 2ob–3.
113. Ibid.
114. RGB, f. 246, k. 18, ed. 1, l. 62ob.
115. RGB, f. 246, k. 6, ed. 6, ll. 36–36ob.
116. For example, see, *Slovo Tserkvi*, 1915 No. 9, 207–10, and No. 10, 230–31,
117. Ibid.
118. Archbishop Ioann first publically expressed his desire for an Old Rite Metropolitan in a public letter to Rogozhskoe Cemetery on September 26, 1906. He continued urging recognition of a new Old Rite Metropolitanate until his death in April 1915. RGB, f. 246, k. 6, ed. 6, ll. 39–39ob.
119. Ibid.
120. RGB, f. 246, k. 18, ed. 4, ll. 60–60ob.
121. Rieber, *Merchants and Entrepreneurs*, 146.
122. Ibid., 146–47.
123. A number of historians compare Old Believer communities and individuals to the idea of the Protestant Work Ethic. See, Crummey, *Old Believers and the World of Antichrist*, Hudson, "Lords of the Urals," Michels, *At War with the Church*, Rieber, *Merchants and Entrepreneurs*, and Ruckman, *The Moscow Business Elite*.
124. See for example, Z. V. Grishina and V. P. Pushkov, "Moscovskii nekropol': o staroobriadcheskom kypechestve kontsa XVIII – nachala XX vekov." in *Mir staroobriadchestva*, Vol. 2 (Rossiiskoe universitetskoe izdatel'ctvo, Moscow 1995), 75–96.
125. See, William Blackwell, "The Old Believers and Private Enterprise," and Jo Ann Ruckman, *The Moscow Business Elite*.
126. Blackwell, "The Old Believers and Private Enterprise," 151–2.
127. Riabushinskii, *Kupchestvo moskovskoe*, 176.
128. Roy R. Robson, "Of Duma or Antichrist: Old Believers and Russian Politics, 1905–14," in *Church and Society in Modern Russia*, Elise Wirtschafter and Manfred Hildemeir, eds, (Wiesbaden: Harrassowitz Verlag, 2015), 173–83, and James L. West, "Philosophical Idealism and Utopian Capitalism: The Vekhi Authors and the Riabushinskii Circle," *Russian History*, Vol. 38, No. 4 (2011), 493–513.
129. See catalogue in Iukhimenko, *Staroobriadcheskii tsentr*, 163–5.
130. One of the Morozov's family-run factories, the Nikolskaia factory near Vladimir, alone produced an annual profit of between 3 million to 4 million rubles a year since the early 1890s. Ruckman, *The Moscow Business Elite*, 65–6. The Riabushinskiis also accumulated much of their fortune in textiles and Pavel Mikhailovich Riabushinskii, the father of the more famous Riabushinskii brothers, accumulated a personal fortune of over 20 million rubles, which he left to his sons, before his death in 1899. Violetta Sedova, "'Vse dlia dela – nichego dlia sebia': Brat'ia Riabushinskie," In *Tret'iakovskaia Galereia*, 2003 No. 1, 110–11.

131. "Moral capitalism" is the term used by both Linda Bowman and Mark Steinberg. See, Bowman, "Seeking Salvation," 323. Also, see, Mark D. Steinberg, *Moral Communities: The Culture of Class Relations in the Russian Printing Industry, 1867–1907*, (Berkeley, CA: University of California Press, 1992).
132. For more on Timofei's management, and the origins and outbreak of strikes in 1885, see, Bowman, "Seeking Salvation."
133. V. S. Lizunov, *Staroobriadcheskaya Palestina: Iz istorii Orekhovo-Zuevskogo kraia*, (Orekhovo-Zuevo, 1992), 58.
134. Ibid., 58–9.
135. Ibid., 62–7.
136. Savva Morozov, quoted in ibid., 66.
137. For greater detail on Savva's political views and ties to and even funding for Vladimir Lenin's *Iskra* periodical, see, Morozova and Potkina, *Savva Morozov*, Bowman, "Seeking Salvation," and Ruckman, *The Moscow Business Elite*.
138. Savva Morozov, quoted in ibid., 66.
139. See, Morozova and Potkina, *Savva Morozov*, 152–66.
140. P. V. Vlasov, *Blagotvoritel'nost' i miloserdie v Rossii*, (Moscow, 2001), 76.
141. Ibid., 76–7.
142. RGB, f. 246. k. 18. ed. 1. ll. 62–62ob.
143. Ulianova, "Not for Wealth but for God," 46.
144. Rieber, *Merchants and Entrepreneurs*, 291.
145. Ibid.
146. Sedova, "'Vse dlia dela – nichego dlia sebia': Brat'ia Riabushinskie," 110–11.
147. Ibid.
148. Ibid., 111–12.
149. Ibid., 114–15.
150. Ibid., 113–14, 117.
151. V. P. Riabushinskii, *Staroobriacdchestvo*, 171–2.
152. See, Blackwell, "The Old Believers and Private Enterprise," 144, 150–2, and Ruckman, *The Moscow Business Elite*, 155–9.
153. Morozova and Potkina, *Savva Morozov*, 183–8.
154. Ibid. Savva losing his post at the Nikolskoi plant remains one of the theories to the cause of a mental breakdown that eventually led to his committing suicide three months later in France. However, as previously noted, another theory suggests the Social Democrats and even Lenin targeted Savva for his refusal to continue funding them and shutting down their paper, *Iskra*, and ordered Savva's murder. See, Morozova and Potkina, *Savva Morozov*, 167–99.
155. Rieber, *Merchants and Entrepreneurs*, 293–6 and James L. West, "The Riabushinskii Circle," 42–3.
156. Rieber, *Merchants and Entrepreneurs*, 295.
157. Ibid. and West, "The Riabushinskii Circle," 45.
158. West, "The Riabushinskii Circle," 43.

159. Ibid., 45–6.
160. T. I. Butkevich, quoted in Alexandra S. Korros, "Nationalist Politics in the Russian Imperial State Council: Forming a New Majority, 1909–1910," *Emerging Democracy in Late Imperial Russia*, Mary Schaeffer Conroy, ed., (Niwot, CO: University Press of Colorado, 1998), 209.
161. West, "The Riabushinskii Circle," 44–7.
162. Rieber, *Merchants and Entrepreneurs*, 295 and West, "The Riabushinskii Circle," 45.
163. James L. West, "The Riabushinskii Circle: Burzhuaziia and Obshchestvennost' in Late Imperial Russia," In Edith W. Clowes et al., eds, (Princeton: Princeton University Press, 1991), 45–6.
164. Riabushinskii, *Staroobriadchestvo*, 12–20.
165. Ibid., 41.
166. Ibid.
167. Ibid.
168. RGB, f. 246, k. 6, ed. 6, l. 2, and V. F. Kozlov, "Moscovskoe staroobriadchestvo v pervoi treti XX v. (khrami, molel'ni, obshestvennie organizatsii i uchezhdeniya," In *Staroobriadchestvo v Rossii (XVII–XX vv.)*, (Moscow 1999), V. 2, 223–4.
169. *Tserkov'*, 1908 No. 22, 787.
170. Ibid.
171. Kozlov, "Moskovskoe staroobriadchestvo," 228.
172. *Tserkov'*, 1914 No. 35, 801–5.
173. RGB, f. 246, k. 17, ed. 15, l. 49ob.
174. See for example the founding of the new Old Rite church for the Vvedenskaya community, a priestly community located near the priestless Preobrazhenskoe Cemetery, *Tserkov'*, 1908 No. 3, 100.
175. *Tserkov'*, 1908 No. 19, 655, and No. 42, 1292–7.
176. *Tserkov'*, 1908 No. 46, 1404.
177. Ibid.
178. *Tserkov'*, 1909 No. 14, 485.
179. RGB, f. 246, k. 17, ed. 16, l. 21.
180. *Tserkov'*, 1914 No. 35, 801–5.
181. *Slovo Tserkvi*, 1915 No. 8, 177–8.
182. RGB, f. 246, k. 6, ed. 6, l. 82.
183. *Tserkov'*, 1911 No. 39, 951.
184. For more see, Robson, *Old Believers in Modern Russia* and James L. West, "The Neo-Old Believers of Moscow: Religious Revival and Nationalist Myth in Late Imperial Russia," *Canadian-American Slavic Studies*, Vol. 26, No. 1–3, 1992, 5–28.
185. See, Crummey, *The Old Believers and the World of Antichrist*, Paert, *Old Believers, Religious Dissent and Gender in Russia*, and "Regulating Old Believer Marriage," Robson, *Old Believers in Modern Russia*, Zenkovsky, *Russkoe staroobriadchestvo*, and De Simone, "An Old Believer 'Holy Moscow.'"

186. See Filaret, Metropolitan of Moscow, *Sobranie mnenii*, Vol. 4, 84. Quoted in N. I. Subbotin, ed., *Bratskoe Slovo*, 1891, 445, and N. I. Subbotin, "Iz istorii Rogozhskago Kladbisha," 446–7.
187. For more on Old Rite publishing efforts, see for example, Gary Marker, *Publishing, Printing, and the Origins of the Intellectual Life in Russia, 1700–1800*, Princeton Legacy Library Series, (Princeton: Princeton University Press, 2014), Paert, *Religious Dissent and Gender in Russia*, Roy Robson, "The Old Believer Press: 1905–1914," in *Russia's Dissenting Old Believers*, Georg Michels and Robert Nichols eds, (Minneapolis, MN: Minnesota Mediterranean and East European Monographs, 2009), 277–90. and Ulianova, "Old Believers and New Entrepreneurs."
188. Subbotin, "Iz istorii Rogozhskago Kladbisha."
189. See Iukhimenko, *Staroobriadcheskii tsentr*, Makarov, *Ocherk istorii, and* Robson, "The Old Believer Press."
190. *SobranieMVD*, 142–3.
191. *Narodnaia gazeta*, No. 184, August 10, 1906, 1.
192. See for examples from *Tserkov'* see publications from: February 17, 1908, 240; December 20, 1909, 1432; and March 28, 1910, 338.
193. *Tserkov'*, 1908 No. 29, 929.
194. Ibid.
195. Feodor Permiakov, *Vypiski iz Sviashchennago i sviatootecheskago pisaniia, i tvorenii sviatykh ottsov i uchitelei tserkov: o vnesenii patriarkh Nikonom i ego priemnikami novizn i lozhnago ucheniia; chast I*, (Moscow: P. P. Riabushinskii, 1910), viii.
196. Ibid., 21–3.
197. Ibid., 23ob–27ob.
198. Ibid., 23ob.
199. For more on the Uniate Church, see Note 20. Also see, Fr. John Meyendorff, *Rome, Constantinople, Moscow*, 108–10, 134–6, Stremooukhoff, "Moscow the Third Rome," 87–9, and Alef, "Muscovy and the Council of Florence," 399–401.
200. Permiakov, *Vypiski*, 28–34.
201. Ibid., 30.
202. Ibid., 63.
203. St. Peter of Damascus, quoted in ibid., 64.
204. For the details of the beard tax see, *PSZ*, Ser. I, Vol. 6, 641–2, 720, and Vol. 10, 624–6.
205. St. Jerome, quoted in Permiakov, *Vypiski*, 175ob.
206. RGB, f. 246, k. 156, ed. 2, ll. 5–6.
207. Ibid., L. 1–6. For published photographs, see, *Snimki drevnikh ikon i staroobriadcheskikh khramov rogozhskago kladbisha v Moskve.*
208. See, *Tserkov'*, 1908 No 10, 367.
209. RGB, f. 246, k. 6, ed. 6, l. 32.
210. Iukhimenko, *Staroobriadcheskii tsentr*, 145–6. For some works completed with Rogozhskoe's materials see: N. K. Nikol'skii, *Rukopisnaia knizhnost'*

drevnerusskikh bibliotek (XI–XVII vv.): Materiali dla slovaria vladel'tsev rukopisei, pistsov, perevodchikov, spravshikov i knigokhranitelei (Saint Petersburg, 1914); V. G. Druzhinin, *Pisaniia russkikh staroobriadtsev* (Saint Petersburg: M. A. Aleksandrova, 1912); and the collected essays by F. E. Mel'nikov-Piercheskii recently published by Rogozhskoe Cemetery, in 2007, *Chto takoe staroobriadchestvo* (Moscow: Russkoi Pravoslavnoi Staroobriadcheskoi Tserkvi, 2007).

Epilogue and Conclusion Tragedy and New Challenges

1. Vladimir V. Putin, quoted in *100-letnii iubilei raspechataniia altarei khramov staroobriadcheskogo Rogozhskogo kladbisha v Moskve* (Moscow 2005), 1.
2. Metropolitan Kornily of Moscow and All Russia. Quoted in "V Moskve idet vosstanovlenie obitli staroobriadtsev – Rogozhskoi slobodi," *TV Tsentr,* April 18, 2009.
3. Iukhimenko, ed., *Drevnie i dukhovnie sviatini staroobriadchestva,* No. 6.
4. With the Bolshevik takeover of Moscow on November 3, the note makes clear that Rogozhskoe remained well aware of events throughout Russia, and the very real threat that the Bolsheviks posed for the community. Ibid.
5. OPI GIM, f. 54, ed. 825, l. 110, and TsGAMO, f. 966, op. 4, d. 1036, l. 9.
6. TsGAMO, f. 966, op. 4, d. 1036, l. 8.
7. TsGAMO, f. 966, op. 4, d. 1059, ll. 165–65ob.
8. Dmitrii Yrushev, "Iz kolena Avvakumova: Mitropolit Alimpii pervishe vsego tsenil molitvu i bogosluzhenie," *Nezavisimaia gazeta,* 18 January 2006, http://religion.ng.ru/printed/91765.
9. Ibid.
10. Ibid.
11. Ibid.
12. *TV Tsentr,* "Rogozhskoi slobodi."
13. *RIA Novosti*, "Vlasti Moskvi reshili ne restavrirovat' Rogozhskuiu slobodu," 18 November 2011, http://ria.ru/moscow/20111118/491773651.html.
14. Ibid.

BIBLIOGRAPHY

Primary Sources

Archival Sources

Hilandar Research Library and Resource Center for Medieval Slavic Studies, Columbus, OH (Noted as HRL)
  Pimen M. Sofronov Collection

Otdel Pis'mennikh Istochnikov Gosudarstvennogo Istoricheskogo Muzeia, Moscow (Noted as OPI GIM)
  Fond 54

Rossiiskaia Gosudarstvennaia Biblioteka, Moscow (Noted as RGB)
  Otdel Rukopisei Fond 246, Rogozhskoe Cemetery
  Otdel Rukopisei Fond 247, Rogozhskoe Cemetery

Rossiiskii Gosudarstvennyi Arkhiv Drevnikh Aktov, Moscow (Noted as RGADA)
  Fond 1183, Moscow Secret Committee on Old Believers

Tsentral'nyi Gosudarstvennyi Arkhiv Moskovskoi Oblasti, Moscow (Noted as TsGAMO)
  Fond 966, Otdela muzeev Glavnauki Narkomprosa

Laws and Regulations

Polnoe sobranie zakonov Rossiiskoi Imperii. Series I, 1647–1825 (Saint Petersburg, 1830), Vols. 1–45.

Polnoe sobranie zakonov Rossiiskoi Imperii. Series II, 1825–1881 (Saint Petersburg, 1911), Vols. 1–27.

Polnoe sobranie zakonov Rossiiskoi Imperii, Series III, 1881–1913 (Saint Petersburg, 1916), Vols. 1–33.

Sobranie postanovlenii po chasti raskola (Ministry of the Interior, Saint Petersburg, 1875).

Sobranie postanovlenii po chasti raskola sostoiavshikhsia po vedomstvu Sv. Sinoda (Saint Petersburg 1860), Vols 1–2.

Newspapers

Narodnaia gazeta (1905–6)
Russkoe Slov (1914)
Slovo tserkvi (1914–17)
Tserkov' (1908–14)

Published Sources, Articles, Memoirs, and Documents

Arsenii, Bishop of the Urals. *Zhizn' i podvigi Antoniia, staroobriadcheskogo arkhiepiskopa Moskovskogo i Vladimirskogo*. Moscow: MP "Pechatnik," 1995.

Bartenev, P. I., ed. *Osmnadtsatyi vek: istoricheskii sbornik*, Vol. I. (Moscow, 1868).

Belliustin, I. S. *Description of the Clergy in Rural Russia: The Memoir of a Nineteenth-Century Parish Priest*. Gregory L. Freeze, trans. (Ithaca, NY: Cornell University Press, 1985).

Bulgakov, S. *Handbook for Church Servers*. (Kharkov, 1900).

de Shamborant, A. V. *Raspechatanie altarei v khramakh staroobriadcheskogo Rogozhskogo kladbisha 16 apr. 1905 g.* (Moscow 1905).

Drozdov, Metropolitan Filaret. *Sobranie mnenie i otsyvov Filareta, mitropolita Moskovskago i Kolomenskago, po dielam pravoslavnoi tserkvi na Vostokie.* (Saint Petersburg: 1888).

Filofei, "Filofei's Concept of the 'Third Rome.'" *Medieval Russia: A Source Book, 850–1700*. Basil Dmytryshyn, trans., ed., (Gulf Breeze, FL: Academic International Press, 2000), 259–61.

Giliarovskii, V. A. "Raspechatanie altarei Rogozhskogo kladbisha." *Staraia vera: Staroobriadcheskiia Khrestomatiia*, A.C. Ribakov ed., (Moscow: I. D. Sytin, 1914).

Ivanova, T. A. ed., *Iz istorii Belokrinitskoi Ierarkhii: sbornik.* (Moscow: VIKTAN-poligraf, 2007).

Katkov, M. N. ed., "Iz rasskazov i zapisok V. A. Sapelkina." *Russkii vestnik*. No. 11, (Moscow, 1864).

Kirillov, I. A. *Tretii Rim: Ocherk istoricheskogo razvitiia idei russkogo messianizma.* (Moskva: Izdatel'stvo "Tretii Rim," 1996).

Lanskoi, Sergei. *Iz istorii Rogozhskago kladbishcha.* (Moscow: Tip. E. Lissnera I IU. Romana, 1892).

Levshin, Archimandrite Platon. *Polnoe sobranie sochinenii mitropolita Platona*, (Saint Petersburg: P. P. Soikina, 1913).

Marinicheva (Oleneva), G. *Istoriia Rogozhskogo poselka–tsentra staroobriadchestva*. (Moscow, 2004).

Materialy k istorii Prokhorovskoi trekhgornoi manufaktury i torgovo-promyshlennoi dieiatel'nosti sem'i Prokhorovykh: gody 1799–1915. (Moscow: "Terra": Izdatel'skii dom "Ekonomicheskaia gazeta," 1996).

Mel'nikov, P. I. *Istoricheskie ocherki popovshini.* (Moscow: Katkov, 1864).

Meshcherskii, V. P., *Ocherki nyneshnei obshchestvennoi zhizni v Rossii: Pis'ma iz srednykh Veliko-Russkikh gubernii*. (Saint Petersburg: Ministry of the Interior, 1868).

Nestor-Iskander. *The Tale of Constantinople, Of its Origin and Capture by the Turks in the Year 1453*. (New Rochelle, NY: A.D. Caratzas, 1998).

Permiakov, F. *Vypiski iz Sviashchennago i sviatootecheskago pisaniia, i tvorenii sviatykh ottsov i uchitelei tserkov: o vnesenii patriarkh Nikonom i ego priemnikami novizn i lozhnago ucheniia; chast I*. (Moscow: P.P. Riabushinskii, 1910).

Petrov, Avvakum. *Archpriest Avvakum the Life Written by Himself*, Kenneth N. Brostrom, trans. (Ann Arbor, MI: Michigan Slavic Publications, 1979).

Popov, N. I. *Sbornik iz istorii staroobriadchestva.* (Moscow, 1866) Vol. I–III.

Riabushinskii, Vladimir P. *Staroobriadchestvo i russkoe religioznoe chuvstvo.* (Moskva-Ierusalim: "Mosti," 1994).

———. *Kupchestvo moskovskoe.* (Moscow: Rodina, 1992).

RIA Novosti. "Vlasti Moskvi reshili ne restavrirovat' Rogozhskuiu slobodu." November 18, 2011, http://ria.ru/moscow/20111118/491773651.html.

Russkaia Pravoslavniia Staroobriadcheskaia Tserkov', *100-letnii iubilei raspechataniia altarei khramov staroobriadcheskogo Rogozhskogo kladbisha v Moskve.* (Moscow: Vestnik mitropolii, 2005).

———. "Na Rogozhskom sostoialos' zasedanie Moskovskoi eparkhii," March 19, 2012.

Senatov, V. G. *Filosofiia istorii staroobriadchestva.* (Moscow: Biblioteka zhurnal "Tserkov'," 1995).

Snimki drevnikh ikon i staroobriadcheskikh khramov rogozhskago kladbisha v Moskve. (Moscow: Tipo-lithografiia T-vo I.N. Kushnerev i Ko., 1913).

Subbotin, N. I., ed., *Bratskoe Slovo: zhurnal, posviashennii izuchenii raskola.* (Moscow, 1891).

———. *Istoriia Belokrinitskoi ierarkhii.* (Moscow: T. Ris, 1874).

———. *Materiali dlia istorii tak nazivaemoi avstriiskoi, ili belokrinitskoi ierarkhii.* (Moscow: E. Lissnera i Iu. Romana, 1897).

TV Tsentr, Moscow, "V Moskve idet vosstanovlenie obiteli staroobriadtsev – Rogozhskoi slobodi," April 18, 2009.

Xenos {I. G. Kabanov}, *Okruzhnoe poslanie Rossiiskikh arkhipastirei Belokrinitskoi ierarkhii*, Feb. 24, 1862.

Yrushev, Dmitri. "Iz kolena Avvakumova: Mitropolit Alimpii pervishe vsego tsenil molitvu i bogosluzhenie." *Nezavisimaia*, 18 January 2006.

Secondary Sources

Alef, Gustave. "Muscovy and the Council of Florence." *Slavic Review*, Vol. 20, No. 3 (October 1961), 389–401.

Alexander, John T. *Emperor of the Cossacks: Pugachev and the Frontier Jacquerie of 1773–1775.* Lawrence, KS: Coronado Press, 1973.

———. *Bubonic Plague in Early Modern Russia: Public Health and Urban Disaster.* (Baltimore, MD: Johns Hopkins University Press, 1980).

Andreev, V. V. *Raskol i ego znachenie v narodnoi russkoi istorii.* (Osnabruck: Otto Zeller, 1965).

Anisimov, Evgeni V. *The Reforms of Peter the Great: Progress through Coercion in Russia.* John T. Alexander, trans. (Armonk, NY: M.E. Sharpe, Inc., 1993).

Ascher, Abraham. *The Revolution of 1905*, Vols 1 and 2 (Stanford: Stanford University Press, 1992).

Bartenev, A. N. *Staraia vera kazakov* (Moscow: Spolokhi, 2001).

Blackwell, William L. "The Old Believers and the Rise of Private Industrial Enterprise in Early Nineteenth Century Moscow." *Slavic Review*, Vol. 24 No. 3 (Sep. 1965), 407–24.

Bowman, Linda. "Moral Economies and Management at the Morozov Mills, 1885–1905." *Social History*, Vol. 28, No. 3 (October 2003), 322–45.

Bradley, Joseph. *Voluntary Associations in Tsarist Russia: Science, Patriotism, and Civil Society.* (Cambridge, MA: Harvard University Press, 2009).

Breyfogle, Nicholas. *Heretics and Colonizers: Forging Russia's Empire in the South Caucasus*. (Ithaca, NY: Cornell University Press, 2005).

———. "Prayer and the Politics of Place: Molokan Church Building, Tsarist Law, and the Quest for a Public Sphere in Late Imperial Russia." *Sacred Stories: Religion and Spirituality in Modern Russian Culture*. ed. Heather Coleman and Mark Steinberg. Indiana University Press, 2007, 222–52.

Bushkovitch, Paul. *The Merchants of Moscow, 1580–1650* (Cambridge: Cambridge University Press, 1980).

Cherniavsky, Michael. "The Old Believers and the New Religion." *The Structure of Russian History: Interpretive Essays*. Michael Cherniavsky, ed., (New York: Random House, 1970, 140–90).

———. "The Reception of the Council of Florence in Moscow," *Church History*, Vol. 24, No. 4 (December 1955), 347–59.

Clay, John Eugene. "Russian Peasant Religion and its Representation: The Christ-faith (Khristovshchina) and the Origins of the 'Flagellant' Myth, 1666–1837," (Ph.D. diss., University of Chicago, 1989).

Coleman, Heather. *Russian Baptists and Spiritual Revolution, 1905–1929*. (Bloomington, IN: Indiana University Press, 2005).

Cracraft, James. *The Revolution of Peter the Great*. (Cambridge, MA: Harvard University Press, 2003).

Crummy, Robert O. *The Old Believers and the World of Antichrist*. (Madison, WI: University of Wisconsin Press, 1970).

———. *Old Believers in a Changing World*. (DeKalb, IL: Northern Illinois University Press, 2011).

———. "Old Belief as Popular Religion: New Approaches." *Slavic Review*, Vol. 52 No. 4 (Winter 1993), 700–12.

de Madariaga, Isabel. *Ivan the Terrible, First Tsar of Russia*. (New Haven: Yale University Press, 2005).

De Simone, Peter T. "An Old Believer 'Holy Moscow' in Imperial Russia: Community and Identity in the History of the Rogozhskoe Cemetery Old Believers, 1771–1917." (Ph.D. diss., Ohio State University, 2012).

Dergachev, V. V. *Ikonopisnaia masterskaia N.M. Sofonova, Palezh: materiali k istorii roda palekhskikh ikonopistsev Sofonovikh, ikh khudozhestvennogo naslediia i deiatel'nosti po restavratsii drevnerusskikh pamiatnikov, antologiia, al'bom*. (Moscow: Glasnost', 2010).

Druzhinin, V. G. *Pisaniia russkikh staroobriadtsev*. (Saint Petersburg: M. A. Aleksandrova, 1912).

Dudley, Guilford III. *Religion on Trial: Mircea Eliade and His Critics*. (Philadelphia, PA: Temple University Press, 1977).

Durkheim, Emile. "The Elementary Forms of Religious Life." W.S.F. Pickering, ed., *Durkheim on Religion*. (Atlanta, GA: Scholars Press, 1994).

Engelstein, Laura. *Castration and the Heavenly Kingdom: A Russian Folktale*. (Ithaca, NY: Cornell University Press, 1999).

Esin, B. I. *Reportazhi Giliarovskogo*. (Moskva: Moskovskogo universiteta, 1985).

Evseeva, L. M. and Kate Cook, eds, *A History of Icon Painting: Sources, Traditions, Present Day*. (Moscow: Grand Holdings Publishers, 2005).

Field, Daniel. *Rebels in the Name of the Tsar*. (Boston, MA: Houghton Mifflin, 1976).

Firsov, N. N. *Pugachevshchina: Opyt sotsial'no-psikhologicheskoi kharakteristiki*. (Moscow: Gos. izd-vo, 1921).

Gill, Joseph. *The Council of Florence.* (Cambridge: Cambridge University Press, 1959).

Grishina, Z. V. and V. P. Pushkov. "Moskovskii nekropol': o staroobriadcheskom kupechestve kontsa XVIII–nachala XX vekov." in *Mir staroobriadchestva*, Vol. 2. (Moscow: Rossiiskoe universitetskoe izdatel'stvo 1995), 75–96.

Habermas, Jurgen. *The Structural Transformation of the Public Sphere: An Inquiry into a Category of Bourgeois Society.* Sixth Edition. (Cambridge, MA: The MIT Press, 1991).

Hedda, Jennifer. *His Kingdom Come: Orthodox Pastorship and Social Activism in Revolutionary Russia* (DeKalb, IL: Northern Illinois University Press, 2008).

Heretz, Leonid. *Russia on the Eve of Modernity: Popular Religion and Traditional Culture under the Last Tsars* (Cambridge: Cambridge University Press, 2008).

Hintermaier, John M. "The First Modern Refugees? Charity, Entitlement, and Persuasion in the Huguenot Immigration of the 1680s." *Albion*, Vol. 32 No. 3 (Fall 2000), 429–49.

Hudson, Hugh D., Jr. "Lords of the Urals: The Demidov Entrepreneurial Family and the Rise of the Iron Industry in Eighteenth-Century Russia," (Ph.D. diss., University of North Carolina at Chapel Hill, 1981).

———. "Religious Persecution and Industrial Policy in the Reign of Anna I: V.N. Tatishchev and the Old Believers Reconsidered." *Jahrbücher für Geschichte Osteuropas*, Vol. 50 No. 1 (2002), 22–36.

Hughes, Lindsey. *Russia in the Age of Peter the Great.* New Haven: Yale University Press, 1998.

Iasevich-Borodaevskaia, V. I. *Bor'ba za veru.* (Saint Petersburg, 1912).

Iukhimenko, E. M. *Staroobriadcheskii tsentr za Rogozhskoi zastavoiu.* Moskva: Iazyki slavianskoi kul'tury, 2005.

Iukhimenko, E. M. et al., eds, *Drevnosti i dukhovni sviatini staroobriadchestva: Ikoni, knigi, oblacheniia, predmeti tserkovnogo ubranstva Arkhiereiskoi riznitsi i Pokrovskogo sobora pri Rogozhskom kladbishe v Moskve.* (Moskva: Interbuk-biznes 2005).

Kadson, I. Z. "Vosstanie Pugacheva i Raskola." *Ezhegodnik muzeia istorii religii i ateizma.* Vol. 4. (Moscow and Leningrad: Akademia nauk SSSR: Muzei istorii religii i ateizma, 1960), 222–38.

Kappeler, Andreas. *The Russian Empire: A Multiethnic History.* (Harlow, England: Pearson Education Limited, 2001).

———. "Czarist Policy toward the Muslims of the Russian Empire." *Muslim Communities Reemerge: Historical Perspectives on Nationality, Politics, and Opposition in the Former Soviet Union and Yugoslavia*, Edward Allworth, ed., (Durham, NC: Duke University Press, 1994).

Katunin, Iu. A. and A. V. Belskii. "Etapi bor'bi za sozdanie tserkvi u staroobriadtsev," *Kul'tura narodov prichernomor'ia.* No. 81, 2006.

Korros, Alexandra S. "Nationalist Politics in the Russian Imperial State Council: Forming a New Majority, 1909–1910." In, *Emerging Democracy in Late Imperial Russia*, Mary Schaeffer Conroy, ed., Niwot, CO: University Press of Colorado, 1998, 198–227.

Kozlov, V. F. "Moskovskoe staroobriadchestvo v pervoi treti XX v. (khrami, molel'ni, obshestvennie organizatsii i uchezhdeniia)." *Staroobriadchestvo v Rossii (XVII–XXvv.)* Vol. 2. Moscow 1999.

Lebedev, E. E. *Edinoverie v protivodeistvii russkomu obriadovomu raskolu: Ocherk po istorii i statistike edinoveriia s obzorov sushestvuoshich o nem mnenii i prilozheniiami.* Novgorod, 1904.

Lindenmeyr, Adele. *Poverty is Not a Vice: Charity, Society, and the State in Imperial Russia.* (Princeton, NJ: Princeton University Press, 1996).

Lizunov, V. S. *Staroobriadcheskii Palestina: Iz istorii Orekhovo-Zuevskogo kraia.* Orekhovo-Zuevo, 1992.

Makarov, V. E. *Ocherk istorii Rogozhskogo kladbisha v Moskve (K 140-letiu ego sushestvovaniia: 1771–1911 gg.).* (Moscow: BARC, 1994).

Maloney, George. *A History of Orthodox Theology Since 1453.* (Belmont, MA: Nordland Publishers, 1976).

Marker, Gary. *Publishing, Printing, and the Origins of the Intellectual Life in Russia, 1700–1800.* Princeton Legacy Library Series. (Princeton, NJ: Princeton University Press, 2014).

Marsden, Thomas. *The Crisis of Religious Toleration in Imperial Russia: Bibikov's System for the Old Believers, 1841–1855* (Oxford: Oxford University Press, 2015).

Martin, Alexander M. *Enlightened Metropolis: Constructing Imperial Moscow, 1762–1855.* (Oxford: Oxford University Press, 2013).

———. *"Moscow Society in the Napoleonic Era: Cultural Tradition and Political Stability."* (Washington, DC: National Council for Eurasian and East European Research, 2004).

Matejic, Predrag. "Rediscovered Texts from the *Life of St. Sergius of Radonezh:* Understanding Russia and Russian Orthodoxy in the 16th Century." *The Trinity-Sergius Lavra in Russian History and Culture.* Vladimir Tsurikov, ed., (Jordanville, NY: Holy Trinity Seminary Press, 2005), 251–98.

Mel'nikov, F. E. *Chto takoe staroobriadchestvo* (Moscow: Russkoi Pravoslavnoi Staroobriadcheskoi Tserkvi, 2007).

———. *Kratkia istoriia drevlepravoslavnoi (staroobriadcheskoi) tserkvi.* (Barnaul: Barnaul State Pedagogical Institute, 1999).

Merridale, Catherine. *Red Fortress: History and Illusion in the Kremlin* (New York: Metropolitan Books, 2013).

Meyendorff, John. *Rome, Constantinople, Moscow: Historical and Theological Studies* (Crestwood, NY: St. Vladimir's Seminary Press, 1996).

Meyendorff, Paul. *Russia, Ritual, and Reform: The Liturgical Reforms of Nikon in the 17th Century* (Crestwood, NY: St. Vladimir's Seminary Press, 1991).

Michels, Georg. *At War with the Church: Religious Dissent in Seventeenth-Century Russia.* (Stanford: Stanford University Press, 1999).

Michels, Georg and Robert L. Nichols, eds. *Russia's Dissident Old Believers, 1650–1950* (Minneapolis: University of Minnesota Press, 2009).

Morozova, T. P. and I. V. Potkina. *Savva Morozov* (Moscow: Russkaia kniga, 1998).

Nathans, Benjamin. *Beyond the Pale: The Jewish Encounter with Late Imperial Russia* (Berkeley, CA: University of California Press, 2002).

Nikol'skii, N. K. *Rukopisnaia knizhnost' drevnerusskikh bibliotek (XI–XVII vv.): Materiali dlia slovaria vladel'tsev rukopisei, pistsov, perevodchikov, spravshikov i knigokhranitelei.* (Saint Petersburg, 1914).

Nil'skii, I. F. *Semeinaia zhizn' v russkom raskole* (Saint Petersburg: Pechatano v tip. departmenta Udielov, 1868).

O'Rourke, Shane. *The Cossacks* (Manchester: Manchester University Press, 2007).

Ostrowski, Donald. "'Moscow the Third Rome' as a Historical Ghost," *Byzantium: Faith and Power (1261–1557): Perspectives on Late Byzantine Art and Culture*, Sarah T. Brooks, ed., (New York: Metropolitan Museum of Art, 2006) 170–9.

Paert, Irina. *Old Believers, Religious Dissent and Gender in Russia, 1760–1850* (Manchester: Manchester University Press, 2003).

———. "Regulating Old Believer Marriage: Ritual, Legality, and Conversion in Nicholas I's Russia." *Slavic Review*, Vol. 63 No. 3 (Fall 2004), 555–76.

———. "'Two or Twenty Million?' The Languages of Official Statistics and Religious Dissent in Imperial Russia." *Ab Imperio*, 3 (2006), 75–98.

Pera, Pia. "The Secret Committee on the Old Believers: Moving away from Catherine II's Policy of Religious Toleration." *Russia in the Age of the Enlightenment, Essays for Isabel de Madariaga.* Rodger Bartlett and Janet M. Hartley, eds, (London: MacMillan and University of London Press, 1990), 222–41.

Pervushin, M. V. "Edinoverie do i posle mitropolita Platona (Levshina)." http://www.bogoslov.ru/text/315404.html, February 15, 2009 (accessed November 18, 2011).

Poe, Marshall. "Moscow, the Third Rome: The Origins and Transformations of a 'Pivotal Moment,'" *Jahrbucher fur Geschichte Osteuropas*, Vol. 49, No. 3 (2001), 412–29.

Polunov, A. Iu. *Pod vlastiu ober-prokurora: gosudarstvo i tserkov' v epokhu Aleksandra III* (Moscow: AIRO-XX, 1996).

Posochin, Mikhail V. *Pamiatniki architektury Moskvy. Okrestnosti staroi Moskvy (iugo-vostochnaia i iuzhnaia chasti goroda)* (Moscow: Iskusstvo, 2007).

Pospielovsky, Dimitry. *The Orthodox Church in the History of Russia* (Crestwood, NY: St. Vladimir's Seminary Press, 1998).

Provorikhina, A. S. "Moskovskoe staroobriadchestvo," *Moskva v ee proshlom i nastoiashchem*, 10th edn (Moscow, 1912).

Raskov, D. E. *Ekonomicheskie instituty staroobriadchestva.* (Saint Petersburg: Saint Petersburg State University, 2012).

Riasanovsky, Nicholas V. *Nicholas I and Official Nationality in Russia, 1825–1855* (Berkeley, CA: University of California Press, 1959).

Rieber, Alfred J. *Merchants and Entrepreneurs in Imperial Russia* (Chapel Hill, NC: University of North Carolina Press, 1982).

Robson, Roy R. *Old Believers in Modern Russia* (DeKalb, IL: Northern Illinois University Press, 1995).

———. "An Architecture of Change: Old Believer Liturgical Spaces in Late Imperial Russia." Stephen K. Baldwin, ed., *Seeking God: The Recovery of Religious Identity in Orthodox Russia, Ukraine, and Georgia* (DeKalb, IL: Northern Illinois University Press, 1993).

———. "Of Duma or Antichrist: Old Believers and Russian Politics, 1905–14," Elise Wirtschafter and Manfred Hildemeier eds, *Church and Society in Modern Russia: Essays in Honor of Gregory L. Freeze.* (Wiesbaden: Harrassowitz Verlag, 2015).

———. "The Old Believer Press: 1905–1914," Georg Michels and Robert Nichols, eds, *Russia's Dissenting Old Believers* (Minneapolis, MN: Minnesota Mediterranean and East European Monographs, 2009, 277–90).

Rogers, Douglas. *The Old Faith and the Russian Land: A Historical Ethnography of Ethics in the Urals* (Ithaca, NY: Cornell University Press, 2009).

Romaniello, Matthew Paul. "Absolutism and Empire: Governance on Russia's Early-Modern Frontier," (Ph.D. diss., The Ohio State University, 2003).

———. "The Profit Motive: Regional Economic Development in Muscovy after the Conquest of Kazan." *The Journal of European Economic History*, Vol. 33 No. 3 (Winter 2004), 663–85.

Rose, Fr. Seraphim. *The Northern Thebaid: Monastic Saints of the Russian North*. (Plantina, CA: Saint Herman Press, 1995).

Rowland, Daniel B. "Moscow – The Third Rome or the New Israel?" *Russian Review*, Vol. 55, No. 4 (Oct. 1996), 591–614.

Ruckman, Jo Ann. *The Moscow Business Elite: A Social and Cultural Portrait of Two Generations, 1840–1905* (DeKalb, IL: Northern Illinois University Press, 1984).

Sedova, Violetta. "'Vse dlia dela – nichego dlia sebia': Brat'ia Riabushinskie," *Tret'iakovskaia Galereia*, 2003 No. 1, 108–17.

Shchapov, A. *Russkii Raskol staroobriadstva, razsmatrivaemyi v sviazi s vnutrennim sostoianiem russkoi tserkvi i grazhdanstvennosti v XVII veke i pervoi polovine XVIII*. (Kazan: Izdanie knigoprodavtsa Ivana Dubrovina, 1859).

Shevzov, Vera. *Russian Orthodoxy on the Eve of Revolution* (Oxford: Oxford University Press, 2004).

———. "Letting the People into the Church: Reflections on Orthodoxy and Community in Late Imperial Russia," Valerie A. Kivelson and Robert H. Greene, eds, *Orthodox Russia: Belief and Practice Under the Tsars* (University Park, PA: Pennsylvania State University Press, 2003, 59–77).

Slobodskoi, Archpriest Seraphim. "Bells and Russian Orthodox Peals." *The Law of God* (Jordanville, NY: Holy Trinity Monastery, 1996).

Smirnova, Engelina. "The Icons of Moscow and Local Artistic Schools, 15th – early 16th centuries." L. M. Evseeva and Kate Cook, eds, *A History of Icon Painting* (Moscow, 2005).

Steinberg, Mark D. *Moral Communities: The Culture of Class Relations in the Russian Printing Industry, 1867–1907*. (Berkeley, CA: University of California Press, 1992).

Strayer, Brian E. *Huguenots and Camisards as Aliens in France, 1598–1789: The Struggle for Religious Toleration*. (Lewiston, NY: The Edwin Mellen Press, 2001).

Stremooukhoff, Dmitri. "Moscow the Third Rome: Sources of the Doctrine." *Speculum*, Vol. 28, No. 1 (January 1953), 84–101.

Tarasov, Oleg. *Icon and Devotion: Sacred Spaces in Imperial Russia*, Robin Milner-Gulland, trans. (London: Reaktion Books Ltd., 2002).

Ulianova, Galina. "Not for Wealth but for God." *Russian Studies in History*, Vol. 39, No. 2 (Fall 2000), 28–51.

———. "Old Believers and New Entrepreneurs: Religious Belief and Ritual in Merchant Moscow," In *Merchant Moscow: Images of Russia's Vanished Bourgeoisie*, James L. West and Y. A. Petrov, eds, (Princeton: Princeton University Press, 1998).

Urushev, Dmitri A. "Tisiachi ikh bili ubiti ...," http://biyskrpsc.narod.ru/Ist_Ger.html

Vasil'evskii, M. N. *Gosudarstvennaia sistema otnoshenii k staroobriadtsam v tsarstvovanie imperatora Nikolaia I*. (Kazan: Tsentr. tip., 1914).

Vlasov, P. V. *Blagotvoritel'nost' i miloserdie v Rossii*. (Moscow: Centrpoligraf, 2001).

Vorontsova, Lyudmila and Sergei Filatov. "Paradoxes of the Old Believer Movement." *Religion, State and Society*, Vol. 28, No. 1, 2000, 53–67.

Waldron, Peter. *The End of Imperial Russia, 1855–1917* (New York: St. Martin's Press, 1997).

———. "Religious Reform after 1905: Old Believers and the Orthodox Church," *Oxford Slavonic Papers*, Vol. 20 (1987): 110–39.

———. "Religious Toleration in Late Imperial Russia," Olga Crisp and Linda Edmondson, eds, *Civil Rights in Imperial Russia* (Oxford: Clarendon Press, 1989, 103–20).

Wartenweiler, David. *Civil Society and Academic Debate in Russia, 1905–1914* (Oxford: Clarendon Press, 1999).

Werth, Paul W. *At the Margins of Orthodoxy: Mission, Governance, and Confessional Politics in Russia's Volga-Kama Region, 1827–1905* (Ithaca, NY: Cornell University Press, 2002).

———. "Orthodoxy as Ascription (and Beyond): Religious Identity on the Edges of the Orthodox Community." *Orthodox Russia: Belief and Practice under the Tsars*, Kivelson, Valerie A. and Robert H. Greene, eds, (University Park, PA: Pennsylvania State University Press, 2003).

———. *The Tsar's Foreign Faiths: Toleration and the Fate of Religious Freedom in Imperial Russia*. (Oxford: Oxford University Press, 2014).

West, James L. and Iuri A. Petrov, eds, *Merchant Moscow: Images of Russia's Vanished Bourgeoisie*. (Princeton, NJ: Princeton University Press, 1998).

———. "Philosophical Idealism and Utopian Capitalism: The Vekhi Authors and the Riabushinskii Circle," *Russian History*, Vol. 38, No. 4, 2011, 493–513.

———. "The Neo-Old Believers of Moscow: Religious Revival and Nationalist Myth in Late Imperial Russia," *Canadian-American Slavic Studies*, Vol. 26, No. 1–3, 1992, 5–28.

———. "The Riabushinskii Circle: Burzhuaziia and Obshchestvennost' in Late Imperial Russia," Edith W. Clowes et al., eds, (Princeton: Princeton University Press, 1991) 41–56.

White, James Mathew. "A Bridge to Schism: Edinoverie, Russian Orthodoxy, and the Ritual Formation of Confessions, 1800–1918," (Ph.D. diss., European University Institute, 2014).

Wortman, Richard. *Scenarios of Power: Myth and Ceremony in Russian Monarchy*, Vol. II. (Princeton: Princeton University Press, 1995).

Zenkovsky, Serge A. *Russkoe staroobriadchestvo: Dukhovnye dvizheniia semnadtsatogo veka*. (Munich, 1970).

———. "The Russian Church Schism: Its Background and Repercussions," *Russian Review* Vol. 16, No. 4, (Oct., 1957): 37–58.

Zernov, Nicolas. *Eastern Christendom: A Study of the Origin and Development of the Eastern Orthodox Church*. (New York: Putnam, 1961).

Zhuk, Sergei I. *Russia's Lost Reformation: Peasants, Millennialism, and Radical Sects in Southern Russia and Ukraine, 1830–1917* (Baltimore: Johns Hopkins University Press, 2004).

Zitser, Ernest. *The Transfigured Kingdom: Sacred Parody and Charismatic Authority at the Court of Peter the Great*. (Ithaca, NY: Cornell University Press, 2004).

INDEX

Alexander I, 50, 79
  policies on Old Believers, 71–2
Alexander II, 93, 95–6
  assassination and Rogozhskoe response, 138–9
  Old Rite reform, 121–5
Alexander III, 118, 138–42, 145
  ukaz of May 3, 1883, 118, 142–3
Alexis, 2, 14, 20, 139, 205
Alimpii, Metropolitan of All Rus' of the Russian Orthodox Old Rite Church, 212
All-Russian Congress of Old Believer Peasants, 192–3, 200–1
almshouses, 26, 46–7, 62–3, 75–7, 82, 90–2, 114–17, 171, 174, 198, 207
Ambrose, Metropolitan of the Belokrinitskaya Hierarchy, 85–7, 101–2, 104
  Okruzhnoe poslanie debate, 108, 111–12
Antichrist, Old Rite perception of, 3, 14, 18, 32, 104, 108, 122–3, 139, 193, 205
Antonii, Belokrinitskaya Archbishop of Moscow and All Rus', 101–2
  Okruzhnoe poslanie debate, 108, 110–12
  Rogozhskoe Cemetery, 102–3
architecture
  Rogozhskoe use of, 48–52, 163, 166–8, 214 *see also* bell tower; Intercession Cathedral; Nativity Cathedral
Arseniev, Alexander, Rogozhskoe priest, 81, 84
art, 188–90, 194, 207
Avvakum, 16, 54, 56

banking
  Rogozhskoe influence in, 116, 186, 189
barin, 194
beards,
  as part of Old Rite identity, 16, 33, 38, 42, 92, 119, 184, 194, 206
beglopopovtsy, 112, 177
Bekleshov, Alexander, Governor-General of Moscow, 50
Belaia Krinitsa Monastery, 85–6, 112, 122
  as center of Belokrinitskaya Hierarchy, 100–4, 182
beliefs,
  Old Rite effort to define *see* corruptions of Orthodoxy; Nikonian Reforms; *Vypiski* of 1910, defining the Old Rite

bell tower, 163–8
Belokrinitskaya Hierarchy, 7, 26, 78–9, 96, 98, 120, 146, 148, 175, 211–12
  Creation, 7, 71, 85–7
  debate on spiritual validity, 100–1, 103–13, 199
  role in Rogozhskoe after 1905, 170, 172–3, 176–7, 182, 198
  role in Rogozhskoe Cemetery, 4, 8, 26, 86–8, 100, 102–4, 108–13
  State response to, 87–8, 90, 122, 142–45
bespopovtsy, 4, 103–4, 128 *see also* Old Believers, priestless movement
Bibikov, Dmitri, Minister of Internal Affairs, 70, 90
bishops
  Old Rite, 86, 104–5, 109–12, 175–6
  Russian Orthodox, 11, 39, 41, 107, 182, 211–12
Bloody Sunday, 147, 150
books,
  Old Rite reverence for, 13–14, 16, 19–21, 109, 118, 151, 178, 194, 198–200, 204–5, 207–8, 211
Borisovo Old Believer community, 196
boundaries, 5–6, 45–46, 56–57, 61, 89–92, 211
bubonic plague, *see* Moscow, Plague of 1771
Butikov, Ivan, 115, 129, 138, 142
Butkevich, Timofei
  views on Old Believers, 192
Byzantine Empire
  legacy in Russia, 2, 9–12, 17, 54

capital (financial),
  Rogozhskoe Old Believers' view of, 20–3, 61–2, 98, 117–18, 132, 171, 181, 184, 186–7, 191, 213, 215
Catherine the Great, 41, 121
  creation of *Edinoverie*, 39–40
  policies on Old Believers, 28–9, 38–9, 42–3
  response to Pugachev Rebellion, 39
  Rogozhskoe Cemetery, 48–9, 154
  views of Moscow, 43–5, 57
chapels, 36, 40, 46–52, 72–4, 82–4, 94–5, 116, 120, 125, 127, 152
charity, 8, 20–1, 45, 47, 58–64, 75–8, 98, 113–19, 136, 146, 163–5, 184, 186–9, 212–13, 215
children, 66, 77–8, 151, 172, 176–8, 183, 195
Church interiors, 74–5, 130–4, 144, 153, 162 *see also* boundaries; chapels; iconostases; icons
churches *see* chapels
clergy
  in Rogozhskoe, 5, 19–20, 65–6, 78–9, 82–3, 99–105, 113, 138, 141, 144, 151–5, 166–7, 170, 172–8, 197, 215 *see also* bishops; Rogozhskoe
Constantine XI, Byzantine Emperor, 9
Constantinople, 85
  and Council of Florence, 9–11
  and Russian Orthodoxy, 12–13, 204–5
  Sack of 1453, 9–11, 16
conversion
  to *Edinoverie*, 7, 71–2, 83, 88–9, 93, 120
  of Old Believers, 18, 32–3, 71, 88, 140
  to the Old Rite, 61–2, 77–8, 85–6, 128, 150–1
corruptions of Orthodoxy
  Old Believer views of, 2, 5–6, 13–22, 37, 53–6, 62, 74, 77, 90, 98, 104–5, 175, 200, 213, 215
cossacks, 64
Council of Florence, 10–11, 32

influence on Russian Orthodoxy, 13, 15–17
cultural destiny,
Old Rite as defender of, 1–3, 13, 17, 20–3, 103, 193–4, 201–7
Russian, 9–13

Divine Liturgy, 47–8, 64–5, 72–3, 79, 87, 95, 141, 143, 165
Dolgorukov, Vladimir,
relationship with Rogozhskoe Old Believers, 114–15, 126–7, 137–8, 140–2
donations
of materials, 163–5
of money, 62–3, 65–6, 115–18, 132, 163–5, 181, 188, 213
of sacred items, 52, 55, 141, 188, 190, 210

economics
Old Believers' role in, 2–4, 7–8, 24, 32–5, 43–4, 61, 81–2, 114, 122, 129, 132, 140, 147–8, 172, 183–95, 213 *see also* Old Believers, role in Moscow merchantry; Rogozhskoe, members in Moscow merchantry
Edinoverie, 7, 39–40, 97
and Rogozhskoe Cemetery, 75, 78–85, 87–90, 93, 95–6, 120
state efforts to convert Old Believers to, 70, 72, 75, 87–8, 92–3
state-sponsored Old Rite, 40–2
edinovertsy See Edinoverie
education,
Old Believers' approach, 66–7, 77, 118–19, 126, 151, 174–81, 183–4, 187, 189, 198
see also Old Believer Theological Institute; schools
Russian state approach, 16, 37, 118, 194, 200

emancipation, 98, 117
entrepreneurs, 6, 22, 35, 59, 98, 117, 140, 183–90 *see also* Morozov family; Prokhorov family; Riabushinskii family; Soldatenkov family

factories, 59, 62, 119, 187–91
Filaret, Metropolitan of Moscow, 72–3, 96, 101, 124, 138, 145, 199, 211, 214
conflict with Rogozhskoe Cemetery, 70–3, 75, 77, 79–80, 82–4, 87, 89–90, 93–5, 121–2
use of Edinoverie against the Old Rite, 70, 72, 78, 84
Filofei of Pskov, 11–12
and the Third Rome Doctrine, 12, 204

Giliarovskii, Vladimir
account of Rogozhskoe Cemetery, 153–9
Golitsyn, Dmitri, 152, 158
Gol'skii Family, 53, 55, 59
Great Reforms, 97–8, 146, 195
and Old Believers, 113, 124
and Rogozhskoe Cemetery, 98–9, 117–20, 126–30, 138–9, 214

historiography, 3–4, 18–26, 199–207 *see also* Subbotin, Nikolai; Riabushinskii, Vladimir; *Vypiski* of 1910
Holy Moscow, ideals of, 19–20, 103–4, 110–11
after 1905, 152, 158, 162–3, 172–3, 185, 197–8
before 1905, 3, 5, 8, 25–6, 29, 47–9, 57–60, 64–5, 70, 78–83, 88, 93–4, 113–20
Holy Synod, 32
legislation against Old Rite services, 74, 80–3, 143–5

and the Old Rite, 40–1, 130, 134, 142
and Rogozhskoe Cemetery, 52, 71–2, 75, 77–8, 84, 89, 93, 95, 128
hospitals, 8, 63, 73, 76–7, 90, 117–18, 171, 187–8
Huguenots
comparative oppression, 31

Iastrebov, Ivan, 58, 80–1
resistance to *Edinoverie*, 84, 88
iconostases, 52, 55, 116, 127, 141, 144, 160–2, 181
icons, 12, 16, 26, 50–6, 58–9, 65, 80, 84, 91, 107, 114–16, 125–7, 130, 138, 141, 144, 153, 156, 160–2, 174, 180–1, 188–90, 194, 196–7, 207, 210, 212,
industrialization, 98, 149, 183–4, 188 *see also* Morozov family; Prokhorov family; Soldatenkov family; Riabushinskii family
Innocent, Metropolitan of Moscow, 138
Intercession Cathedral, Rogozhskoe Cemetery, 47–52, 55, 114, 141–2, 166–7, 174, 210
photographing, 132–4
reopening of altars, 152–5, 158–9
repair and restoration, 114, 125–7, 144, 161–2
sealing of altars, 95, 116, 121
Ivan III, 9
Ivan IV, 12, 56

January Uprising, 109
Jesus
spelling of, 14, 54, 107, 206 *see also* Nikonian Reforms, *Okruzhnoe poslanie*; *Vypiski* of 1910, defining the Old Rite
John VIII Palaeologus, Byzantine Emperor Council of Florence, 10

Kabanov, Ilarion, "Xenos"
author of *Okruzhnoe poslanie*, 105–9
Kirill, Metropolition of Belokrinitskaya Hierarchy, 101–2
Okruzhnoe poslanie debate, 109–12
and Rogozhskoe Cemetery, 103–4
Kirillov, Ivan, 20–1
Kozlov, Alexander, Governor General of Moscow, 162–3
Kuznetsov, Matvei, 160, 163, 171, 174
Kuznetsov, Sergei, 171, 174

laity
role in formation of Old Rite, 2, 5, 13–14, 25
role in Rogozhskoe, 113, 148–9, 174 *see also* MSORK; Rogozhskoe family; trustees
Lanskoi, Sergei, Minister of Internal Affairs, 94–5, 124
Lobanov-Rostovskii, Aleksei, Deputy Minister of Internal Affairs, 126
Lobanov-Rostovskii Commission, 126, 128, 130, 132–5, 138

Makarov, Vladimir, 3, 21, 53, 55, 64, 159
marriage, 18, 65, 73–4, 151
Martinov, Rodion, 129
Maximov, Ivan, Rogozhskoe priest, 81, 84
Mel'nikov, Peter, 114, 122, 125–6, 129
migration, 24, 59 *see also* Catherine the Great, policies on Old Believers
Milorad, Alimpii, monk, 85
Milovanov, Dmitri, 114, 125–6, 129
moral capitalism *see* capital, Rogozhskoe view of
moral community *see* Rogozhskoe Cemetery, as ideal of Orthodox Russia
Morozov family, 8, 23, 53, 59, 63, 67, 76, 183–6, 195, 213
and charity, 187–90

Morozov, Arsenii Ivanovich, 171, 181, 186–8
Morozov, Ivan, 164
Morozov, Savva Timofeyevich, 186
  charity, 187–8
  charity in memory of, 164–5, 188
  company workers, 187–8, 191
  politics, 190–1
Morozov, Savva, Vasilievich, 59, 64
  Savva Morozov Company, 187
Morozov, Sergei, 186–8
Morozov, Timofei, 122, 129, 142, 164, 187
Morozova, Fedosiia, 164–5
  funding Rogozhskoe bell tower, 167
Morozova, Maria, 164–5, 187
  as benefactress, 188
  Morozov factories, 191
Moscow
  as capital of Russia, 7–10
  Fire of, 1812, 29, 57–9, 61–3, 68
  Old Believer economic influence *see* Old Believers
  as "Old Capital", 2–3, 44, 47–8, 57–8
  Plague of 1771, 3, 29, 44–6, 61–2
  population growth, 34, 43–4
  Rogozhskoe Cemetery's influence in *see* Rogozhskoe Cemetery Old Believer Community, members of the Moscow merchantry
  state views of, 5, 44, 49, 57–9
  in Third Rome Doctrine, 12, 17
Moscow Secret Committee, 26
  and Rogozhskoe almshouses, 76
  and Rogozhskoe Cemetery, 75, 84, 92–3
  and Superintendent of Rogozhskoe, 90
Moskovskaya Staroobriadcheskaya Obshina Rogozhskogo Kladbisha (MSORK), 170–5, 198, 207
  leadership of Rogozhskoe, 170–2, 185, 207–8
  oversight of Rogozhskoe charities, 170–2, 195
  relationship with Russian state, 176, 195
  Rogozhskoe schools, 179–81, 195
  Rogozhskoe spiritual life, 172–4, 182, 196
Mozzhakov, Nikita,
  persecution of Rogozhskoe Old Believers, 90, 92–4
  Superintendent of Rogozhskoe Cemetery, 90
muzhik
  Old Believers as, 194

Narodnaia gazeta, 201–2
Nativity Cathedral, Rogozhskoe Cemetery, 50–2, 58, 79, 116, 166–7, 211
  opening of altars, 152, 154–8
  photographing of, 132
  renovation and restoration, 125, 144, 161–2, 212
  sealing of altars, 95, 121
Nazarov, Timofei, 129
newspapers *see Narodnaia gazeta*; *Tserkov'*
Nicholas I, 7, 69, 84–5, 96, 119, 199, 214
  policies toward Old Believers, 70, 72–4, 78–80, 88, 92–3, 162
  targeting of Rogozhskoe Cemetery, 70–3, 75, 78–80, 87–9, 101, 121–2, 135
Nicholas II, 143, 149, 153, 192
  religious toleration, 8, 147, 150–2, 169–70, 208, 214
  Rogozhskoe Cemetery, 146, 149, 152, 159, 176, 197
Nikon, Patriarch of Moscow, 2, 13–14, 16

Old Believer views of, 2, 9, 14–16, 18–21, 36, 52–4, 203–5
Nikonian Reforms, 8–9, 13–16
Old Rite rejection of reforms, 2, 8–9, 13–21, 52–4, 139, 203–5
Novikov, Ivan, 174

October Revolution, 189
and Rogozhskoe Cemetery, 209, 211–12
Okruzhnoe poslanie, 105–13
debates in Rogozhskoe Cemetery, 108–13
legitimization of the Belokrinitskaya Hierarchy, 105–8, 111–12
neokruzhniki, 109–12, 177
okruzhniki, 108–12, 177
views of Russian Orthodoxy, 106–8
Old Believers
community formation, 17–26
cultural ties to Moscow, 2–3, 17–20, 28–9, 36, 43–4, 58–60, 64–7
and *Edinoverie see Edinoverie*
Great Reforms, 113, 124 *see also* Great Reforms
literacy, 66–7, 199–200
model of Russian identity, 13–17, 20–1, 48, 193–5, 202–7 *see also* Old Believers, self-identity
oppression of, 2–4, 31, 37, 70–8, 81–4, 136, 143–4, 149
preservation of Pre-Nikonian Russia, 13–22, 34, 37, 48, 52–5, 74, 82, 203–5
priestless movement, 4, 18, 35–6 *see also* Preobrazhenskoe Cemetery; Vyg Old Rite Community
priestly community formation, 35–6 *see also* Rogozhskoe Cemetery Old Believer Community
publishing, 26, 198–201
the *raskol'*, 13–17
religious toleration *see ukaz* of 1905
role in Moscow merchantry, 2–3, 6, 28–30, 34–5, 58–61, 63–8, 117–19, 148, 183–90 *see also* Rogozhskoe Cemetery and members of Moscow merchantry
self-identity, 1–3, 15–17, 20–1, 36, 128, 193–5, 199–207
state definitions of, 15, 35–42, 127, 151–2, 128, 199
Third Rome Doctrine, 17, 20, 193–5, 201–5
Old Believer Theological Institute, 179–81, 196
Onuphrius, Belokrinitskaya Archbishop of Moscow, 103
and *Okruzhnoe poslanie*, 103, 109–10
Orlov, Grigori, 45
orphans, 76–8 *see also* almshouses

parishioners
role in Rogozhskoe, 24, 47–8, 52–8, 62, 65, 79–80, 85, 113–14, 118, 131–2, 172, 174, 180–1, 196–7
Patriarchate of Moscow, 12–13
patriotism
Rogozhskoe displays of, 61, 67–9, 98, 194, 215 *see also* Rogozhskoe Cemetery Old Believer Community, oath of loyalty; World War I
patronage, 20, 43, 61–4, 98, 186, 188, 191–3, 207–8, 214–15
Paul I, 40–1
Pavel, Bishop of Kolomna, 14
Peter the Great, 7, 28, 32, 39
and Old Believer Response to, 22, 32, 37, 55, 139
policies on Old Believers, 7, 33, 42, 140, 206
Peter III, 28, 38, 42

petitions
Rogozhskoe's use of, 29, 41, 45, 47–8, 50, 84, 89, 93, 116, 124–6, 128–33, 141–6, 149, 162–5, 176, 182, 195
Philip II, Metropolitan of Moscow, Iconography of, 56
photography, 131–5
Platon, Metropolitan of Moscow
origins of *Edinoverie*, 40–1
Pobedonostsev, Konstantin, 143
repression of the Old Rite, 145, 150, 214
and Rogozhskoe Cemetery, 143, 145–6, 149
politics
Rogozhskoe participation in, 110, 118–19, 126, 129–30, 137–9, 147–8, 170–2, 184–97, 200–2 *see also* Morozov, Savva Timofeyevich; Riabushinskii, Pavel; Riabushinskii, Vladimir; Shibaev, Ivan
views of the Old Rite, 38, 42, 70, 87–8 *see also* Moscow Secret Committee; Pobedonostsev; Konstantin; Saint Petersburg Secret Committee
pravoverie, 37
Preobrazhenskoe Cemetery Old Believers, 29, 36, 40, 75, 102, 184
priests
edinovertsy, 40–1, 90, 93, 95
Rogozhskoe, 65–7, 73, 75, 79–89, 93–5, 99–102, 141, 160–1, 172–5, 181, 196 *see also* clergy
runaways, 19–20, 44, 71–2, 78, 80, 83–4, 90, 112, 177
Prokhorov Family, 61–3
Prokhorov, Timofei, 21
Prokhorov, Vasili, 61
property
conflict with *edinovertsy*, 92–4
Rogozhskoe use of, 64–5, 83–4, 114, 170, 212
Prozorovskii, Alexander, Governor-General of Moscow, 47–9
public sphere
misrepresentation of Old Rite *see* Old Believers, state definitions of; Subbotin, criticism of the Old Rite
Old Rite efforts to participate, 19, 22–3, 98, 128, 148, 190, 194–202, 207
Pugachev's Rebellion
state view of Old Believers, 39
Pugovkin, Ivan, 160, 171, 174, 176, 195
purity
as trait of Old Rite Orthodoxy, 2–3, 9–10, 13, 15–18, 22, 37, 54–6, 59, 65, 95–6, 99, 112, 158, 175, 178, 213–4
Putin, Vladimir, 210

Rakhmanov family, 23, 53, 59, 207, 213
Rakhmanov, Grigori, 160, 195
Rakhmanova, Agniia, 210
raskol'niki, 15, 37–8, 82–3, 127, 151 *see also* Old Believers, state definitions of
Rastorguev, Petr, 160, 176, 195
religious dissent
state approach, 31–2, 38 *see also* Old Believers, oppression of
religious services, 21, 29, 44–8, 64–6, 72–3, 79, 82, 94–5, 99, 102, 116, 120, 130–1, 140–3, 151–2, 157–8, 161–2, 166, 172–3, 175–6, 196–7, 212 *see also* clergy; Divine Liturgy; priests
Revolutions of 1905, 147, 149–51
and religious toleration, 147, 150–2
and Rogozhskoe Old Believers, 147, 152, 191
Riabushinskii family, 6, 8, 23, 53, 59, 67, 148, 183–6, 189–90, 207–8, 213–15,

politics after 1905, 184–5, 191–5, 200–1, 207–8
Riabushinskii, Dmitri, 186, 189
Riabushinskii, Feodor, 186, 189
Riabushinskii, Mikhail, 186, 189
Riabushinskii, Nikolai, 186, 189
Riabushinskii, Pavel Mikhailovich, 189
Riabushinskii, Pavel Pavlovich, 26, 160, 170, 186, 189, 191–5, 200–3
Riabushinskii, Sergei, 174, 186, 189–90
Riabushinskii, Stepan, 163–4, 170–1, 186, 189–93, 207
Riabushinskii, Vlaidimir, 1, 20–2, 26, 61, 184, 186, 189–95, 200–1
rituals *see* beards; *Okruzhnoe poslanie*; sign of the cross; *Vypiski* of 1910, defining the Old Rite
Rogozhskoe Cemetery Old Believer Community
  founding of, 45–6
  as ideal of Orthodox Russia, 1, 20–2, 46–8, 52–4, 65–7, 71, 74, 78–87, 104, 167–8, 189–90, 193–208
  influence of Belokrinitskaya Hierarchy, 4, 8, 26, 86–8, 100, 102–4, 108–13 *see also Belokrinitskaya Hierarchy*
  influence on Old Rite movement, 1, 64–7, 127–30, 159–68, 177–8, 193–208
  members of the Moscow merchantry, 6, 8, 21–3, 29–30, 45–53, 58–61, 63–5, 67–8, 82–3, 88–9, 116–19, 131–2, 148, 183–95
  oath of loyalty, 139–42
  relationship with Russian state after, 1917, 210–12
  role in Old Rite publishing, 26, 198–201
  sealing of cathedral altars, 34, 95, 116, 121
Rusanov, Peter, Rogozhskoe priest, 81, 84
Russian
  identity of culture *see* cultural destiny; Rogozhskoe Cemetery Old Believer Community, as ideal of Orthodox Russia; Third Rome Doctrine

sacred space, 5–6, 22–5, 46–55, 74, 91, 95–9, 114–16, 124–5, 130–2, 140, 144–5, 162–3, 171, 214
Safonov, Nikolai, 161
Saint Petersburg Secret Committee
  closure of Rogozhskoe altars, 95, 121, 123
Sapelkin, Vladimir
  conversion to *Edinoverie,* 89–90
schools, 62, 66–7, 73, 77, 99, 170–2, 177–8, 181, 195 *see also* Old Believer Theological Institute
Senatov, Vasili, 20–1
serfs, 43, 59, 61, 64, 98
Shibaev, Ivan
  and the Great Reforms, 122–4, 126, 128–32
  publishing, 166
  relationship with state authorities, 126–8, 138–9, 142
  and Rogozhskoe Cemetery, 120, 122–4, 126–32, 138–9, 142
  Tserkov', 166, 201–2
sign of the cross, 13–14, 54, 107, 109, 205–6 *see also Okruzhnoe poslanie*; *Vypiski* of 1910
soglasie, 36
Soldatenkov family, 53, 59, 213
Soldatenkov, Kozma, 118, 120, 123, 129, 141–2
Solovyov, Sergei, 176
Sophroni, Belokrinitskaya Bishop, 87
Sorokin, Prokopi, 160, 174

staroobriadtsy, 2, 15, 36, 38, 127, 151, 170 *see also* Old Believers, self-identity
Stoglavy Sobor, 12–13
Subbotin, Nikolai, 26
  criticism of the Old Rite, 108, 199–200
  criticism of Rogozhskoe Cemetery, 75, 90–1, 108, 127, 199–200
Suvorov, Alexander Abramovich, 138
Suvorov, General Alexander Vasilyevich, 138

Tatishchev, Vasili,
  policies toward Old Believers, 139
taxes,
  on Old Believers, 33, 38, 42, 140, 206 *see also* Peter the Great, policies on Old Believers
textiles, 30, 35, 59, 63, 115, 164, 189 *see also* Morozov family; Prokhorov family; Riabushinskii family
Third Rome Doctrine, 12, 17
  and Old Believer views of, 17, 193, 201–5
  and Rogozhskoe views of, 20, 25, 99, 193, 201–5
Timashev, Alexander, Minister of the Interior, 114, 133
Tolstoi, Dmitri, Minister of the Interior, 145
Trustees, 62–3, 66–7, 79, 113–16, 121, 124–6, 137–8, 141–2, 160, 170–1
tsar-*batiushka* phenomenon, 123, 159
Tserkov', 26, 201–2
  defining the Old Rite after 1905, 201–2
  and Old Rite publishing, 201–2
  and Rogozhskoe, 166, 177, 201, 207
ukaz of May 3, 1883, 118, 142–4
ukaz on religious toleration, April 17, 1905, 22–3, 147, 150–2, 159–60, 163, 167, 169, 172, 174, 176–7, 182, 192, 198, 208, 212, 214

Valuev, Peter, Minister of Internal Affairs, 124
Vasili II
  and Council of Florence, 10–11, 32
Vasili III
  and the Third Rome Doctrine, 12, 204
Velikodvorskii, Pavel
  and Belokrinitskaya Hierarchy, 85, 102
Vyg Old Believer community, 17–18, 34–6, 140
Vypiski of 1910
  defining the Old Rite, 1, 203–6
  Old Rite self-identity, 206–7

wealth
  Rogozhskoe members' views of, 20–2, 61–3, 82, 98, 117, 132, 171, 184, 186–7, 213, 215
Westernization
  Old Believer view of, 20–2, 37, 54–5, 98, 119, 139, 183–4, 194, 206, 215
Witte, Sergei, 168
workers, 64, 149, 180, 187–8, 191
World War I, 181–2, 197, 209

Yermilov, Peter,
  conversion to *Edinoverie*, 90